Stendhal

for Elena

Stendhal

Michael Wood

Cornell Paperbacks

Cornell University Press

ITHACA, NEW YORK

First published 1971
First printing,
Cornell Paperbacks, 1971

International Standard Book
Number 0-8014-9124-X
Library of Congress Catalog Card
Number 73-164669

PRINTED IN GREAT BRITAIN

Contents

I should like to thank the Master and Fellows
of St John's College, Cambridge for three unhurried
and now rather distant years during which
a good deal of the groundwork for this book was done.

Chronology

23 JAN. 1783
Marie-Henry Beyle born rue des Vieux-Jésuites, Grenoble.

NOV. 1796–SEPT. 1799
Attends newly opened Central School of Grenoble.

SEPT. 1800–DEC. 1801
Commission in the cavalry of Napoleon's army in Italy.

APRIL 1802–MAY 1806
Paris. Resigns commission, plans to become the greatest comic poet since Molière. Brief spell in Marseille as a grocer's apprentice. Affair with Mélanie Guilbert, an actress.

OCT. 1806–APRIL 1814
Brunswick, Paris. Administrative posts under Napoleon. Mistresses, money, travels, the life of a dandy. Takes part in the Moscow campaign.

AUG. 1814–JUNE 1821
Italy. Publishes *Vies de Haydn, de Mozart et de Métastase* (1815), *Histoire de la Peinture en Italie* (1817); *Rome, Naples et Florence en 1817* (1817). Works on a life of Napoleon. Unhappy passion for Mathilde Viscontini.

JUNE 1821–NOV. 1830
Paris. Publishes *De l'Amour* (1822), *Racine et Shakespeare I* (1823), *Vie de Rossini* (1823), *Racine et Shakespeare II* (1825), *D'un nouveau complot contre les industriels* (1825), *Armance* (1827), *Promenades dans Rome* (1829), *Le Rouge et le Noir* (1830). Articles on Italian opera, on the Paris Salon of 1824,

regular contributions to English reviews, some short fiction. Trips to England, Italy, the south of France. Stormy love affairs, reputation as a wit.

APRIL 1831–NOV. 1841
French consul in Civita-Vecchia, near Rome. Writes but does not publish *Souvenirs d'Egotisme* (1832), *Lucien Leuwen* (1834–1835), *Vie de Henry Brulard* (1835–1836). Long and productive leave in Paris, 1836–1839. Publishes *Mémoires d'un Touriste* (1838), *La Chartreuse de Parme* (1839) and three Italian tales under the title *L'Abbesse de Castro* (1839). Works on his life of Napoleon, begins *Lamiel*. An old love-affair continues; there is a last shadowy romance with a lady in Rome.

NOV. 1841–MARCH 1842
Leave in Paris. Attack of apoplexy in the evening of 22 March 1842. Dies the following morning without regaining consciousness.

Part One   Towards Fiction

1. SHAPES

'Par un petit sentier détourné et
auquel un buisson cache la plaine immense . . .'
LUCIEN LEUWEN

By another road : there is an odd paragraph in one of Stendhal's early notebooks under this heading. The phrase brings back 'laughing and delicious' memories. Stendhal thinks of an English garden near Milan, where a twisting path which seemed to be taking him to unknown parts would suddenly deposit him in front of a familiar shrub or statue. It would be very different, he adds melodramatically, if a man were searching for his stolen wife on a December night in the driving rain, or running from the police with a price on his head, and if after two hours of following what he thought was the right road he were to find himself even further from his wife or even closer to the police. 'Think carefully about all that,' Stendhal tells himself, 'the whole secret of style in verse and prose, of painting etc. is there . . .'[1]

The whole secret of style looks like a secret of structure, and Stendhal may have been exaggerating the range of his idea. He was young, and given to exaggeration in those years. He had resigned his commission in Napoleon's cavalry, and was setting out to eclipse Molière and possibly Shakespeare too. 'What is my aim?' he asked himself, and answered promptly, 'To be the greatest poet possible.'[2] He lived in a fifth-floor room in Paris with a view of the colonnades of the Louvre, he went to the theatre, read voraciously, made pompous notes, took English lessons with an Irish priest. He was 'wild about *Hamlet*', in his own later words, and he was as 'mad and lonely as a Spaniard' (*Brulard* 10). But the great plays were shy. The young poet had trouble with his verse. At one stage he calculated that he was averaging a line every two hours fifty-six minutes (*Journal* 466). 'All things considered,' he was soon to comment, 'I don't think I have a flair for tragedy.'[8] His attempts at comedy were not much more fruitful : scraps, plans, fragments of dialogue.

Stendhal decided to postpone his literary fame and devote himself to a scheme for becoming an important banker : six months in Marseille, six months in Bordeaux, four months in Nantes, eight months in Antwerp and then, with the aid of a fat loan from his father, an establishment in Paris by 1807. 'I shall be twenty-four by then' (*Journal* 511). Stendhal managed the first part of this scenario, a gloomy year in Marseille as a grocer's assistant, but his father had no intention of lending him money, and he was in any case, through the influence of his cousins Daru, caught up in the whirl of the late Empire. The fall of Napoleon in 1814 brought Stendhal down too. He consoled himself by pillaging a book on Haydn and publishing the results, and by leaving for Italy, where he stayed for seven years, and where his literary career began in earnest.

Yet exaggeration apart, the structure suggested by the phrase *by another road* is strikingly prophetic. It indicates precisely the movement of the novels Stendhal was to write some twenty and thirty years later. Julien Sorel, the hero of *Le Rouge et le Noir*, is a fierce Dick Whittington, a poor young man driven by an angry desire to make his fortune. The fortune once made, he breaks it irrationally, and learns that all he really wanted was what he left behind him months ago : quiet evenings in an orchard and the love of a provincial lady. The wrong road. But the lady herself comes to visit him in prison as he awaits his execution for an attempted murder, and there are thus moments of bliss after all, *by another road*, before he dies. Similarly Fabrice, the protagonist of *La Chartreuse de Parme*, is haunted by a fear of the gaol which has been predicted for him. The prediction turns out to be correct, but in gaol Fabrice meets the gaoler's daughter, the love of his life, and having escaped, in great danger and at great cost to his friends, returns voluntarily to his prison in order to see the girl.

The structure comes close to Stendhal's formula for comedy, where there is a comparable mixture of geometry and romance. Passionate people, he says, must take the wrong road to happiness. They must make their mistake 'in an amusing manner' (*Racine* 61).

'Amusing' ('plaisant') in Stendhal's vocabulary almost always means neatly ironic, just as 'miserable' means not so much wretched as hopelessly complicated, distressing to the reasonable mind—Stendhal inherits many of his linguistic habits from the eighteenth century. Comedy will come, then, from the symmetry of the comic figure's errors. The road will be precisely and beautifully the wrong road.

Yet such symmetries are not always amusing. In *Oedipus the King*, for example, a man, alerted by a horrendous prophecy, flees from the people he believes to be his father and mother. Arriving in a foreign country, he unwittingly kills his real father and sleeps with his real mother. The wrong road in no uncertain terms. Or there is this other moral and metaphysical tale. Death visits a rich merchant of Baghdad, and tells him he will call for him in the evening. The merchant packs his bags, takes to his horse, rides as far as he can go, and reaches Samarra by nightfall. In the afternoon of the same day, Death meets the merchant's servant in the market-place of Baghdad and is surprised to see him there. I should have thought, Death says, that you would have gone with your master. I have an appointment with him this evening in Samarra.

Ironies of this kind may be comic, tragic, pathetic and doubtless any number of other things. But in each case they work magic, they turn a fear into a fable, bring together ideas which are more often painfully separate in our minds. We are afraid both of the meaninglessness of our lives and of the possible meanings they may have. Stories of the wrong road which is *perfectly* wrong or which in some gruesome or sinister or comic sense turns out to be the right road after all, are means of displaying the dilemma while holding it at bay. The random decisions of Oedipus, including his flight from the oracle, are the patterned plot of the gods—but the plot destroys him. The merchant's journey is foreseen in Death's design —but at least there is a design. Life appears to us simultaneously in its aspects of freedom, disorder, chance, and in its aspects of pattern, intelligibility and shape. It is as if we were able, by a fold in our perception, to see both sides of a finely woven carpet at once : the figure on the face, the tangled threads behind. We are left staring at a satisfying but unresolved conflict, dazed by a form of double vision.

This ironic structure serves Stendhal in much the same way as the metaphysical schemes of his later years served Yeats. 'Some will ask,' Yeats wrote at the end of his introduction to *A Vision*, 'whether

I believe in the actual existence of my circuits of sun and moon.'
His answer was that finally he saw them rather as 'stylistic arrangements of experience'. 'They have helped me,' he ended eloquently
and powerfully, 'to hold in a single thought reality and justice.'

Stendhal's reversing plots allow him to play off his sense of life
against his taste for philosophy, his fidelity to a bewildering world
against his delight in patterns, what he knows against what he wants
—and yet to produce something more than an elementary collision.
He is able to set up a 'competition of equilibriums', in Robert
Adams' fine phrase.[4] He converts contradictions into a flexible
form, his work is an ordered emblem of a disordered territory, a
rational model of unreason, like a labyrinth. Yet unlike a labyrinth,
it is more than a mockery. Stendhal's novels are never cynical or
sarcastic. Across their complex irony they bear a faint secular
theology, a wistful Enlightenment dream of a hidden reason, of a
secondary, displaced order in a universe of visible, strident confusion.

The structures of Stendhal's novels are closer to logic than to literature. They take the form of puzzles, paradoxes, not 'stories' in the
usual sense. There are no master images, as in Henry James or
Ibsen; there are no webs of metaphor, as in George Eliot or Claudel.
Nothing is hidden, the art lies on the surfaces. When Stendhal uses
a symbol its meaning is so obvious that even his heroes are
embarrassed.

Julien Sorel, longing to escape from Verrières, his stifling provincial birthplace, finds himself on a high rock on a mountainside,
and *smiles* at the allegorical nature of his position (*Rouge* 276).
Later in the novel, he is about to climb up a ladder to a lady's bedroom for the second time within a matter of months. He laughs at
the literalism of his social ascents and tells himself that destiny seems
to have decreed the use of ladders for him (*Rouge* 537). So that
when Stendhal notes in the margins of a story more or less contemporary with *Le Rouge et le Noir*, 'Criticism: ladder again'
(*Romans* 447), he is reflecting not only his own but Julien's feelings.

Mathilde de la Mole, Julien's Parisian passion, flings a written
message at him as he sits working in her father's library. They are
living in the same house, could talk to each other easily. Julien
thinks, 'It looks as if this is going to be a letter-novel' (*Rouge* 531).
Stendhal mocks his heroes a good deal, but they have their moments
of revenge. They grin slyly at the lives they lead, and thereby at
their author's clumsiness or poverty of invention—Stendhal him-

self, during a love-affair with a lady called Clémentine Curial, had scrambled up Julien's ladder.

Stendhal thus offers very little handhold to 'thematic' critics like Victor Brombert or Stephen Gilman.⁵ The 'themes' tend to turn into heavy paraphrase of what Stendhal has already elegantly said. With Julien smiling on his rock, we hardly need to be told about the 'translation of spiritual exaltation into ascensional images'.⁶

Stendhal's symbols are caricatures. In and out of his fiction, exemplary simplifications are his mark. 'I have spent my life falling from horses' (*Souvenirs* 1396). The form, like a lampoon, hints at a stylized truth while mocking its own failure to reach it. At the beginning of *La Chartreuse de Parme* we learn of the death of Prince Eugène's minister in Italy, Count Prina, who was killed in a right-wing revolt. He was assassinated, Stendhal says, 'à coups de parapluie', beaten to death with umbrellas (*Chartreuse* 41). Apparently the fact is historical. The count was attacked, and after five hours of agony, finished off with umbrellas. It doesn't matter that Stendhal didn't invent this death. What matters is its eloquent characterization of the right wing in Italy after the fall of Napoleon, and its kinship with the body of Stendhal's other images. Most of them are like this. They represent beautifully, but they exaggerate, they deprecate, they seem to apologize for their crassness. They ridicule both their objects and themselves—delicately and without explanation. What makes Stendhal difficult to write about is not the depth or complexity of his prose but the lightness of his touch, and the stringency of his refusal of emphasis.

There is more : a curious playfulness. Julien Sorel stands on his mountainside. An August sun inflames the sky, cicadas sing in the fields below. He sees twenty leagues of country 'at his feet'. A sparrowhawk circles above his head, he envies the bird's strength and isolation, and wonders, 'It was the destiny of Napoleon, would it one day be his?' (*Rouge* 276–277).

It seems to me hard to take this passage quite seriously. Yet there is no explicit comment from Stendhal, no sign marked : Here be irony. This *is* how Julien sees himself and the world and his future. The sparrowhawk becomes his metaphor, not Stendhal's. In this sense the passage is serious. Our other sense comes from the faint inflation of the prose, the grandeur of Julien's dream, the arrogance and silliness of his symbolic appropriation of the countryside. The sparrowhawk is a portent for Julien but a caricature for us. Like the assassins' umbrellas, it is an emblematic truth delivered as a discreet joke. Julien is perfectly capable of seeing his silliness here, indeed he is hamstrung for a good part of the novel by his fear of seeming a fool, so that plainly he is letting himself go on the mountain. He is alone, for once he doesn't care how ridiculous he is. This is one of his rare moments of free and natural and juvenile sentiment, a day of hookey from the programme of hypocrisy he has set for himself. It is an expressive, and even moving scene, a glimpse of the child's universe through the child's glasses. But it *is* also ridiculous, and the ridicule remains as a context, an enclosing commentary on whatever we feel, a smile at the edges of our sympathy. This is Stendhal's peculiar talent : he can fill out a caricature with humanity, and yet not blur its clean and critical outline.

Stendhal is a quick, discursive, associative writer, careless about keeping sight of his characters, about the linear development of his plots. But he is rigorous about his arrangement of plot and character in conceptual or logical space. The heroes of his novels are tightly trapped in paradoxes which turn their every move into an irony— wrong roads lead off in all directions. In Stendhal, as Maurice Bardèche says, the situations create epigrams.[7] One could also say that epigrams create the situations, that the novels are like epigrams fleshed out and set in movement.

A remark attributed to Polidori, Byron's doctor and secretary, appears at the head of Chapter XIV, in the First Part of *Le Rouge et le Noir* : 'A girl of sixteen had the complexion of a rose, and she wore rouge' (*Rouge* 293). In the following chapter Stendhal comments on his young hero's 'incredible efforts to spoil whatever was likeable about him'. Julien has just slept with his first mistress for the first time, but has ruined the best moments of the night by his attention to himself, to his sad notions of love as military conquest and sex as a form of guard-duty, a nocturnal parade for worldly soldiers. 'He is a girl of sixteen,' Stendhal says, 'whose colours are charming and who is silly enough to wear rouge to the ball' (*Rouge* 298). The same idea, in different words, with a different emphasis and given this time to Sainte-Beuve, serves as an epigraph to the second, Parisian part of the novel : 'She's not pretty, she doesn't have any rouge' (*Rouge* 433). In *Armance*, Octave de Malivert's manners in society put him in the position of a 'young woman arriving without rouge in a salon where the use of rouge is general; for a few moments her paleness makes her seem sad' (*Armance* 41).

Plainly Stendhal is attached to this epigram, and indeed *Le*

Rouge et le Noir, the whole novel, may be described as a gloss on the moral possibilities it opens up. The girl doesn't need the rouge, but the world may demand it. Julien Sorel poses, paints his face at the wrong time—when he is with Mme de Rênal, his first mistress, in the provinces. He thereby misses the chief or perhaps the only compensation there is, in Stendhal's eyes, for not living in Paris : the chance to be natural. But in Paris itself, everyone uses rouge, you can't show your face without it. Julien, who is not as noble or as wooden or as unreal as Octave, masks his features there, dresses up, takes lessons in deportment, confronts the world on the world's terms. His attention to himself, precisely, which marred his night with the provincial lady, now wins for him an aristocratic beauty— he conquers Mathilde de la Mole by a sustained act of will, by a severe self-discipline. This is a remarkable cosmetic achievement, a triumph of social disguise and control for the carpenter's son. But it is also a flirtation with evil, with a secular, peculiarly Stendhalian peril : the face may be ruined by the make-up. Stendhal whisks Julien away to the provinces just in time, saves him from his dazzling success, and sends him clear-complexioned to his redeeming death.

This makes Stendhal sound like a writer of moral romances, which he is. In a sense, the epigram about the girl and the make-up summarizes all Stendhal's novels, not only *Le Rouge et le Noir*. Sincerity is tempted by seductive disguises but sincerity, in the end, is saved. Stendhal's 'story' is thus the reverse of Musset's, in *Lorenzaccio*. There, a man assumes the mask of evil in order to get close to a bad ruler and destroy him. By the time he is close enough, the mask has become the face, he is as evil as the man he planned to kill. At first glance, Musset's version seems truer, nearer to the world we know, while Stendhal's reading looks wishful, a fantasy tilting towards fairy-tale. But if it is true that a mask is always a danger, that we may become what we pretend to be, it is also true that some people manage to drop their disguises when they need to, that the role does not inevitably and always absorb the actor. Both Musset and Stendhal dramatize the risks of deception, the nature of a particular threat to the self. But Stendhal goes on to suggest a possible purity.

It is a strange purity he offers us, however. It is a possible but unlikely one, a moral freak in a muddy and complex world, a condition which can only appear as a paradox, even as a perversity, to our dimmed, spoiled eyes. Julien saves himself by attempted homicide, which is redemption *by another road* indeed. The symmetry suggested by Stendhal's phrase, by the story of Oedipus or the merchant of Baghdad, is a vision of order, but it is an exceptional vision of an order which is normally invisible, a revelation which, precisely, does not come every day.

An epigram is an imitation of such a vision: clear truth, rich simplicity, an improbable neatness. It may be faintly or fully apologetic about its neatness. If faintly, it is a picture of order presented with irony, a touch of doubt. If fully, it is a use of the instruments of reason to show where reason ends—a linguistic analogue of the labyrinth. In Stendhal, curiously, the epigrams are both. He turns them into paradoxes whose moving parts reflect each other endlessly but also reflect the world and a vision of the world. He construes them as novelistic propositions which baffle logic and yet which simultaneously create a logic of their own. All Cretans are liars, said the Cretan. It is as if that famous puzzle were to become a spiral rather than a circle, and managed to tell us something after all about the inhabitants of Crete.

Epigrams suggest separation, divorce. The map of the wrong roads is drawn as a maze. But there is also the other ending to Stendhal's story: the wrong road is the right road, the young man comes home to a familiar place in the English garden near Milan. This is an irony too, although it rests on surprise rather than symmetry. It is closer to *double-entendre* than to paradox. Distance is seen as an illusion, a contradiction closes into a pun, a multiple meaning. To express this irony in his novels Stendhal uses a quibble, a form of linear equivocation which we find in Jane Austen and which becomes a positive *tic* with Henry James.

A word, a phrase, a reading of a situation is offered, and shown to be wrong. Then the same word, phrase or reading, displaced, amplified or redefined, is seen to be right after all. Catherine Morland, in *Northanger Abbey*, thinks General Tilney is a monster, guilty of all kinds of extravagant Gothic crimes. He is not. But he *is* a monstrous snob, and Catherine comes to feel that 'in suspecting General Tilney of either murdering or shutting up his wife, she had scarcely sinned against his character or magnified his cruelty'. In James' *The Ambassadors* Chad Newsome's affair with Mme de Vionnet is certainly not virtuous in the sense which the upright Strether gives to the word. But Strether arrives at a new meaning for virtue, and like Catherine, decides that his first feelings, although immensely enriched now, were correct. The affair *was* virtuous. Verbal forms of this odd trick appear in all James' late work.

In *Le Rouge et le Noir* Julien Sorel, as tutor to the children of the mayor of Verrières, is horrified to learn that his employer's men are changing the beds throughout the house. He has a portrait of Napoleon hidden in his mattress. He begs Mme de Rênal, his employer's wife, to save his reputation by rescuing this portrait for him. He asks a further favour : she is not to look at the portrait, its subject is a secret. Mme de Rênal, who has just begun to scrutinize her increasingly tender feelings for Julien, is in an agony of jealousy. She believes she is fetching the portrait of the woman Julien loves. But she brings it bravely, and she doesn't look. Julien snatches the picture from her and rushes off to burn it, reviewing his narrow escape in his mind. The portrait of Napoleon was bad enough in itself, in the house of a small-town aristocrat in edgy Restoration France. But Julien had recorded on the portrait the 'excesses' of his admiration for the fallen emperor. In his concern Julien thinks : 'and each of these *transports of love* is dated' (*Rouge* 273, my italics). Stendhal is extraordinarily casual for a good deal of his writing time, but he lays his clues very carefully if he needs to. When he comes to create the now famous phrase 'Every true passion thinks only of itself' (*Rouge* 439) he is talking about Julien's feelings for Napoleon. Mme de Rênal in her error was right. Napoleon is and will remain, almost to the end, her rival.

Stendhal's novels are full of such double meanings. Judgements are regularly seen to be both right and wrong, redefinition is a major mode. In *Lucien Leuwen* the ambitious and scheming Mme Grandet goes through the motions of love in order to get her husband a ministry. But the mechanical motions work like Pascal's prayer, and her simulated love becomes the real, the sincere thing. The passion of Mathilde de la Mole for Julien Sorel, in *Le Rouge et le Noir*, starts in a different place but, as we shall see, follows a parallel track. And Lucien Leuwen himself, confronted with an abrupt and spectacular family success, even borrows the young Stendhal's metaphor of the other road : 'By a little side path, and from which a bush blocked the view of the immense plain we now look down on, my father has brought me to the peak of fortune' (*Lucien* 1345).

The wrong roads reveal balanced designs. Sometimes they are the right roads in disguise, unperceived paths to a sudden truth. Stendhal's world, like the world of *Tom Jones* or *Finnegans Wake*, is a place of patterns—although the patterns in Stendhal spring from the logical location of the hero, his position in a paradox, and not from the plot, as in Fielding, or from the language, as in Joyce. With all three writers the patterns are primarily functional, technical—devices for holding brittle and delicate novels together. But they are also ironic, self-consciously intricate, a reminder that our minds are tidier than our lives. They are slightly wishful too, attempts at oblique, discreet, sympathetic magic by sceptical men. If errors can become enlarged truths, as with Mme de Rênal's mistake about the portrait of Napoleon, then perhaps patterns may attract patterns, and the world may yet show itself to be more ordered than we think. The maze of coincidence often looks like the work of a designing mind.

As a schoolboy, Stendhal tells us, he sought the equation for what he called the 'metaphysics of mathematics' (*Brulard* 253). 'Apply mathematics to the human heart' was a piece of his early advice to himself.[8] He likes to see events arranged in geometrical space. His autobiographical *Vie de Henry Brulard* is riddled with drawings of rooms, houses, streets, stretches of countryside, almost all seen in plan, from above, and at a distance of forty years, with astonishing precision. He indicates where he stood, where his grandfather stood, where guests stood or sat. The young man in the garden near Milan, the hypothetical fugitive or pursuer in the symmetrical melodrama, are caught in just this kind of diagram. The surveyor watches over them with a god's eye. He sees shapes where they see only gravel, hedges or December rain.

2. THEFTS

'... j'ai sur le coeur ce mot sot : deviné ...'
SOUVENIRS D'EGOTISME

Stendhal's first attempt at a novel was called simply 'Novel'—
'Roman'. The title is partly ironic, since in one sense the work is not
a novel at all. It is a masked peace-offering, an apology in fiction for
an offence committed in the world of fact. It is a letter to Mathilde
Viscontini, a continuation of the painful correspondence which
followed Stendhal's unfortunate trip to Volterra in 1819.

Mathilde had gone there and Stendhal, madly in love, went too.
He hoped to be near her, get a glimpse of her, talk to her perhaps.
His reasons were not clear. He was heavily disguised in green
glasses and an improbable overcoat, but alas, he was recognized.
Mathilde was furious, accused Stendhal of an unpardonable lack of
delicacy in trailing after her. His letters labour at his justification,
offer a stammering defence against the charge. 'Roman' is a new
tack.

The plan is simple. A young French officer loves Métilde (the
name is Stendhal's personal form of Mathilde), a suffering, melancholy beauty whose bruised and exhausted heart is no longer capable of a serious passion. Friendship is all she can offer. She is about
to grant this to the young man when he, carried away by his extreme
feelings for her, commits a series of bad blunders—'follies and im-
prudences' (*Romans* 87). As if this were not enough, he has an
enemy, Métilde's jealous friend, the duchess, who persuades the
girl to drive the young officer to despair. (Stendhal himself had, or
thought he had, a comparable enemy in the person of a female

19

cousin of Mme Viscontini's.) Finally, however, there is a reconciliation all round, even between the officer and the duchess—'I have a tender affection for you,' he says nobly, 'because you are her friend' (*Romans* 87). Métilde and the hero spend their declining years together, among joys 'unknown to common people' (*Romans* 87).

The fragment we have consists of this brief, pale plan and a first chapter. The writing in this chapter is lively and intelligent, and the opening focus is characteristically oblique. We see the jealous duchess pacing the garden of her country house, worrying about the future of her 'strange friendship' (*Romans* 91) for Bianca (Métilde's name in the first chapter). Bianca is inside, talking to Poloski (the French officer has become a young Pole). 'So I am going to lose everything that I love,' the duchess mutters to herself. 'Poloski, Poloski, how you hurt me and how I hate you!' (*Romans* 88). We then find Poloski in conversation with a friend, who offers him contradictory and ineffective discouragement: Bianca can't love him because she can't love anyone, and in any case she is falling in love with the rich Zamboni. Poloski's own fear is that the awesome duchess will ruin him—she will never forgive him for daring to love Bianca.

'Roman' was never sent to Mathilde. Stendhal wrote *De l'Amour* instead. I have described the fragment because I think it helps us to see some important features in Stendhal's later fiction. The novel begun here is potentially an attractive and delicate work—a bit bloodless and wistful, perhaps—but it is not a novel Stendhal will ever write. It is too close to his own life, of course, but that is not really the point. It is even closer to his romantic sensibility, and Stendhal always comes down hard on that sensibility whenever it shows itself without protection. 'I make every possible effort to be *dry*,' he writes in *De l'Amour*. 'I want to silence my heart, which imagines it has a lot to say. I am always afraid of having written only a sigh, when I think I have noted a truth' (*Amour* 58, Stendhal's italics). His most intimate taste is for reverie, for quietly lyrical or even painful moments—'I see that I have preferred my reveries to everything' (*Brulard* 14). 'Roman' is too close to this taste, it is not a novel but a daydream. Poloski's love is a solitary feeling, brooding, thwarted, unrequited, pure reflection. The passion of the novel, had it been written, could only have come from the jealousy of the Lesbian duchess.

There is a profound intuition at work, then, drawing Stendhal to his later violent themes: a passionate crime in *Le Rouge et le Noir*, gory adventures in the Italian Stories, cloaks, ropes and daggers in *La Chartreuse de Parme*. He has a taste for sensation and melodrama, certainly, and he has a rough sociological theory of 'energy'—he is fond of saying that energy is found only among the poor, 'in the class which has to struggle with its real needs' (*Brulard* 19). Hence Julien Sorel, bandits and Renaissance thugs. But more important than this is Stendhal's sense of a bad habit which demands its counter-balance: blood and action to give consistency to feeling and introspection. 'One can acquire everything in solitude,' he writes, 'except character' (*Amour* 266).

A similar intuition takes him from the vague and wishful outline of 'Roman' to the apparent rigour and tightness of *De l'Amour*. The rigour is only apparent, Stendhal's pretended scientific method is only a scientific metaphor, but it serves its purpose. I insisted earlier on the logical symmetry of Stendhal's plots, because his logic is entirely a structural matter, and the immediate impression his novels make is quite different. 'Where the devil are the *masses* in these games of my pen?' he writes (*Souvenirs* 1469, Stendhal's italics), and he may well ask. His great talent is for multiplication, for refinement, for the unsettling of affairs which looked as if they were settled. 'Life is simpler than that,' Zola used to growl on the subject of Stendhal.[9] 'Roman' is the perfect introduction here. Poloski is at fault, loses Bianca's love through his own rashness and indelicacy. The duchess is to blame, she destroys Poloski's chances. Poloski had no chances, because Bianca could not love him or anyone. Too many reasons, too many motives. Stendhal needs his neat geometry to sustain his incorrigibly scattered thinking, his shifting sympathies and points of view. In his major novels he finds it. In his autobiographical works it doesn't matter that he doesn't.

Stendhal had a very early sense of his twin vocation: women and literature, in that order. Yet the would-be Don Juan, to the day of his death and in spite of a fair amount of sexual and romantic success, remained mortally timid with women he cared about. The would-be Molière never finished a play.

Stendhal's talent was precocious too. At eighteen we find him in possession of many of his major insights—'I shall almost always be wrong when I think of a man's character as all of a piece' (*Journal* 419)—and well on the way to a mastery of his mature prose style. The following passage owes something to Montaigne, and possibly to later moralists, but the slipping syntax and the nervous, energetic voice are recognizably Stendhal's own :

'Let us make haste to enjoy, our moments are numbered, the hour I have spent grieving has not the less brought me closer to my death. Let us work, for work is the father of pleasure; but let us never grieve. Let us reflect sanely before taking a decision; the decision once taken, let us never change our minds. With stubbornness, one can master anything. Let us give ourselves talents; one day, I should regret the time I wasted.' (*Journal* 414)

Yet this insistent young man publishes his first novel, *Armance*, at the age of forty-four, and publishes it even then half as a scabrous joke, a contribution to the currently fashionable subject of impotence.

More surprising still, at the age of thirty-one, liberated by the fall of Napoleon from all occupations save those of writer, lover and man of leisure, Stendhal did not return to fiction, to the manuscript of a play he had dragged with him to Moscow and back, for example. His first book, published in 1815, was plagiarized from the writings of four or five more or less mediocre music critics. The *Lettres écrites de Vienne en Autriche, sur le célèbre compositeur Haydn, suivies d'une vie de Mozart, et de considérations sur Métastase et l'état présent de la musique en France et en Italie*, to give them their full title, soon to be abbreviated to *Vies de Haydn, de Mozart et de Métastase*, were a flagrant rearrangement of a group of recent works, padded out by bits of contemporary musical gossip. Stendhal himself later called the book a trickle of tepid water.

At the time, however, he was unrepentant, and went on to lift his next book, *Histoire de la Peinture en Italie*, from a further selection of relevant scholars. While writing his first clearly personal work, *Rome, Naples et Florence en 1817*, he was planning another pillage, principally from *The Edinburgh Review*, for a life of Napoleon. *Rome, Naples et Florence* itself is a traveller's diary which rarely strays far from the facts, except into the occasional stolen anecdote. The timid 'Roman', as we have seen, is scrapped in favour of a treatise on love. Between that effort and *Armance* there is plenty of critical writing and a life of Rossini, but no fiction, apart from one or two stillborn schemes for the theatre. Stendhal's approach to the novel is as devious and dilatory as his heroes' approach to happiness.

It is undoubtedly true, as Jean Prévost says,[10] that Stendhal in his youth worked too hard at becoming a writer. Too hard, and too scientifically. He read too much, made too many notes, was overly addicted to the analytical view—as if plays were bridges and you could learn how to make them by taking old bridges apart, running the film backwards.[11] But this is not the whole story. It is also true that he didn't work hard enough. Stendhal, for all his love of systems, was anything but a systematic writer. He loved the *metaphor* of the system, the image of a clean, ordered, properly explicable world. But it was only the metaphor he loved. In his failure to write the great plays he planned, not only is he on the wrong track, he is not following even that track with sufficient concentration. He could not have become a major playwright by his stiff methods. Too many ingredients were missing from the recipe. But he could have become a competent one, even by those methods. Many less talented people do. He is like Julien Sorel, who chooses an ugly road to the top—hypocrisy, clerical intrigue, the theological seminary as the backdoor to power—and doesn't get far even on that road. 'He was having no success, and in an ugly career at that' (*Rouge* 392). Julien in the end succeeds mainly by his mistakes, which is Stendhal's way of echoing his own haphazard development, stumbling into the novel via a joke (*Armance*) and a lucky inspiration, a good story in a newspaper (*Le Rouge et le Noir*).

Stendhal is too earnest, he is not earnest enough. There is another reason for his curious reluctance or inability to finish any of his plays: a flaw in the ambition itself. 'I'm tired of being unknown', he groans in 1804, when he is twenty-one (*Journal* 452), but there is no evidence that he felt this strongly, or that he had at that period or indeed at any point in his life the drive it normally takes to become a writer of any distinction. He wanted to get a reputation in acting circles as an author of comedies, but this is a familiar enough young man's fantasy, a social dream disguised as a literary project. Stendhal the successful writer would be surrounded by swooning actresses, all his for the choosing. Alternatively, or perhaps in addition, he would be rich. He was planning a trip to Philadelphia on the (unforthcoming) proceeds of the *Vies de Haydn, de Mozart et de Métastase*.

All Stendhal's early schemes have this quality of speculation and romance about them. At twenty he draws up an elaborate schedule for his writing future (*Journal* 435–436), beginning with a three-year break after knocking off a couple of plays. He will not bother with two further promising subjects because the works to be drawn

23

from them are not likely to last more than two hundred years at the most. He is going to write an art of loving, in verse, but he will have to learn about women first, he says acutely, and he will not start this opus until he is twenty-six. When he is fifty, he will write his *Poetics*, also in verse. At thirty-five, he will begin work on his three big historical books about Napoleon, the Revolution and the great men of the Revolution. What is surprising about this hopeful outline is not the faintly prophetic nature of it—Stendhal did write about Napoleon, and he did write something like an art of loving, albeit in prose—but that a young man with such fantasies should have ever become a writer at all. Those projects have all the marks of a sad future failure on them. People who plan such things at twenty are lawyers or academics by the time they are thirty.

Stendhal's plagiarisms belong here, the borrowed *Vies de Haydn, de Mozart et de Métastase*, and *Histoire de la Peinture en Italie*. Critics are embarrassed by them, and offer brave defences, running from the slack manners of the age on the subject of authorship to Stendhal's own rather more swashbuckling line : how can a person who uses a pseudonym be a plagiarist? We are told that Stendhal may not have known what he was doing because he was in the habit of taking such copious notes as he read, and that in any case, if our doubts remain, Stendhal redeems his thefts by the originality and verve of the views he slips in between them. It all seems beside the point. Stendhal didn't pretend to originality in these works, he was out to make money and conquer his own timidity and wavering motivation. His worst crime is to assume that other people share his cavalier notions on the subject of literary property.

Joseph Carpani, the author of the lifted letters on Haydn which provided the bulk of the *Vies*, protested vigorously, not so much at Stendhal's unacknowledged translation and rearrangement of his work as at his borrowing personal details, like Carpani's acquaintances and adventures in Vienna. For example, Stendhal has Carpani's influenza, miraculously cured by hearing a Haydn mass. Worse still, perhaps, Stendhal antedates all those stolen memories, so that Carpani's book, which appeared in 1812, is made to look like a copy of its own copy. Stendhal published his book under the unlikely name of Louis-Alexandre-César Bombet—an allegory of tyrants tumbling into the middle class—and Carpani managed to round up a group of Viennese friends mentioned in the book who were ready to swear they had never set eyes on any Bombet, and certainly had not given him information about Haydn. To this Stendhal replied, in the person of Bombet's younger brother, with a challenge. Let M. Carpani set thirty pages of his own alongside thirty pages of M. Bombet's and the public will judge who is the plagiarist. The joke is worthy of Sterne, has a flavour of Borges about it. Why can't M. Bombet answer for himself? He is in London —'very old, very gouty, very little bothered with music and still less with M. Carpani . . .'[12]

Plainly, borrowed works and unfinished plays are part of the same psychological pattern, expressions of a large diffidence which is also a form of pride. Stendhal will not be seen to fail, and the plagiarisms are his alibi, a means of appearing in public while escaping the public's judgement. They are haughty, gleeful jokes, oblique night attacks on the city of literature. They were meant to bring him fame and riches (they didn't) without compromising his vocation as a writer of 'works of imagination', as he later put it (*Souvenirs* 1448). They were also, in their small way, works of imagination themselves.

Plagiarisms provoke and legitimize disguises. Stendhal's borrowings from Carpani and others are good grounds for becoming Bombet, just as the political opinions expressed in *Rome, Naples et Florence en 1817* create the need for Stendhal's second and lasting mask: the name of M. de Stendhal, itself lifted from a small town in Prussia. These opinions are indeed not radical, they are the reverse. But they are so sycophantically sound that they come across as sarcasms. Metternich at least got the message, and refused to have Stendhal as French consul in Trieste because of this book. But then the pseudonym was no protection after all?

In fact, Stendhal deceives for the sake of deceiving, his life is a network of minor lies, a library of miniature fictions. Certainly the secret police of the time in both France and Italy was extremely efficient and powerful, and Stendhal was well known for his liberal and imprudent views. But what exactly does he gain by noting his age in code on the waistband of his best trousers (*Brulard* 6)? Or by telling us he did?

Bombet and Bombet's brother, like M. de Stendhal, like the philosophical characters in *De l'Amour*, like the imaginary interlocutors in *Racine et Shakespeare*, like all Stendhal's future heroes, are fresh faces for the author, fronts, disguises, extensions of his movable identity. 'Will anyone believe me?' he writes in *Souvenirs d'Egotisme.* 'I would wear a mask with pleasure, I would love to change my name. *The Arabian Nights* which I adore occupy more than a quarter of my head . . .' (*Souvenirs* 1415–1416). Towards the end of his life he drew up a curious document awarding himself various kinds of magical powers, 'privileges' as he called them, including that of becoming another person, 'provided that the creature exists' ('Privilèges' 1525). Stendhal began his career as a novelist by becoming Joseph Carpani, complete with 'flu.

Stendhal lies instinctively, then, joyfully. But he also lies timidly. In *Rome, Naples et Florence* he describes the re-opening of the reconstructed San Carlo opera house in Naples. He had seen San Carlo, but he wasn't there when it re-opened. He mentions a meeting in Venice with Byron, whom he had met, but in Milan and not in 1817. M. de Stendhal, the supposed author, is a cavalry officer. Stendhal had been a cavalry officer, briefly, but his name wasn't Stendhal. The retentions and modifications of fact are quite gratuitous, an exercise of the ordering and investing mind's power over reality. But they are trivial too, as if Stendhal were afraid of reality's revenge.

He wants to inhabit both history and fiction, both his own life and the lives of others. He wants to tell us and not tell us what happened, or how he feels. He wants us to guess: 'I'm haunted by this stupid word: *guessed*' (*Souvenirs* 1461, Stendhal's italics). If we guess we shall have passed the qualifying quiz, earned his intimacy.

The M. de Stendhal who writes *Rome, Naples et Florence* is saddened by the thought of leaving Italy and returning to his job in a ministry in Berlin. His heart contracts at the 'ugliness of the north' glimpsed at Frankfurt-am-Main on the way home (*Rome* 215). Only Stendhal himself has no job in Berlin, and is not leaving Italy. His delight at staying, characteristically, is evoked by his double's distressed departure. 'Everything tells me that the happy days of Italy are over for me . . . I must confess frankly, this is one of the most miserable moments of my life' (*Rome* 215).

There is a way then of qualifying Jean Starobinski's brilliant, if overworked piece on Stendhal's pseudonyms. The mask, the fiction, the plagiarism, are not primarily flights from the self, means of becoming someone else. Stendhal never disappeared into his own imaginings in the way Balzac is said to have immersed himself in the world of his novels. It is not, as Starobinski seems to suggest, that Stendhal wants to shed or master his personality but can't.[13]

What he wants is a double personality, his own and another, with perfect lucidity in both incarnations. That is his dream from *The Arabian Nights*. When the prince disguises himself as a beggar, he is both beggar and prince, he is the prince's mind in the beggar's life. This is precisely the pleasure conjured up by Stendhal's magical licenses. He wants to know foreign languages ('Privilèges' 1525), to inhabit the body of an animal, to live two lives at once ('Privilèges' 1526), to guess people's thoughts at short range ('Privilèges' 1529), to see what they are doing at a distance ('Privilèges' 1530). He wants to do these things *really*.

With Balzac or Dickens we have a strong sense of fiction as creation, as exuberance, of the intoxication of the demi-urge making his world. Stendhal has no 'world' in this sense. His world is the world beyond his books, the historical world of newspapers and law-reports and the common conversation of contemporaries. He is not a demi-urge, he is the mind's secret agent, sowing modest, unextravagant lies in the territory of truth, slipping fictions into the realm of fact.

In one sense, of course, he does have a world. All novelists do. His fiction is a particular moral universe inhabited by certain kinds of heroes and heroines and villains, a place of specific values, habits, structures, where his characters can be themselves and not someone else. It is possible to explore and describe his domain, and the present book, I hope, is doing just that.

But the first characteristic of the domain is its incompleteness, its abrupt boundaries, its dependence on history and on echoes in the memories and sympathies of readers. 'Vanina Vanini', a story published a year before *Le Rouge et le Noir*, opens at an elegant ball in Rome. After a page or so of description, Prince Don Asdrubale, the heroine's father, is seen crossing the room towards her— 'Prince Don Asdrubale approached his daughter' ('Vanina' 749). There is a quick and witty sketch of the prince—if you met him in the street you would think he was an old actor. He is worried about Vanina, who doesn't want to get married. She despises the inhabitants of Rome.

The next paragraph begins, 'The day after the ball . . .' Why did the prince cross the room towards Vanina? Did he reach her? What did he say? What happened to that conversation? Stendhal's fiction is full of such missing pieces. His novels are, as he says, mirrors carried along a road (*Rouge* 557), but the mirrors tilt, jump and go dark with alarming frequency. If we want to know more about the foreign king's visit to Verrières, which creates such a stir in *Le Rouge et le Noir*, we can, Stendhal suggests, read the local newspapers (*Rouge* 317). Stendhal's 1830, as we shall see, is a pointed anachronism, a historic year in which nothing historic happens. But the point depends on our sense of what did happen in the France beyond the novel.

History waits at the edges of Stendhal's work, which thereby becomes a form of history itself—a running commentary on the experience of an age. His novels also re-create their age, of course. They are complete in themselves, like all effective works of art. They have intimate and erratic connections with contemporary historical realities, but I am not suggesting that you have to be a historian to read them. I am suggesting, though, that we *guess* ('I'm haunted by this stupid word') at the history in Stendhal. It is not given to us as a picture, or a realized background. It exists as a set of assumptions, not as a panorama, not as a 'world'.

But when Stendhal skips the prince's conversation with his daughter, he is not only pointing beyond his book, referring us to another dimension, to other sources if available, to darkness and mystery if not. He is also reminding us that we are in his hands, hinting at just how arbitrary or how careless he can be. The conversation is his to tell or not to tell. Simultaneously, of course, the incompleteness of the narrative is itself a metaphor. Stendhal sees life that way—as a broken, unequal landscape full of craters and sudden limits to the view.

The shifting perspectives of *Le Rouge et le Noir* create a similar effect. The novel begins in the third person, with a light, neutral description of a small town : 'The little town of Verrières is probably one of the prettiest in Franche-Comté. Its white houses with their pointed red-tile roofs . . .' (*Rouge* 219). There is a deafening nail factory at the entrance to the town, though (*Rouge* 219). We are now lent the eyes and ears of a traveller who is in these parts for the first time (*Rouge* 220). He is from Paris (*Rouge* 220), and he is a distinctly delicate soul, shocked by the air of self-satisfaction of the mayor, seen crossing the street, and stifled by the scent of money and greed in the atmosphere (*Rouge* 220). He has been in the town only a matter of moments. At this point Stendhal suggests that *we* are the traveller—he refers to a sawmill which struck *us* as we entered Verrières ('that sawmill of which the odd location . . . struck you . . .') (*Rouge* 221).

This is a favourite trick with Fielding and Sterne, who like to turn their public, or parts of their public, into characters within the book they are holding in their hands. Early on in *Tristram Shandy* Sterne sends a lady-reader back to look over a chapter again, and continues to talk confidentially to those who are still with him—*about* the lady who is to be imagined several pages away, doing her homework.

After a paragraph she comes back. 'But here comes my fair Lady. Have you read over again the chapter, madam, as I desired you? You have . . .' Plainly, this diligent and docile reader, like Stendhal's sensitive traveller, who is so touchy about money and mayors, is fully as fictional as any of the major characters in the novel.

Stendhal now switches to the first person and becomes a nostalgic narrator who has often been to Verrières—often leaned on the wall of the public promenade and thought of Paris balls left the night before (*Rouge* 223). He lets us know his political opinions (liberal) and explicitly announces his intention of telling us a story—'But although I want to talk to you about the provinces for two hundred pages . . .' (*Rouge* 225). The arriving traveller-reader is thus revealed as a rhetorical front for a narrator who chose to hide himself for a chapter. Even Stendhal's masks have masks of their own.

The narrator continues to appear and disappear throughout the book. For a good part of the time, he simply vanishes into the consciousness of his major characters, and tells us what they think and feel, usually without comment. But he comments too, when he feels like it. 'I must confess that the weakness shown by Julien in this monologue gives me a poor opinion of him' (*Rouge* 348). 'We are sorry to confess, for we like Mathilde, that . . .' (*Rouge* 510). At one stage he casually introduces a conversation he has had with his editor on the subject of politics in the novel. The narrator wanted a page of discreet dots, leaving the rest to the reader's imagination. The editor insisted on detailed political chatter (*Rouge* 575–576). Presumably this 'real' conversation, which breaks into fiction, is fictional too.

I think there is probably an authentic carelessness on the part of Stendhal here—as in the case of the missing conversation in 'Vanina Vanini'. He simply doesn't worry much about narrative point of view. No matter. The result is what counts, and the result is to create a narrator who is less obtrusive than those of Fielding, Sterne and Thackeray and yet less business-like, less professional than those of Balzac or Scott. He is not a character in the book, and he is not a hardened story-teller settling into an old habit. He

29

is a man who knows a particular tale, and who has chosen to put it down on paper just this once, to tell it in his own conversational manner. I am talking, needless to say, about the stance of Stendhal's narrator, not about Stendhal, who wrote novels like everyone else, only faster.

The tone of *Lucien Leuwen* is much closer to that of a conventional narrative, and there are elements of professional story-telling in *La Chartreuse de Parme*, especially near the beginning. Stendhal repeatedly refers to Fabrice as 'our hero', and later asks Balzac's advice on this subject. But *La Chartreuse* quickly returns to the manner of *Le Rouge et le Noir* : the swift, negligent, mobile style of a man publishing a story for his few and subtle friends, and having accesses of occasional panic and caution as he remembers that his book will be for sale, and that even his enemies, especially his enemies, may easily find the money to buy it.

3. *DE L'AMOUR* (1822)

'Mais, me dira quelque Duclos, vous
voyez de l'amour partout?'
HISTOIRE DE LA PEINTURE EN ITALIE

De l'Amour was a sad flop when first published—a sacred text, no doubt, Stendhal's editor mournfully thought, because no one would touch it. Posterity has handsomely caught up, and if anything, *De l'Amour* has come to be rated rather too highly. For a reader arriving fresh from the novels it seems hard, scattered, ill at ease with itself; its voice is less confidently Stendhal's own than that of *Racine et Shakespeare*, say, published a year later.

Partly, of course, *De l'Amour* has simply been swept up into Stendhal's general fame, but modern attention to the book goes further than that. There is the title, perhaps. Does it offer something slightly scabrous, a spot of nicely-mannered pornography from a great writer. In fact, as Victor Brombert has pointed out,[14] *De l'Amour* couldn't be more decorous. It has a risky short chapter on fiascos, to be sure, which Stendhal himself regarded as indecent and thought of making optional in some copies, and in the end decided not to publish. But only the subject was risky, and was risky only at that time, in the prickly Restoration. The treatment is impeccably delicate, makes its way from Mme de Sévigné to Montaigne with great care. More than this, Stendhal's whole vision of love is the reverse of pornography, if by pornography we mean a certain intense brooding on the flesh. Love for Stendhal, as for Proust, is nine-tenths imagination, a leap into the feverish secrecy of the mind with a name and a pretty face as a pretext.

31

No, the chief charm of *De l'Amour* lies elsewhere, in its invitation to step behind the scenes, to see the other, tender Stendhal, the quivering heart beneath the mocking, urbane façade. Stendhal himself starts this rush backstage, describes his tears as he corrects the proofs of this book scribbled in pencil in Milan in the days of his distressed love for Mme Viscontini (*Souvenirs* 1428). He can't revise the text because the wound it represents is too fresh, has hardly begun to heal (*Souvenirs* 1473). Surrounding *De l'Amour* itself are restrained but feeling-filled comments. When Mme Viscontini dies in May 1825 Stendhal writes dryly on his copy, in English : 'Death of the author (*Amour* 405). On a draft for a new preface he lets himself go in Italian : 'Ah! rimembranza!' (*Amour* 407). Moving moments, and there was a time when Stendhal's reputation was such that we needed to be firmly reminded of them, when the cynical supporter of delinquents like Julien Sorel had to be shown to have a heart. But that time has gone. In an age which demands less fulsome professions of sentiment, indeed which is suspicious of fulsome professions, Stendhal's *sotto voce* feelings speak loudly enough even in his least personal writing, and there is something slightly archaic about defences of *De l'Amour* as a document. We see Stendhal there 'body and soul', Martineau said in 1959 (*Amour* 11, Martineau's introduction); we have here, in Del Litto's even more recent words, 'the key to Stendhal's true personality'.[15] Well, we don't. Stendhal is much more himself in his novels. And in any case talk of a key or a portrait takes us away from *De l'Amour* as a book, from whatever was missed by those people in 1822 who decided to spend their money on something else.

I have already quoted the shortest chapter of *De l'Amour* :

'I make every possible effort to be *dry*. I want to silence my heart which imagines it has a lot to say. I am always afraid of having written only a sigh, when I think I have noted a truth' (*Amour* 58, Stendhal's italics).

The lines are characteristic, and for a moment, touching. Suppressed emotion is seen to beleaguer the severe, unbending writer. But then one begins to wonder about the unbending, about the 'every possible effort'. Why? What are the benefits of dryness, finally? Why not listen to the heart? The question is not a psychological one, although doubtless an urgent habit and preoccupation are expressed above. It is a question of method, a question of tone and approach and tools and emphasis, of what kind of writer Stendhal is to be. The answer is : not this kind. In *De l'Amour* all Stendhal's early intellectual baggage hangs heavily on him, the book is a false start, a move in a direction which was not to be his. More interestingly, it illustrates, awkwardly, painfully, the least resolved aspects of his literary ambition, his double desire to be both Lamartine and an eighteenth-century ideologue.

De l'Amour is not a novel, Stendhal tells us (*Amour* 25, 47), hence can't evoke love; we have to know what love is to start with :

'Imagine a fairly complicated geometrical figure drawn in chalk on a large blackboard : well, I am going to explain this geometrical figure, but if I am to do this, it must *be already* on the blackboard; I can't draw it myself' (*Amour* 25).

Later (*Amour* 275, 278) he even casts doubts on the capacity of novels to draw what he is talking about. All the more reason then for stern, cold language, for 'exact and scientific description' (*Amour* 21). *De l'Amour* is a monograph on a certain sickness (*Amour* 27, 35), an attempt to speak mathematically about a passion (*Amour* 25). It is a discourse on feeling as the work of the ideologues was a discourse on ideas (*Amour* 47–48). Now clearly Stendhal is not quite serious about all this, his tongue is at least moving towards his cheek. But he is not humorous about it either, his respect for science and mathematics, for the work of philosophers like Tracy and Cabanis and Helvétius will not let him find his unlikely enterprise as funny as he knows it is. He is half-serious, in other words, always a bad thing. His book is a journey, he says in a looser, less strangling metaphor, into 'little known regions of the human heart' (*Amour* 22). A journey, though, with stethoscope and taxonomy in hand. Stendhal distinguishes four loves : passion, taste (by which he means the decorous, pink, pastoral love of high society and well-bred novels), physical pleasure and provoked vanity. At one point he sets out an ambitious plan for the study of love in terms of six temperaments (sanguine, bilious, melancholy, phlegmatic, nervous, athletic) and six possible political conditions (eastern despotism, absolute monarchy, veiled oligarchy, federal republic, constitutional monarchy, revolution). The thing to do would be to put the four loves through the six temperaments and then put the results through the political options (*Amour* 159–160).

Mercifully, he does none of this. In effect, *De l'Amour* is a notebook, a collection of thoughts, memories, anecdotes, epigrams, patches of analysis. It is almost always delicate, often brilliant, a book to keep quoting from. Stendhal is a keen feminist, has interesting things to say about women's education. 'I admit that girls are not physically as strong as boys : that is conclusive evidence for the quality of their minds, because we know that Voltaire and d'Alembert were the leading men in their century when it came to throwing a punch' (*Amour* 223). He strikes out at marriage as 'legal prostitution' (*Amour* 79): 'It is much more immodest to go to bed with a man one has seen only twice, after three words in Latin said in a church, than to yield in spite of oneself to a man one has adored for two years' (*Amour* 80).

He begins the book in an attempt to exorcise the spectre of Mathilde Viscontini, he has his 'day of genius' at the end of 1819 (*Amour* 15, quoted in Martineau's introduction), thinks of his plan for converting a moping passion into the materials of study; but then he adds to his work in all directions, continues the theme of love into Arab poetry and the courtly lyric of Provence and goes on accumulating ideas, quotations, stories about almost everything. 'One of my regrets is not to have seen Venice in 1760 . . .' (*Amour* 298), 'In Europe desire is inflamed by constraint, in America it is deadened by liberty' (*Amour* 282), 'Prudishness is a form of avarice, the worst form of all' (*Amour* 267).

In spite of his firmly announced scientific programme, Stendhal's book is an erratic miscellany, and although he has sentimental reasons for not reworking it, he has moral and artistic reasons too. He knows that truth is often fragmentary, that *De l'Amour*, as he later saw for *Souvenirs d'Egotisme* (*Souvenirs* 1428), may ultimately say more for being less composed, less like a rounded, well-made essay, for being drastically unfaithful to its stiff intentions. Stendhal at his best always wrote this way : the unity of *Le Rouge et le Noir* and *La Chartreuse de Parme* is not the reflection of a careful plan, of a balanced arrangement of plot, character or image, it is the result of a firm intuitive grasp on the novel's most intimate subject, of a placing of the self at the centre of the web; everything, down to the smallest detail, follows from there. But we can't defend *De l'Amour* along these lines because the web has no centre, its threads hang loose. The fragments are not fragments *of* anything.

A distraught paragraph gives the game away.

'I have just reread a hundred pages of this essay; I have given a very poor idea of real love, of the love which takes over the whole soul, filling it with images which are at times of the happiest and at other times hopeless, but always sublime, and leaving it insensitive to everything else which exists. I don't know how to express what I see so well; I have never felt the lack of talent more painfully' (*Amour* 111).

So he does want to evoke love, to draw the figure on the blackboard, and not merely name it, explain it, anatomize it. What has happened to the 'scientific austerity of language' (*Amour* 21), to all the plans for a dry monograph? Were they bluff, an evasion, an early apology for not trying to do what he knows he should be doing? A refusal to write a novel because a novel is precisely what he wants to write, and is afraid of mishandling? Too much hindsight in such a view, perhaps.

In any case, whatever unity *De l'Amour* possesses comes to it from its movements towards fiction. The book is nominally not by Stendhal, it is offered to the public by an anonymous editor and translator who mentions the author, an Italian called Lisio Visconti. The young man has just died, in June 1819 at Volterra, leaving behind him a mass of notes on scraps of paper and the backs of playing cards. 'The oldest notes are dated Berlin 1807, and the most recent were written a few days before his death . . .' (*Amour* 161). We recognize the sad scenario of 'Roman', the echo of Mathilde's name, and the place where, in retrospect, Stendhal saw his hopes as having died. There are other incarnations of Stendhal in the book, notably Salviati and Delfante, who are lent several of Stendhal's difficulties with Mathilde. There is even an extract from Salviati's diary, which he wrote on his copy of Petrarch. Mathilde herself appears as Léonore. But Visconti, the supposed author, invites our especial attention. He has read much the same books as Stendhal (*Amour* 331),[16] and although his editor lists no ideologues among his sources, their influence is palpable in the text, so we are entitled to see *De l'Amour* as a shy, half-started novel about a man failing to write a treatise.

Here as in *Rome, Naples et Florence* Stendhal is flirting with fiction—as if fiction were simply lying, altering truth, inventing false names. Later he was to learn that there is more to it than that, although his novels retain the marks of his sly beginnings, are in many ways qualified by the road Stendhal took to them. But for now he is only flirting, indeed his attempt at a cold essay is as much a flight from a fully realized novel as it is from the memory of

Mathilde. A novel on this subject would have to quicken it again, reopen the wound, it would not serve in any way as an unguent. The essay on the other hand may help.

Perhaps it did. But an evasion will not sustain a book, can only leave a hollowness, the empty, broken web. It is not an accident that Stendhal's most forceful and moving evocation of what he felt for Mathilde should come in *Lucien Leuwen*, when he had learned that fiction was more than lies, and had just finished facing up directly, in *Souvenirs d'Egotisme*, to his despair over her. Of course, it was later too.

Stendhal/Visconti, when he is not making airy promises about the scope and nature of his book, shows an engaging modesty, a willingness not to ride his ideas too hard, or even not to ride them at all, if the intellectual weather looks bad. Having identified four kinds of love, he admits calmly that there might just as well be eight or ten kinds (*Amour* 41), and then goes on, without batting an eyelid, to list seven stages of infatuation. He has a theory of climates, whereby love is a fruit of the south, a version of orange-blossom, not seen much in Paris, but recognizes that more women kill themselves for love in Paris than in all the towns in Italy put together. This fact bothers him, and he hasn't an answer for the moment, but he doesn't change his opinion (*Amour* 164). He adduces an even more extreme case, Burns and Mary Campbell. He hasn't the space to tell the sad story, he says. 'I shall only remark that Edinburgh is at the same latitude as Moscow, which might upset my system of climates a little' (*Amour* 323). He makes another, handsome, moving confession of incompetence : '. . . a man can say almost nothing that will be sensible about what goes on in the heart of a tender woman' (*Amour* 56).

Leaving the achievements of the book aside, then, even its intentions begin to look thinner than they did. Stendhal is not writing about feelings in the way the ideologues wrote about ideas, he is writing about *a* feeling; and essentially about a man's experience of that feeling. In fact the whole work breathes a sense of limitations, for these and other reasons. Love is rare, for a start. Rare in France, Stendhal likes to suggest (*Amour* 21), but in fact, rare anywhere, as all passions are (*Amour* 171, 191, 202). And then more than this, Stendhal's conception of the passion is itself a rare one. In spite of his frequent protestations, love for him is neither profound emotion nor light pastime, he is neither Romeo nor Lothario, neither

Werther nor Don Juan. His love is above all agitation, a commotion of the substance, as Claudel, another egoist, later put it.

The lover Stendhal portrays for us in *De l'Amour* is a kind of hurt buffoon, strange contemporary for so many dignified romantic melancholics. He is a man locked into his imagination, able only to stumble when he comes out into the world. The key-term in Stendhal's analysis is *crystallization*—the image has become almost synonymous with his book—'a certain fever of the imagination' (*Amour* 69) which works on a given object in the same way that salt crystallizes around the bare branch of a tree, turning its poverty into a set of infinite jewels (*Amour* 43). This is what we do to people we love. Indeed the imagination *is* love for Stendhal, love is the imagination crowding out reality, converting whatever happens into a part of its own predisposed story. 'The smallest things suffice, for everything is a *sign* in love . . .' (*Amour* 158, Stendhal's italics). This is to say that there is nothing which is *not* a sign, there are no probabilities any more, nothing is left to chance (*Amour* 63). Worse, there are ultimately no limits to what the imagination can do, whatever it thinks up has the power to wound or move us as if it were a full, concrete reality : *'an imagined thing is an existing thing'* (*Amour* 129, Stendhal's italics). Madness, then, paranoia.

No, because beyond these fevers the loved person pursues an independent life in the material world, has to be seen, met, talked to. And here the lover is a clown, can offer only banalities, or clumsy, pathetic exaggerations of his true feelings. 'Love hides in its excess' (*Amour* 89). This is so true that a man may take his embarrassment with a woman as an index of his interest in her (*Amour* 252). One has courage with a woman one loves only when one loves her less (*Amour* 86, 278).

It is all very extreme and doesn't sound sublime, doesn't sound like the elevating passion it is made out to be. And it isn't. Stendhal, for all the romantic dash of a lot of his pronouncements, is never mystical, metaphysical or even particularly soulful about love. When he says heart he usually means nerves. What are the joys of the love he offers us? '. . . a man who trembles isn't bored' (*Amour* 260). 'Only the imagination escapes for ever from satiety' (*Amour* 256). 'Each step of the imagination is rewarded by a moment of delight' (*Amour* 132–133). These are thoughts for a man mortally afraid of stillness, a man for whom boredom is not a pose and not a passing mood but a familiar, threatening monster wearing the faces of death and old age. Love is the talisman, a hope of youth, a promise of eternal upset, and Stendhal paraded it bravely to the end of his life, even when he saw it fading—the odd, tender story of that is elliptically told in 'Earline'. *De l'Amour* is a small, self-absorbed book, a mirror, its view of love scanty and mean. But it worked for Stendhal. It brought him closer to his novels, helped to throw off some cherished masters, who are here seen to fail him. And it kept the monster from breaking in during a bad spell. Later his fiction, his clear view of his writing vocation, would kill it altogether.

4. THE NEW MOVEMENT

*'Je n'hésite pas à avancer que
Racine a été romantique . . .'*
RACINE ET SHAKESPEARE

Stendhal's books and conversations are full of beast-fables designed to illustrate the limits of comprehension. You're a cat and I'm a rat, he would say abruptly, when an argument tired him. A man trying to explain Italy to northerners, he says, is like a tiger trying to explain to a stag how much he likes drinking blood. 'It is part of that internal doctrine which one must never divulge' (*Rome* 65). Again, on the subject of differences of taste in the arts, he offers a dialogue between a mole and a nightingale: the one doesn't understand how the other can live in the wind and the dazzling light, the other hates the thought of darkness.[17] Both are wrong, Stendhal adds. In a later comparison between the English and the French (*Romans* 96–97), he obligingly turns the invidious nightingale into a sparrow, thereby levelling things out a bit—but not much. The mole, needless to say, is English.

This view is at least as much a fruit of Stendhal's reading as of his experience—and is perhaps even more a fruit of his dedication to eighteenth-century psychology, 'the science of the movements of the soul', as he calls it.[18] We are a race of separate psyches, ticking at different speeds, and Stendhal's question is always: What happens in your head (*Racine* 36)? 'Your feelings,' he writes, 'are not a material thing which I can extract from your heart and lay before your eyes to refute you' (*Racine* 42). Or as he says elsewhere: I can't prove that you have a cramp.[19]

39

Stendhal's aesthetic is always running into this kind of philosophical dead end : art is emotion, and if I say you should feel this and you say you don't, we can go no further. 'I have arrived at the last limits of what logic can apprehend in poetry' (*Racine* 43). 'How can I speak of music without giving the history of my feelings? People will deny that I had them. I think my adversaries will often be in good faith : so much the worse for them' (*Rome* 117).

He is frequently aggressive about possible disagreements of this kind. After a long psychological description of Leonardo's 'Last Supper', he suggests that most people will probably not see the painting as he does, and if they don't, will they please close his book —they can admire the way Da Vinci renders the folds in his tablecloth.[20] On the other hand, he is aware that his brand of irritated relativism can become a principle of tolerance. We are the prisoners of our habits, of individual differences. 'I see a fund of literary tolerance in this phrase' (*Racine* 115). His polemical Romanticism is able to respect a sincere classicism (*Racine* 117). People and pigeons see the Tuileries from different angles (*Armance* 25).

Stendhal's tolerance, however, is patchy, often marred by a determined desire to be offensive, just as his aggressions are usually diluted by sudden slips into sympathy. He is a man of endlessly moving viewpoints. Indeed, this kind of alternation between blows and caresses is a major characteristic of his style, and a further reason for his failure to write the comedies he wanted to write. He can't simplify enough, or rather he can't sustain his simplifications, can't resist refinements—abruptly showing us the world from his target's point of view, for example. There is a very funny scene in *Le Rouge et le Noir*, where M. de Rênal receives an anonymous letter accusing his wife of infidelity to him. He falls into a paroxysm of jealousy, fear, embarrassment, indecision, all beautifully but broadly rendered, and finally, leaning back into an old habit, reaches a solution : he'll consult his wife. Then he remembers that his wife is the one person he can't consult. A few paragraphs further on, Stendhal is telling us that M. de Rênal is a man 'really to be pitied' (*Rouge* 333), and broad comedy will simply not support this kind of uncertain perspective. Stendhal quickly tries to re-establish M. de Rênal's nastiness, but it's too late. He has become human, resistant to rough laughter, like a modern portrayal of Shylock, or the Jew of Malta. He is one of the rare figures in Stendhal who realizes just how alone he is.

Stendhal accepts fully the romantic notion of isolation, responds to it with a conscious intensity which is quite alien to anyone writing before Sterne. All his heroes and heroines are radically lonely even if they don't often know how lonely they are. But he presents the idea with an old-fashioned rational toughness which his contemporaries found very disconcerting.[21] They thought he was being immoral because he tried to remain reasonable. Balzac saw in *Le Rouge et le Noir* the 'conception of a cold and sinister philosophy', and his anger moved him to a brilliantly acute remark. Reading the novel, he said, he thought he heard 'the laughter of a demon, delighted to discover that men are separated from each other by abysses of personality where all benefits are lost'.[22] Just so. The sense of loneliness which frightened and attracted and redeemed the romantic artist is presented by Stendhal as just one of those logical things, a premise not a predicament. Worse still, perhaps, it is presented as a source of comedy. His novels are full of a sour and delicate joy at the symmetrical combinations of our solitary errors.

Stendhal held rather mean and mechanical views on comedy, but his best scenes go against everything ever written on the subject, from Hobbes to Bergson, and including Stendhal himself. Julien Sorel, returning to see the woman who loves him, weeps when she tries to throw him out of her bedroom, but gradually his habit of calculation takes over, and he schemes his way into the lady's bed. 'Thus,' Stendhal comments, 'after three hours of dialogue, Julien obtained what he had so passionately desired during the first two' (*Rouge* 426). This is hard comedy, certainly, especially when one thinks of what the meeting means to both protagonists, but comedy is what it is. Castex has pointed out that M. de Rênal, reappearing as the suspicious husband and rattling at the door of his wife's bedroom literally echoes a line from the *Marriage of Figaro* : Why have you locked yourself in? Julien slithers under a sofa, just as Cherubino makes for a dressing-room.[23] There is a similarly mixed moment in *Tom Jones* when Sophia leaves the inn at Upton, having witnessed, or near enough, Tom's casual infidelity. She insists that she is glad to know the truth about Tom at last, that 'she never was more easy than at present', then she bursts into a 'violent flood of tears'. None of the theories of comedy with which I am familiar comes at all close to accounting for the charm of this scene, and most of them are exploded by it—for they tell us that we cannot simultaneously laugh and feel sympathy. 'The only limits to laughter,' Stendhal himself writes: 'compassion and indignation'.[24] Yet we

41

feel a good deal of compassion for Sophia, and an odd blend of compassion and indignation at Julien's performance; and we still think they are funny. Their loneliness, like M. de Rênal's, remains perfectly real.

Stendhal's sudden sympathy for M. de Rênal in his comic jealousy is a mistake only if we are thinking of crude and grotesque humour —of the kind Stendhal had in mind for his plays, unfortunately, of the kind he thought he saw in Molière. Otherwise it is a typical achievement of Stendhal in the novel, and a moment which looks forward to Joyce's *Ulysses*, where mockery and pathos become quite indistinguishable : lonely Bloom in the lavatory planning his writing career.

'In music, as in many other things, alas,' Stendhal said, 'I am a man of another century'.[25] He loved Mozart and Cimarosa, hated the new music of Weber and Beethoven—'German din', as he called it.[26] He prefers voices to orchestras, operas to symphonies, he accuses Haydn of having replaced melody by harmony. He gets these ideas, as Guichard reminds us,[27] from the unfortunate Joseph Carpani, already mentioned, but he makes them his own. There is a difficulty here, of which Stendhal is well aware. How can he, the campaigner for novelty and contemporaneity in the arts, prefer the old music? Well, he says, shuffling, there really was no battle between classic and romantic in music, there couldn't be. All music is romantic. As we shall see, he resorts regularly to arguments of this kind when in trouble. What he means is that while his tastes in music are perfectly classical, his responses are thoroughly romantic.

Music is sentiment for Stendhal : what you feel when you hear music. 'The degree of delight to which our soul is transported is the only thermometer of beauty in music' (*Rome* 27).

The juxtaposition of *soul* and *thermometer* alone says volumes about Stendhal's place in the intellectual history of the last two hundred years. He wants to *feel* like Shelley and to *measure* like D'Alembert. But music is *about* sentiments too. 'We have long been agreed that music cannot depict the mind . . . Music can depict only passions, and only tender passions' (*Rome* 47). Music softens the hearts of tyrants,[28] it is the art which, without offending our dignity, makes us believe in human pity (*Rome* 47). In all this, clearly, Stendhal was very much a man of the early nineteenth century.

But in many other things, as he says, he wasn't. In his rational, common-sense approach to loneliness, as I have suggested. And in the wider fidelity to a set of ideals which is implied by that approach. The years after 1815 were years of a huge revolt against reason. Catholicism became attractive again, not in spite of its conflicts with philosophy and science, but because of them. The more irrational the better. We are accustomed to seeing Mary Shelley's *Frankenstein* (1816) as a prophetic parable about the atom bomb. But its first application remains the most potent. Whether Mary Shelley knew what she was doing or not, her monster was the French Revolution, and Frankenstein was the mad thinker who had let it loose. Reason had conjured up a mob, and the mob had destroyed reason. There was a need then, for a stronger principle of authority, something beyond doubt, beyond argument, beyond talk of constitutions and contracts: church and king. Only in this way can we make any sense of the fury for legitimacy which seized Europe after the Napoleonic Wars, and put the disliked Bourbon family back again on three thrones: Louis XVIII in France, his cousin Ferdinand VII in Spain, and *his* uncle Ferdinand I in Naples and Sicily. It was a magical gesture, a means of denying the Revolution and erasing the memory of Napoleon—an upstart whose concrete achievements paled before the mystery of the royal blood, of the linear and unbroken transmission of kingship. It should be noted, though, that the Bourbons did not return easily to France—a good underground movement, and the town of Bordeaux's declaring for the king swayed the still hesitating allies, who were toying with the idea of putting Napoleon back in the seat they had just driven him from.[29]

In any case, Stendhal would have none of this. He was as romantic as anyone in his insistence on feeling, on the moral primacy of intense personal experience. But he shows no inclination to throw reason overboard. The Catholic Church remains for him the corrupt old conspiracy which the Enlightenment philosophers saw in it. He describes the Bible as a collection of poems and songs (*Amour* 197), and in *Lucien Leuwen* refers obliquely to Christ as a man 'picked up by the police for his political opinions' (*Lucien* 1349). A jaunty, unrepentant atheism, mixed with a good deal of superstition and a fascination for the refined machinations of priests, was his only religion. He was an eighteenth-century man. He was sceptical, logical, scientific. But he had a nineteenth-century heart, which was none of those things.

Romanticism for Stendhal is above all contemporaneity, a body of works which belong to their own period, which are 'adapted to the needs of the age' (*Racine* 172, 174). He had reservations about music and sculpture—he thought sculpture couldn't be romantic, while music had to be—but he was very clear about painting and literature. Winckelmann's conception of a classical form of beauty, ideal, universal, valid at all times, was anathema to Stendhal, and the more personal parts of his *Histoire de la peinture en Italie* are a running refutation of that famous notion—although, as Martineau points out, Stendhal maliciously pretends never to have heard of it. Following Dubos, whose *Réflexions critiques sur la poésie et la peinture* he received as a school prize in Grenoble, he insists on a view of art as conditioned by climate and culture. Beauty is the 'unexpected fruit of a whole civilization', it is the 'expression of the useful',[30] and since the Greeks were another civilization and had their own notions of utility, they cannot serve as our models. 'We must copy no one', Stendhal wrote later on the same subject.[31] All great artists are romantic in their own time. They become classical when we begin to imitate them. So that the opposition of Racine to Shakespeare—the eternal Punch and Judy of Stendhal's literary demonstrations, as Hemmings neatly puts it[32]—is something of a false front. Racine was a romantic too, and it is hard to see how imitating Shakespeare is to be recommended if imitation is necessarily sterile. Stendhal realizes that he has put himself in a spot, and tries some fancy footwork : 'The romantics are not advising anyone to imitate Shakespeare's plays directly . . . By chance, the new French tragedy will be very similar to that of Shakespeare. But this will be solely because our circumstances are the same as those of England in 1590 . . .' (*Racine* 69–70). To no avail. Stendhal's footwork is bad history, and worse literary theory. No. Stendhal's merit was to insist on the need to break with a bloodless and stifling tradition, and he was way ahead of Hugo and Vigny in this. His definitions still have a fine ring :

> '*Romanticism* is the art of offering to the people those literary works which in the present state of their habits and beliefs are likely to give them the greatest pleasure possible.
> *Classicism*, on the other hand, offers them the literature which gave the most pleasure to their great-grandfathers.' (*Racine* 62)

He anticipates both Baudelaire, writing some twenty years later— 'For me, romanticism is the most recent, the most contemporary expression of the beautiful'[33]—and Delacroix, who carried the idea of actuality as far as wanting to paint a man falling as he fell. He was sounder than many of his romantic followers, though, and wanted to connect art with history, not with fashion or the newsreel. 'Romanticism in all the arts is the representation of men of today, and not those of some heroic age which seems so far from us, and which probably never existed . . .'[34]

There is a political colouring to all this. In 1821, Stendhal returned to Paris from Italy, where romanticism meant liberal or radical views. It meant Byron, who called the Congress of Vienna a 'base pageant', and said, 'I have simplified my politics to a detestation of all existing governments'. It meant Alfieri, Foscolo, Monti, Pellico, a dispersed and oppressed country making its first faint movements towards a national consciousness. In Paris, romanticism meant something else, another nationalism. Chateaubriand, Hugo, Lamartine and Vigny, were all hovering close to the extreme right in 1821, and romanticism was a reactionary theme, an excuse for reaching back to the glories of France, to a world which had not been spoilt by revolution. Even Stendhal, in *Racine et Shakespeare*, makes concessions to this sentiment when he proposes topics like Joan of Arc and the English, or the death of the Duke of Guise, as a suitable matter for the new drama. Within four or five years, of course, Chateaubriand himself would have moved towards the left, within ten years Hugo would be saying that romanticism in literature meant liberalism in politics, and the paradox of defending the régime while attacking the academy would have vanished.

In 1822, however, when an English troupe presented a 'romantic' *Othello* in English at the Porte Saint-Martin theatre, things had not gone quite so far. The play was hissed off the stage, the actors were greeted with cries of 'Speak French', pelted with eggs and apples, and the show didn't get beyond a second performance. The liberal papers supported this anti-romantic display, while the right-wing press on the whole came to Shakespeare's defence. The royalists were the romantics.

Naturally, these responses have very little to do with Shakespeare's dramatic manner, or with the style of the visiting production, and everything to do with Shakespeare's language and nationality. England for the royalists was the country which, more than any of its allies, was responsible for the downfall of Napoleon. It had sheltered their king and a large part of their aristocracy during the emigration. For the rest of the French, whatever their feelings about

Napoleon, England was a recent, and violently hated enemy. The liberals, whose political dream was a place more or less like contemporary Britain, found themselves opposed to the owners of their dream, while the royalists, for whom the idea of a constitution along English lines was a recurring apocalyptic horror, found themselves supporting old friends.

At this point Stendhal picks up his pen to put his countrymen straight. It was not simply a question of demonstrating to the liberals that they ought to be romantics, and that their nationalistic egg and apple throwing was a stupid mistake, 'a fine triumph for the honour of the nation,' as he acidly says (*Racine* 169). It was a question of showing the young of all political colours that romanticism was a movement for them.

In fact, both parts of *Racine et Shakespeare*, in spite of their considerable political content, are profoundly anti-political. They are attempts to rescue literature from party squabbles of all kinds.[35] Stendhal's famous remark about politics in literature, repeated later in *Armance, Promenades dans Rome, Le Rouge et le Noir* and *La Chartreuse de Parme*, appears here for the first time : 'They are a pistol shot in the middle of a concert' (*Racine* 134). He means this. He is not of course excluding political perspectives from literature. He is himself perhaps the most political novelist of his century—in terms of insight, if not of intention. What he wants to exclude from literature is *talk* of politics, just as Proust, taking a stab at Zola, insisted on the exclusion of talk of literary theory from the novel. Fortunately, neither Stendhal nor Proust were purists about their position in practice, but the position is sound enough aesthetically. It is a case against unabsorbed material in fiction, and could be illustrated by a comparison between Joyce's *Stephen Hero*, which is full of theory, and his *Portrait of the Artist as a Young Man*, where the theory is put to work.

And specifically, of course, Stendhal means to exclude particular politics, the sad, drab debates of his own day, which he sees as characterized by 'impotent hatred, that fatal disease of the nineteenth century' (*Racine* 135). He is pitiless with liberals and royalists alike. And if he attacks the French Academy in a brilliantly funny version of a hypothetical session—the academicians agree that the best way to deal with romanticism is to pretend that it doesn't exist—he comes down hard on opposition writers in an ironic defence of the censorship—'Ungrateful people that you are,' he writes, sounding like Mme de Staël, 'do not then persist in your complaints against this kind of censorship, it performs the greatest of favours to your vanity, it allows you to persuade others, and perhaps yourselves, that you would do something if . . .' (*Racine* 144).

Above all, then, *Racine et Shakespeare* is a manifesto for youth, a rebuke and a programme for the young people who had 'gone astray' (*Racine* 31) and had hissed *Othello* at the Porte Saint-Martin. Stendhal's point is that young people can still have feelings and feelings are the basis of the new art. A drama which conforms to the three unities appeals to our sense of logic and tradition, to our taste for structure and fidelity to old forms. The new drama will appeal to our emotions. It will depend on the intensity of the brief moments of 'perfect illusion' (*Racine* 41) it is able to create for us—obviously Stendhal's thoughts on what happens in the theatre are more or less the same whether he is there for an opera or a play. He enjoys an opera for its dramatic situations, he enjoys a play for its scattered moments of emotional intensity. And to respond this way in the theatre, one has to be young, 'one must still have a soul receptive to vivid impressions, one must be under forty' (*Racine* 45).

The new tragedy will be written for *us*, Stendhal asserts, 'serious, argumentative and slightly envious young people of the year of grace 1823' (*Racine* 25). The *us* deserves some attention. To the day of his death Stendhal remained a spiritual cousin of Falstaff, much given, as Robert Adams remarks, to murmuring against those who would repress 'us youth'.[36] He was so firm about this that we find one of his editors speaking of Stendhal's 'youthful writings', published between 1814 and 1829.[37] In 1814, Stendhal was thirty-one, in 1829 he was forty-six. In 1817, when he was suggesting that, for him, the happy few would be a group of moderately well-off young people under thirty-five,[38] he was thirty-four. In 1823, as he writes in *Racine et Shakespeare* of the death of sensibility at forty, he is forty. All Stendhal's definitions are run up on loose slide-rules, he is constantly getting caught between his mathematics and his metaphors. In this case, he likes the idea of fixed numbers, of clear and irrevocable deadlines, but he knows that age is a state of mind, and not a mark on a calendar. The years never overtake his susceptible soul, and at fifty-seven, engaged in a non-affair with a lady in Rome, he behaves like a boy in love for the first time.

You are old in Stendhal's view, when your opinions freeze, when you can't escape your habits. The new drama, then, in spite of

Stendhal's taste for numbers, is for young people of all ages. And in this sense, Julien Sorel, at twenty, is already an old man compared with Lucien Leuwen or Fabrice del Dongo. His social resentment almost strangles his sensibility, forcing it to express itself in the violent and terminal form of attempted homicide.

But there remains a literal dimension to the notion of youth. Restoration France, unlike the Ireland of Yeats' *Sailing to Byzantium*, was a country for old men. The threshold of old age at that period was generally thought to be forty—Stendhal was right about that—and by 1830 half the French administration was well over the threshold.[39] A pamphlet directed against the ministry of Villèle (1822–1828) was called *De la Gérontocracie*, and Stendhal has a wry reference to this state of affairs in *Le Rouge et le Noir*. Julien surprises the young Bishop of Agde before a ceremony, practising benedictions with a scowling face. 'I don't want to appear too offhand,' the bishop explains, 'especially because of my age.' He returns to his scowls and his blessings (*Rouge* 316). Later, Julien is dazzled by the bishop's success. 'He had really managed to make himself look old . . . (*Rouge* 317). The admiration of our hero, Stendhal adds laconically, knew no bounds. Stendhal's heroes are young men in an old world, and their first problem is always one of disguise.

In his thirties, Stendhal occasionally held out some hopes for his times—hopes for something closer at hand than the long-term utopias which he habitually placed in the twentieth century. There would be a 'revolution in our minds. We shall talk gaily of gay things, and seriously of serious things; society will retain its simplicity and its grace . . . Great souls will resume their station, strong emotions will be sought again; and we shall no longer be afraid of their supposed coarseness'.[40] 'The nineteenth century then will distinguish itself from everything that went before it by an exact and inflamed depiction of the human heart . . .'[41] The prophecies describe Stendhal's own future work beautifully—its gaiety, seriousness, simplicity, grace—but he couldn't have been more mistaken about the century, which became very queasy on the subject of strong emotions, and preferred scope and sentiment to precision and passion any day.

We must have *novelty*,' Stendhal cries, like a real romantic, 'even if there is none left in the world'.[42] It is the voice of Baudelaire. Yet Stendhal knew even as he wrote his fine phrase that *we* was either too many or too early, that he was more or less alone in his views, champion of a movement which was already heading in a direction he disliked. What is romanticism? his classical antagonist (another avatar of Stendhal himself) asks in *Racine et Shakespeare*. Is it Vigny? Stendhal reviewed that poet's *Eloa* for the *New Monthly Magazine*, and called it an 'incredible amalgam of absurdity and profaneness'.[43] He suggested that the poem, which tells of an angel born of one of Christ's tears, was probably written under the influence of *lachrymae christi*. Lamartine, then? Ah yes, an American says in an imaginary dialogue of Stendhal's written in 1821, Byron with a French hair-do.[44] Hugo? Stendhal thought *Hernani* was a poor rehash of Shakespeare's *Two Gentlemen of Verona*.[45]

Stendhal answers his questioner with the obvious defence: no one has really tried the romantic method yet, that is why there are no really romantic works. But he knew he was on shaky ground. The fact was that the young people who had gone astray and whom Stendhal was trying to bring round, were a hopeless case, soon to be parodied in *Armance*. Octave de Malivert is impotent, Stendhal reminds us, but Paris is full of young men just as morose as he is, with less cause (*Armance* 1426). And in the second *Racine et Shakespeare* we find Stendhal casually undoing all his hard work as a polemicist. If Corneille and Racine had written for the public of 1824, he comments, 'with its mistrust of everything, its complete lack of beliefs and passions, its habitual lying, its fear of being compromised, *the gloomy sadness of its young people*, etc., etc.' (*Racine* 132, my italics), we should have had no tragedy for a century or two. The aesthetic of contemporaneity has been turned full circle, and the wishful trumpet calls of 1817 have come to this: an age gets the art it deserves.

This sounds more like the Stendhal we know, railing against his tepid contemporaries and their hatred of energy, and their anxiety to conform. Returning to Paris in 1821, Stendhal learned the sad truth of Marx's later dictum, that when history repeats itself, it repeats itself as farce. The Restoration in France was a sombre burlesque of the old régime, an attempt not only to put the clock back but to keep its hands still. The left wing was repressed, and the right was angry and agitating, because in their view too many concessions had been made in 1814, when Napoleon's Senate, hanging on for dear life, had tried to dictate terms to the returning Louis XVIII. They had not succeeded, and the Charter promising two houses of parliament, religious toleration, freedom of the press and the inviolability of property, had come as a gift from the king, not as a right of the people restored. It was dated 'in the nineteenth year of our reign'—the reign of Louis XVIII having begun, on this reading, with the death in prison of the infant son of Louis XVI. But it was a charter, nevertheless, and as such distasteful to the extreme right, who clustered round the king's brother, the Comte d'Artois, afterwards Charles X. Louis XVIII himself felt the fate of the French monarchy depended on whether he outlived his brother or not, and he was right. Charles X was an attractive but stupid man who had, the French historian Sorel says, all the qualities needed for gaily losing a battle or for graciously ruining a dynasty, but none of the qualities needed for managing a party or reconquering a country. His ambition was to return France to the 'natural order of things'. He was crowned at Rheims in 1825, amid great pomp, with doves fluttering to the roof of the nave, and the ceremony was followed by a visit to the local hospital, where the king tried his royal hand at healing scrofula by simply touching a few of the unfortunate sufferers. A poem on this fine subject, called *Le Sacre de Charles le Simple*, earned Béranger nine months in gaol and a fine of ten thousand francs. The question comes up in the house of the Marquis de la Mole, in *Le Rouge et le Noir*, and Julien weeps at the violence of a petty social climber's hatred of the poet (*Rouge* 465). The salons of *Armance* and *Le Rouge et le Noir* are packed with jumpy people watching the clock that won't stop, terrified of the revolution which waits round the corner, and *bored*, because they are fenced in by topical taboos on all sides. There is nothing they can talk about.[46] Stendhal, predictably, presents this blight on conversation as a form of liberty :

'As long as one didn't make jokes about God, or about priests, or about the king, or about the people in power, or about artists protected by the court, or about anything which was established; as long as one didn't say anything in favour of Béranger, or the opposition newspapers, or of Voltaire, or of Rousseau, or of any of the elements which allowed themselves to speak with something like frankness; above all as long as one never talked politics, one could discuss everything quite freely' (*Rouge* 457).

It is true, as Auerbach says,[47] that Stendhal's sense of history suffers from an undue emphasis on the idea of conspiracy. But it is also true that he lived in an age of intrigue, and more particularly clerical intrigue. Bishops were political men, parish priests were used as electoral agents. 'The present period will be hard to explain to our descendants,' a contemporary wrote, 'One talks now of nothing but bishops, priests, Jesuits, convents, and seminaries'.[48] Artz suggests that the clerical colouring of Bourbon politics may have aroused more opposition to the régime than anything else. Certainly the only buildings to be sacked during the July revolution of 1830 were two religious houses.

Romanticism was becoming exactly what Stendhal had proclaimed: an art adapted to the needs of the age. It was the age that was the trouble, and Stendhal was not alone in feeling this. 'You created romanticism,' his friend Mme Jules Gaulthier wrote to him in 1832, 'but you created it pure, natural, charming, amusing, naïve, interesting, and they have made a howling monster out of it. Create something else.'[49]

Create something else. Stendhal was the apostle of a romanticism which never was—or rather of which he himself became the lonely exponent.

5. *ARMANCE* (1827)

*'Que de choses vraies qui sortent
des moyens de l'art!'*
CORRESPONDANCE

Armance is Stendhal's awkward goodbye to the other romantic movement, a first hesitant step on his own road.

Octave de Malivert, the hero of the novel, is a gloomy young aristocrat, a graduate of the Paris Polytechnic, the school Stendhal himself was supposed to have attended, and didn't, in 1799 when he arrived in the capital from Grenoble. He made up for this lapse by sending his heroes there whenever his plots allowed. Octave is a passionless man, a martyr to self-consciousness. Coming round from one of his frequent flirtations with suicide, he consoles himself with the thought of fixing up three full-length mirrors in his room (*Armance* 44). He loves only his mother, he dabbles in chemistry and philosophy, reads liberal newspapers then loyally and mechanically reads royalist papers immediately afterwards, not believing in either. He believes in nothing. He is a doll-like figure activated only by an abstract notion of duty, trailing meekly through a life which gives him no pleasure.

On the other hand, and contradictorily, he is all delicacy and nerves, a victim of 'that form of unreasoning sensibility which makes men unhappy and worthy to be loved' (*Armance* 48). He is a person of extreme emotions, not knowing how, we are told, to love or hate by halves (*Armance* 37), and given to brusque outbreaks of violence. He throws a servant out of a window for no very good reason, he picks a pointless quarrel with some soldiers and is wounded. In his youth he was a mild kleptomaniac, in his bad moments he picks out an act of *Don Giovanni* on the piano.

We recognize the two contemporary clichés: the dead soul, the frozen, unfeeling heart, Don Giovanni without the women; and Werther, the extravagant sensibility, the man too fragile or too passionate for the world. Stendhal has no intention of resolving this confrontation in Octave's character, he means to leave him there, caught, predictably enough, between heaven and hell. His 'fine and tender' eyes terrified his mother: 'They seemed sometimes to be looking up to heaven, and to reflect the happiness they saw there. A moment later, one could read in them the torments of hell' (*Armance* 36).

The fact is, and we should still be in the dark about this, had Stendhal not written an extremely explicit letter to Mérimée on the subject, that Octave is impotent, and running romantic clichés into each other is Stendhal's idea of how to communicate the pathology of this problem. We cannot say, as Martineau would have us say (*Armance* 16, Martineau's preface), that Octave is not just another romantic moper because he is suffering from something rather more clinical than *mal du siècle*. *Mal du siècle* is exactly what he seems to have: that form of mournful snobbery which caused his romantic cousins so much trouble. 'He was lacking only a common soul', Stendhal says loftily, tritely, and untruthfully (*Armance* 48). Impotent Octave was lacking more than that. Stendhal claims to have studied the life of Swift for the purpose of getting details on the relevant dilemma, but if he did, it didn't do him much good. There is in any case something very funny about the recruitment of the angry dean for this pale, weepy melodrama.

Octave falls in love, in spite of all his oaths against that passion. The girl is Armance de Zohiloff, a kind of cousin of Octave's. They are a very high-minded pair. They worry endlessly about each other's nobility—'She asked herself unceasingly: Has he a vulgar soul?' (*Armance* 75)—and the whole movement of the novel rests on their principled aversion to lucre. Octave comes into a fortune, and Armance thinks he *changes* because of this. He anxiously tries to persuade her that he hasn't changed at all, and in so doing, imperceptibly falls in love. His love is revealed to him by a chance remark of someone who has been watching them together, and the novel limps over Octave's horror and Armance's bewildered delicacy, through a near-confession on Octave's part (thwarted by the machinations of a wicked uncle) to the inevitable suicide and convent. Octave sails to Greece for his Byronic death, murmurs 'I salute thee, oh land of heroes' when the coastline comes into view, and swallows a mixture of opium and digitalis as the moon rises behind an imaginary classical mountain (*Armance* 189).

Stendhal himself had his doubts about *Armance*. 'This novel is too *erudito*, too learned,' he wrote to Mérimée. 'Does it have enough warmth to keep a pretty French marquise awake until two o'clock in the morning? *That is the question*' (*Armance* 191—the letter forms an appendix). Perhaps that isn't the question, but the answer in any case is no.

More often, Stendhal chose to camouflage his reservations, even from himself. He was normally grateful even for adverse criticism of his work, but about *Armance*, his first novel and a sickly child, he was both touchy and aggressive. 'All my friends hate it,' he wrote, 'and I hate their coarseness' (*Armance* 20, Martineau's preface). It was as delicate, he said, as *La Princesse de Clèves*, and his uncomprehending friends wouldn't understand that remarkable novel either. Yet *Armance*, in the form in which Stendhal published it, is about as comprehensible as a *roman à clef* without the key. How are we meant to know that Octave is impotent?

The essential clue is missing. Stendhal could have called Octave Olivier, and at least contemporary readers would have known what was going on. Mérimée dissuaded Stendhal from this, and the novel trips on its own reticence.

Olivier was the name of a novel about an impotent young man published anonymously in late 1825 or early 1826. The author was Hyacinthe de La Touche, and the book was a joke, a spoof—the point being to suggest that it was by the Duchesse de Duras, a lady-writer known to be interested in 'impossible' situations. She had written *Ourika* (1824), which was about a negress marrying a rich boy, and *Edouard* (1825), which was about a lower-class lad marrying a great lady. Indeed she had written a story about impotence called *Olivier ou le secret*. But she hadn't published it, and it wasn't La Touche's *Olivier*.

Stendhal knew La Touche's book, and reviewed it for the *New Monthly Magazine*. He probably knew Mme de Duras' story too —she herself is briefly mentioned in *Lucien Leuwen*. His own novel, he pretends, is by a 'femme d'esprit', a lady of wit, another avatar, presumably, of the wronged duchess. He is simply correcting the style. Needless to say, he is doing nothing of the kind.

But does *Armance* depend so heavily on the fun and games of the contemporary literary world? If the hero's name is changed, do we understand nothing? In effect, we don't understand much. Of course, there are signs. Octave dreams of a future companion, but is horrified by the thought of falling in love with her: '*I should be in love with her!*' he cries in italics, 'miserable creature that I am! ...' (*Armance* 42). He hates love, is constantly swearing oaths against it, and his response to his discovery of his feelings for Armance is suicidal. Once we are in the know, we can interpret these portents. But if we are not in the know, Octave sounds like a timid young man abnormally afraid of sex, who has turned his fear into a pompous morality. This view is reinforced by the fact that when Octave does fall in love with Armance, his reaction is not: Poor Armance, what do we do? but: Now I've gone and broken all my vows. He struggles to tell Armance of his disability. He has a 'horrid secret', he says, which will explain his 'fatal peculiarities' (*Armance* 174). He is a *monster*, he says later (*Armance* 175). Armance naturally thinks the worst, and imagines he must be an assassin. Why not? There is little evidence in the novel for a better reading.

Stendhal, in spite of his protectiveness about the book, knows something is wrong. On his copy of the published text, by the side of Octave's exclamation ('*I should be in love with her!* miserable creature that I am! ...') he writes, 'Try to suggest *impotence*, put here: *and how could she love me?*' (*Armance* 1435, Stendhal's italics). He knows he needs to hint more clearly, but isn't sure how —isn't even sure that he wants to. He is puzzled by his friends' incomprehension, and on the same copy—rather belatedly, one might think—draws up a plan of the novel which he finds 'irreproachable' (*Armance* 1429).

The plan, in fact, is very loose—there are too many interventions of what Stendhal calls chance, and the uncle's forged letter which prevents Octave from confessing to Armance is outrageously gratuitous. But it does show a certain logistical ingenuity, presumably retained by Stendhal from his days as an imperial administrator, and it does reveal the central problem: how to stretch this thin material to a full-length novel, how to keep these doomed and solemn lovers going?

Behind the text, there is a firm and coherent, if mechanical, structure of thought. In his letter to Mérimée, Stendhal hints at answers to all the awkward questions raised by the novel, once the enigma of impotence has been given to us. How do we know, for example, that Octave would have been impotent with Armance? Could they not find out? No, because timidity is precisely Octave's problem, a failure of self-confidence which comes from his disability and which in turn exacerbates it. He couldn't risk an experiment of this kind with Armance, even supposing she would have agreed—which given the character of the age and the character of Armance, is very unlikely anyway.[50] Why can't he tell her? He can't. That's what's wrong with him. 'This misfortune . . . would be bearable for someone who was perfectly reasonable,' as Stendhal writes elsewhere (*Armance* 1427, note on his copy), but isn't bearable for Octave. Again Stendhal says: 'Personally (but I am forty-three years and eleven months old), I should make a fine confession . . .' (*Armance* 191, letter to Mérimée). But Octave is not Stendhal and he is not forty-three. He comes close to making a confession only when he is perfectly convinced of Armance's total devotion. The forged letter puts an end to this brief spell of confidence, and the novel drifts on to its pathetic conclusion. But there is another, greater difficulty. Before the sad finale, Octave and Armance are married, and spend an eight-day honeymoon in Marseille. How is it that Armance didn't discover the horrid secret then, and do something to cheer Octave up? Stendhal is waiting for us even there. Young girls are very ignorant about sex, he says, and Octave had learned a trick or two of the hand and the tongue from his youthful visits to the brothels of Paris. Armance adored him. She was shy, and modest, and didn't like to say anything.

In short, there is an almost unbelievable gap between the clear crudity of Stendhal's thinking and the flimsy allusiveness of the final text. Stendhal, who thought he was being delicate, managed only to be furtive. In his letter to Mérimée he says he has indicated 'modestly' in the novel that Octave was in the habit of seeing prostitutes—this, we are to imagine, was how he knew he was impotent. Looking for the relevant passage we find that Stendhal's notion of modestly indicating a brothel is to have Armance reproach Octave for his late-night calls in strange places—'strange salons which are little more than gaming houses' (*Armance* 83). For gaming-houses read joy-houses, *maisons de joie* for *maisons de jeu*.

But the failure of *Armance* is not solely the result of Stendhal's timidity, or of his inability to give concrete and novelistic form of his thoughts. There is a sense in which the premise of Octave's impotence is simply irrelevant to the book. For Stendhal, in his life and in his novels, the best part of love is communion, precisely the 'conspiracy of candour', in Hemmings' fine phrase,[51] which Octave and Armance enjoy—'that limitless confidence which is perhaps the sweetest charm of love' (*Armance* 149). 'Because to be in love we need to be understood by the object of our passion', Stendhal writes elsewhere.[52] There are no fat, physical and purely functional affairs in Stendhal, as there are in Proust—or if there are, they don't count. 'Physical pleasure,' Stendhal writes in *De l'Amour*, 'has only a subordinate ranking in the eyes of tender and passionate souls' (*Amour* 41). The precious moments in love are anticipation, or the first touch of a loved lady's hand (*Amour* 284). What has impotence to do with such subtle sensations? It can be at most a tangential difficulty, it won't sustain the whole story. Octave and Armance have the moments all Stendhal's lovers have, their instants of perfect comprehension, and they have no more and no less of them than the others.

What is interesting about *Armance*, to the bright eyes of hindsight at least, is the way in which Stendhal seems to stumble on his future material. For example, Octave has to be unconscious of his growing love. This is the *sine qua non*, Stendhal says, 'since he is a decent man, and I don't want to make him a fool' (*Armance* 1429, Stendhal's note). Yet this unconscious love, introduced here for technical reasons, appears in Stendhal's later work for its own sake, as a favourite phenomenon, a dear theme. Mme de Rênal in *Le Rouge et le Noir* doesn't know she is falling in love with her children's tutor. She is as surprised as Octave when she sees what her symptoms mean: 'Could I be in love with Julien?' (*Rouge* 261). A great deal of the affective force of *La Chartreuse de Parme* rests on Gina Pietranera's unexamined love for her nephew Fabrice. More than this, all Stendhal's heroes, like Octave, 'lack insight and not character' (*Armance* 75), they are brave people but they deceive themselves easily. 'So I was being hypocritical with myself,' Octave exclaims, literally anticipating Julien (*Armance* 116, *Rouge* 692). Julien himself discovers that what he wanted from life was what he had before—when he didn't know what he wanted. Lucien Leuwen is a 'naïve soul who doesn't know himself'—'he didn't know what he would be one day' (*Lucien* 875). Stendhal's heroes never know. This is a fact about their personalities, and about life as Stendhal sees it, an unpredictable, twisting affair, full of unseen alternative routes, *other roads*. There is an echo of his own career here too, which contained similar mistakes: 'Really I have never been ambitious, but in 1811 I thought I was ambitious' (*Brulard* 13). I hardly need to begin to describe the tumbling and haphazard fortunes of Fabrice, in *La Chartreuse de Parme*.

Similarly, the character of Armance is in a technical sense accessory to that of Octave. Yet she becomes a focus for a familiar Stendhalian worry. Her shyness and her doubts, borrowed from *La Princesse de Clèves*, are just there to keep the novel going. Octave confesses his love to her, but 'chance helps him', Stendhal says in his plan (*Armance* 1429), meaning chance helps the struggling author. Armance makes him promise never to ask her to marry him. Hemmings suggests that she is as frigid as Octave is impotent, and that she would rather have him as a companion than as a husband,[53] but Hemmings seems to be thinking of Jane Austen rather than Stendhal here (he compares *Armance* to *Persuasion*). It is true that Armance is frightened of sex, but she is frightened in the manner of Mme de Clèves. She fears that satisfaction will destroy their delicate intimacy—'Do they not say that marriage is the tomb of love?' (*Armance* 95),—she speaks of a happiness which would ruin them both (*Armance* 98) and she is right. In Stendhal, love is always fragile and doomed—if other people don't break it, the lovers themselves will.

Stendhal is extremely kind to his lovers, in one sense. He gives them all moments of bliss, takes them out of time and makes them happy: allows them their revenge on a hard, perplexing life. But then his sense of reality reasserts itself, he counts the moments of his lovers' communions, and quickly hands them back to the hard world. Octave is tricked by his wicked uncle, Julien goes to the guillotine. Lucien is deceived by the grotesque Dr Du Poirier, and Fabrice is kept from Clélia by her marriage and her vow.

Again, Octave's impotence, the technical *given* element of *Armance*, creates in him a chronic lack of confidence which all Stendhal's later heroes inherit to some degree—without the impotence. Octave knows Armance too well to believe in the disabused letter planted for him by the bad uncle. The letter attributes to Armance, quite falsely, all that the Princesse de Clèves feared for the great love of M. de Nemours: her love is dead, because love is brief, the heart is changeable, that's how it goes. Octave tears up the letter, and abandons all thoughts of telling Armance of his disability. 'I needed,' he says, 'the deepest and the wildest passion —for such feelings would have forgiven me my fatal secret'

(*Armance* 183). He needed the passion that Armance really had for him, and which was denied by the letter.

That Octave should fall so easily for this miserable trick, is in one perspective simply bad novelistic management. On another view, the incident is perhaps the most profound moment in the book, a hint at the real novel hidden in the cold romance. Octave believes in the letter because the letter only tells him what he is aways telling himself. He combines a near-pathological lack of self-confidence with a fervent belief in his own exceptional bad luck. Yes, we hear him saying. Of course. How could she continue to love me? It had to happen this way. Lucien Leuwen, likewise, believes the most improbable tales on the subject of the woman he loves. We are given a glimpse of the romantic sensibility as a form of paranoia, and with this in mind we can pick up all kinds of touches added to Octave's character. He thinks of rainstorms as a plot against him (*Armance* 84). When he is reconciled with Armance, the world seems 'less hateful to him, and above all, less dedicated to doing him harm' (*Armance* 81). Armance has to persuade him that people are not always talking about him. 'He realized at last that this world which he had had the crazy pride to imagine was arranged in a manner hostile *to him*, was quite simply badly arranged' (*Armance* 82, Stendhal's italics). This is a long way from the young Lucifer complacently described elsewhere in the book, and Stendhal soon abandons the indulgent approach to his delinquent heroes—at least as far as the tone of his writing is concerned. The sickly pride of his later young men is no longer a distinction, it is the price they pay for their energy, and an element in Stendhal's hard-hearted comedy.

Stendhal not only touches on future themes in *Armance*, he almost discovers a manner. He comments on his characters, as we have just seen ('crazy pride'), and mounts a full-scale campaign against Octave as a 'philosopher', a person who is 'very strong on the theory of life' (*Armance* 59), but only on the theory. He glosses Octave's political naïveté in footnotes, he accuses him, by implication, as Hemmings nicely says, of 'moral pedantry'.[54] Yet Stendhal's remarks of this kind do not, in *Armance*, adds up to a view—they are scattered perspectives on a character who is otherwise drawn with an embarrassing lack of aesthetic or moral distance. It is not until *Le Rouge et le Noir*, that Stendhal finds the manner and the material he wants: a melodramatic plot, with ladders and pistols, locks of hair and lovers hiding in cupboards; protagonists with illusions, tender or otherwise, people who have little knowledge of who they really are; and a narrative *persona* who knows much better, who is half-free, half-involved with his admirable but often silly heroes, heroines and scheming villains. The elements are all there in *Armance* : Octave is wounded in a duel and writes a letter to Armance in his own blood; he is unaware of his love; and Stendhal's dry, knowing voice is heard at times, distinctly if faintly. The elements are not well combined, but one can see, again with hindsight, that the recipe has possibilities. Perhaps the next mix will be better.

The next mix was *Le Rouge et le Noir*, but before leaving *Armance* there is one other facet of the novel to be looked at : Stendhal's interest in the abnormal. Octave's impotence, although it remains, finally, external to the story, must have attracted Stendhal originally for this reason. Like Mme de Duras, he is intrigued by anomalies, marginal cases in a world where the margins are not very wide. 'I transport myself to the frontier', he had written much earlier.[55] But his anomalies are psychological, where hers were largely social; pathologies where hers were broken taboos. Still, in Stendhal's view, a psychological abnormality is often simply the dark side of a social norm, and in this he anticipates the findings not only of Marx but of Frantz Fanon. The behaviour of the individual is a function of the structure of society.

'In my eyes,' he writes in *Souvenirs d'Egotisme*, 'when a thief or a murderer is hanged in England, the aristocracy is sacrificing a victim to its own security, for the aristocracy has forced him to be a rogue . . .' (*Souvenirs* 1450). He adds, prophetically, that this paradoxical truth will probably be a commonplace by the time his book is read. *Souvenirs d'Egotisme* was first published in 1892. In a note on *Le Rouge et le Noir* he suggests that a revolution is bloody in direct proportion to the atrocity of the abuses which provoked it (*Rouge* 711)—which is even closer to Fanon's ideas on the Algerian struggle.

And we can of course see Julien Sorel as he himself invites us to see him at his trial : as a kind of self-seeking Vanzetti of the nineteenth century, sacrificed to the fears of an edgy middle class. 'My crime was atrocious,' he says, 'and it was *premeditated*. I have therefore deserved death, gentlemen of the jury. But even if I were less guilty, I see some men who, disregarding the pity my youth might legitimately inspire, will wish to punish in me and to discourage for ever that category of young men who, born into a lower

class, and to some degree oppressed by poverty . . .' (*Rouge* 674–
675, Stendhal's italics). Julien talks in this strain for twenty minutes.
In one sense it is all true. He is a poor young man who climbs to
the top, and who strikes out blindly at the person who tries to spoil
his final fortune. He discovers that Mme de Rênal has written a
damning letter about him to the Marquis de la Mole, his protector,
and almost his father-in-law. He leaves Paris for Verrières and shoots
her in a church. But in another sense, Julien's poverty and the
class struggle have nothing to do with his crime. He loves Mme de
Rênal, although he can't admit this to himself until after the shooting, and her chance reappearance in his life topples the whole
edifice of his ambition. Like a child or a madman, he wants to
destroy the object of his love because his love itself brings with it a
set of painful, intense and literally overwhelming demands. Yet in
another sense again, there is still a social context even for this private
act, springing from the most intimate and hidden zones of Julien's
mind, because Julien's ambition, his mobilized hatred of the upper
classes, came between him and his love when he and Mme de
Rênal were together, and kept him from returning to her after he
had left. Society itself, that is, the social structure of Julien's France,
was also a component of Julien's mind, internalized there as a resentment, a repression which his passion finally shattered, a barrier
so strong that only an oblique and in some ways inexplicable act
could overcome it. 'There is no private life,' George Eliot wrote in
Felix Holt, 'which has not been determined by a wider public life'.
    Society and the individual crime or passion are two perspectives,
two ways of looking at a single moment. Stendhal in his novel is
too subtle to talk of elementary causality, and even his remark about
English aristocrats and assassins is perhaps an attempt to formulate
the idea of a connection, rather than to indicate the nature of the
connection as literally as it seems to. Stendhal is not, finally, either
Marx or Frantz Fanon. Character in Stendhal, and especially extreme or abnormal character, is the ground where history and
psychology meet and do battle. To borrow his phrase again,
Stendhal transports himself to the frontier. The human heart, the
single and seemingly limited object of his life-long attention, is the
place where the two lives intersect, the vanishing point where the
two perspectives come home, and where the science of the whole
man begins, *anthropology* in Lévi-Strauss' ambitious sense.
    Armance is a long way from this subtlety, this wholeness. There,
the two lovers and their world are set in an automatic, merely

fashionable opposition. Octave and Armance are fantasy figures of incredible beauty, stranded in an ugly and heartless land. They discuss politics, but faintly, stiffly, inadequately. They worry about what people will think of them, and are conscious of society in that sense. But their world remains outside them, and for this reason Octave's impotence is not a symbol of a sterile society, as critics have been keen to suggest. Stendhal does seem to have toyed with the idea (*Armance* 1426, Stendhal's note), but finally Octave's impotence is simply Octave's problem. It is not even an *effect* of his living in a sterile society.

Certainly Octave is marked by his age, all Stendhal's heroes are. 'It is hard to escape from the disease of one's century: Octave thought he was deep, and a philosopher' (*Armance* 82)—Lucien Leuwen too is described as having the 'faults of his century' (*Lucien* 894). But Octave is not scarred by the disease and it is precisely Julien Sorel's profound infection by his times which makes him such a powerful portrait of what it means to live in history. In prison awaiting his execution, he catches himself lying to himself about the source of his fits of sadness. He is not depressed by thoughts of death, or by the damp air of his cell, as he pretends, he is depressed by the absence of Mme de Rênal, who has been visiting him in gaol, and who has been fetched home by her husband. 'The influence of my contemporaries wins the day,' he says aloud, laughing bitterly. 'Talking to myself, only two strides away from my death, I am still a hypocrite . . . Oh nineteenth century!' (*Rouge* 692).

There was another attraction for Stendhal in the theme of impotence. He loved technical difficulties, he was attracted by the thought of the socially or artistically impossible—say a novel about a woman in love with a man who had no arms and legs, as he suggests to Mérimée in his letter about *Armance*. 'So many true things which are beyond the scope of art,' he complains (*Armance* 191). Impotence is not quite so extreme a calamity, but it will do. There is the difficulty of getting away with the subject at all in the touchy and pious times of Charles X. There is the difficulty of making it work aesthetically, there are all the technical problems. How to keep the novel moving, when the hero is, by definition, static on the essential score? How, if he knows he is impotent, can he allow himself to fall in love and not appear to be a scoundrel? How does one end such a novel?

We have seen Stendhal's ingenious if ineffective answers to these questions. The point worth noting is the *gamble* Stendhal knew he was taking. He thought of his books as so many tickets in a lottery, he tells us, and worried only about whether he would be reprinted in 1900 (*Souvenirs* 1436). There is more than a sophisticated theory of communication here. Certainly Stendhal knew that posterity corrects many personal judgements, that Petrarch, as he says, hardly thought of his sonnets as contributing to his fame. He might have added that Cervantes was counting on his unreadable *Persiles y Sigismunda*, rather than *Don Quixote*, to make his name in history. But Stendhal not only takes tickets in the lottery, he is careful to stack the odds against himself, and this accounts, at least in part, for the hit-and-miss nature of his fiction. *Le Rouge et le Noir* and *La Chartreuse de Parme* are inspired gambles which come off. *Lucien Leuwen* is a gamble which almost comes off too, but which bored the punter himself. It is not surprising that a man so given to betting should back a few losers—like *Armance*, and his frequently flimsy short stories.

There is even, probably, in the habit of the wager, the element of a desire to lose—or at least a desire to lose on his own terms rather than win on anyone else's. We can take this back to the unfinished plays and the plagiarisms. Stendhal almost wasn't a novelist either.

He took his fiction seriously, as his working notes indicate abundantly. He always pretended that he read his own works only when he had nothing else to read, and that reading them depressed him. But he read carefully, and worked hard at corrections. The manuscripts of *Lucien Leuwen* are crowded with the most scrupulous thoughts. But what he cannot take seriously is the sight of himself being serious, and his novels are flecked with strange moments of flippancy, gambles against his own chances of success. Julien Sorel, in gaol after his crime, refuses to help the defence to dilute his action. 'I killed with premeditation,' he says. 'Article 1342 of the penal code is quite clear, I deserve death, and I expect it' (*Rouge* 646). The penal code which had been in force in France since 1810 had only 484 articles, as Stendhal must have known.[56]

Mme de Rênal, visiting Julien later in prison, suddenly pronounces an oddly stiff phrase : 'The bounds of austere modesty have been passed,' 'Les bornes de l'austère pudeur sont franchies' (*Rouge* 684). Castex has pointed out that this is a line from Racine's *Phèdre* ('De l'austère pudeur les bornes sont passées'), paraphrased slightly and recast into a more normal prose word order.[57] The line is not irrelevant, but it doesn't belong to Mme de Rênal.

Stendhal may be offering faint legal and literary jokes to the knowing here, but more probably he is reassuring himself of his own detachment—rather as Cervantes, having solemnly described the death of Don Quixote, quickly corrects himself with a cold banality: 'amid the compassion and the tears of those who were there, he gave up the ghost, I mean he died'.

Count Mosca, in *La Chartreuse de Parme*, employs a joking cook on the grounds that a man who makes puns can't be an assassin. He is wrong, and Stendhal's work is a kind of nervous monument to how wrong he is. Assassins do make puns, Stendhal himself makes gags as he leaves his characters to die. His nerves, in other words, become a style, his own self-consciousness is a picture of the jumpy, discontinuous world. For what is striking about Stendhal's mature work is the gambler's caution, not his recklessness. The fiction receives all the complexity and correction and commentary it can take, but no more. The rest remains in the margins. If he allows himself irrelevant jokes, small private consolations, far from rocking the illusion of the work, they add to its consistency. Mme de Rênal is so firmly established as a character that Stendhal can afford to give her a discrepant line. The courage of this dashing treatment of verisimilitude is a compensation for the timidity and reticence of the unfortunate *Armance*.

6. *LE ROUGE ET LE NOIR* (1830)

'Chez l'homme qui, pour se délivrer
de la vie, a pris du poison, l'être moral
est mort; étonné de ce qu'il a fait et de
ce qu'il va éprouver, il n'a plus d'attention
pour rien: quelques rares exceptions.'
DE L'AMOUR

One of the sub-titles of *Le Rouge et le Noir* is 'Chronicle of 1830'. Stendhal was a passionately political man, delighted by the July Revolution in France: 'I saw the bullets from the colonnades of the Théâtre-Francais, very little danger on my part; I shall never forget that fine sunshine, and the first sight of the three-coloured flag . . .' (*Brulard* 11). In July 1830, Charles X, the last Bourbon king, fled in the face of a mild uprising, and Louis-Philippe, a member of the semi-liberal Orléans family, was placed on the shaky French throne. Stendhal was correcting proofs of *Le Rouge et le Noir* at the time, and still writing some of the second part of the novel. Yet there is no mention of any *coup* in the book, in spite of its repeated claims to topicality. In Julien Sorel's July, nothing happens. There is no revolution. The Bourbons stay, the old world hangs on, frightened reactionaries continue to quiver in fear for their lives and their dwindling power and property. Polignac, Charles X's last minister, who was famous for consulting the Blessed Virgin on thorny political issues, appears in the novel as M. de Nerval, a noble fanatic who hears voices from heaven (*Rouge* 583). He is still going strong in August 1830, according to the computations of Henri Martineau. At the end of the book, Mme de Rênal thinks of pleading personally with Charles X at St Cloud for Julien's pardon (*Rouge* 696–7), yet we are now, by the same calculations, in May or July of 1831. Stendhal includes the first night of Hugo's *Hernani* in his novel (*Rouge* 503), but not the end of the Restoration.

Carelessness on Stendhal's part. Laziness, a refusal to adjust his almost completed novel to recent events. A sense that July 1830 would have changed nothing for Julien, and therefore was not worth a mention in the book. Perhaps. But Stendhal's sub-title still stares out at us, insists on saying what it seems to say: this is 1830 and nothing has happened.

Stendhal's references to what *did* happen in 1830 reinforce this reading. A preliminary note to the novel explains that it was just about to be published when the 'great events of July' occurred, and turned people's minds in a direction 'none too favourable to the play of the imagination' (*Rouge* 217). We have reason to believe, the note continues, that the book was written in 1827.

We have of course no reason whatsoever to believe this. We know Stendhal was still writing his book in 1830, and Hugo's *Hernani* was certainly not performed in 1827. Stendhal is covering his tracks, protecting himself. But he is protecting himself in a peculiarly provocative manner. Why should he have to offer this explanation? Is it not then possible to tell from the novel that it is set in Bourbon times? Have the 'great events of July' changed things so little that the new deal is indistinguishable from the old one? Again, in a cagey footnote at the end of the book, Stendhal suggests that democratic régimes give us liberty but interfere with our private lives. Therefore, in order not to interfere with anyone's private life, he has invented a small town (Verrières) and placed his bishop, his jury and his criminal court, when he needed those things, in Besançon, a place where he has never been (*Rouge* 699). So we *are* in post-July France after all, rejoicing in our freedom, but regretting our lost privacy? As Henri Martineau says, Stendhal's evasiveness about dates is not a defence, it is an open invitation to discover connections with contemporary political events.

Similarly, Stendhal's remark about the new developments in France being 'none too favourable to the play of imagination' is distinctly double-edged. The cultural price of democracy, Stendhal was fond of saying, is boredom. Conversely, the political price of a thriving imagination is tyranny—a situation where you *need* your imagination. Hence, the remark is a back-handed compliment to the new régime. But Stendhal came quickly to feel that with Louis Philippe the French had got the worst of two worlds: an age of boredom *and* tyranny. His delight at the July days was extremely short-lived. The middle-class monarchy put an end to his republican dream, and the king appears in *Lucien Leuwen* (1834–1835) as a shifty and vulgar political manipulator given to 'Bourbon refinements' and to trying on the frank and hearty manner of Henri IV (*Lucien*, 1305–6). In *Le Rouge et le Noir* Stendhal expresses his rising disappointment by leaving the Bourbons on the throne.

But more than this, Stendhal wants to locate both the historical 1830 and his book in a longer perspective. The other sub-title of the novel is: 'Chronicle of the nineteenth century'. In this sense it doesn't matter much what the year is, since the year is to be emblematic, typical, the representative year of the age. 1827, the false date of *Le Rouge et le Noir*, is also the real date of *Armance*, subtitled 'Some scenes in a salon in Paris in 1827'. Yet the events which take place in *Armance* plainly belong to 1825, the year of the Indemnity Law for émigrés, which gives Octave de Malivert his fortune and sets the action of the novel moving. Stendhal pretends to move *Le Rouge et le Noir* back by three years, but he really moves *Armance* forward by two. There is a similar tendency at work in Stendhal's habit of dating his short stories by their decade only, leaving the final digit open: 'On a fine morning in the month of May 182– . . .' ('Le Coffre et le revenant',), 'During a dark and rainy night in the summer of 182– . . .' ('Le Philtre'), 'It was a spring evening in 182– . . .' ('Vanina Vanini').

Hence Stendhal's anachronisms in *Le Rouge et le Noir*. The workhouse in Verrières, directed by the greedy Valenod, would not have been there by the late twenties. French workhouses, created on the English model, were initially instituted by Louis XVI. They were then abolished by the Revolution, restored by the Empire, and finally suppressed during the Restoration. By 1830, the Marquis de la Mole would not, apparently, have been able to fix a commission for Julien as he does in the novel. Earlier in the book, Julien is sent with a secret message to a 'great person' in Strasbourg, inviting or seeming to invite the European enemies of Napoleon to reunite and invade France, in order to restore the throne and the altar to their pre-revolutionary power—to silence the workers and to stop the rise of the middle class. Stendhal is thinking here, scholars tell us, of a moment in 1818,[58] when the situation was rather different. A secret note was then sent by an ultra-royalist party to the allies, virtually asking them to continue their occupation of France, so that the forces of order could regroup themselves. This is unpleasant enough from the liberal point of view, but it is not the attempted high treason of *Le Rouge et le Noir*. Without hesitation, and more or less without adjustments, Stendhal moves his political scene back twelve years.

He compresses fifteen years of history into two or three. *Le Rouge et le Noir* is a contracted, concentrated version of the whole Restoration. More than this, the Restoration itself for Stendhal is the start of the typical and defining moment of the century. 'Just as English manners were born between 1688 and 1730, so French manners will be born between 1815 and 1880' (*Amour* 325). Stendhal wrote this in 1822. The revolutionary situation in France, he suggested, began in 1788, was interrupted in 1802 (by Napoleon and the Empire), returned in 1815 with the Bourbons and will end 'God knows when' (*Amour* 160). The Restoration was merely a reactionary swing of the still moving revolutionary pendulum, a crucial but transitional stage in French history. Stendhal came to see the switch to the Orléans family in 1830 as a similarly temporary phenomenon, and he was right in both cases. He died six years too soon to see Louis Philippe topple among the revolutions which flared up all over Europe in 1848, and ten years too soon to see the revolutionary phase finally end in France with the establishment of the Second Empire under Napoleon's nephew in 1852.

One day, Stendhal wrote in the 1820s, we shall emerge from this 'lugubrious farce', we shall be allowed to 'put down our passports, our guns, our epaulettes, our Jesuit's cassocks, and all our (counter-) revolutionary equipment', we shall have an age of 'charming gaiety' (*Racine* 194). True enough. Stendhal foresaw Offenbach and the Paris opera, Meilhac and Halévy. What he didn't foresee was how much he would have disliked the brassy days of Napoleon III.

He was striving for a *type* as Lukács has since defined it :

'a peculiar synthesis which organically binds together the general and the particular . . . What makes a type a type is not its average quality, not its mere individual being, however profoundly conceived; what makes it a type is that in it all the humanly and socially essential determinants are present on their highest level of development . . .'[59]

Stendhal's times are types in the way that Balzac's characters are types.

He treats countries in this manner too. Italy is the land of poetry, of passion, of music, of the grand gesture. Germans are dreamers, the French are spineless hypocrites, activated only by vanity, love of money and the fear of being laughed at. In a sense, of course, these are Stendhal's literal opinions, the belligerent simplicities by means of which he divided his friends from his enemies. But they are also a particular and powerful vocabulary, a form of shorthand used to brilliant effect in much of Stendhal's writing. His moral geography becomes a language of types, an international atlas of caricature.

On the cover of the first edition of the second part of *Le Rouge et le Noir* a vignette shows Mathilde de la Mole, Julien Sorel's aristocratic mistress, holding Julien's guillotined head in her arms. There is, as Robert Adams says, a 'grotesque and almost psychotic pun' here.[60] Mathilde's love for Julien, like his love for her, was an 'amour de tête', a love of the head (*Rouge* 556, 713), a sentiment provoked by an inflamed and self-regarding vanity—'for vanity', Stendhal had written in *De l'Amour*, 'aspires to the thought of itself as a grand passion' (*Amour* 40). This is exactly the movement of Mathilde's feelings for Julien. She reviews all the noble young men who might have a claim to her hand, finds them insipid, thinks of Julien, her father's secretary but a man of energy, a potential force in the coming revolution—has she not heard him conspiring at a ball? (*Rouge* 497). She has an idea. She is in love. 'I'm in love, I'm in love, it's obvious' (*Rouge* 511). She refers mentally to *Manon Lescaut*, and *La Nouvelle Héloïse*, to make sure—it was, of course, Stendhal comments mildly but unkindly, a question only of a grand passion, a heroic sentiment rescued from the days of Catherine de Médicis and Louis XIII. 'Yes,' she says rhetorically, 'it is love with all its miracles which is to reign in my heart . . .' (*Rouge* 512).

But Mathilde's fancy and erratic emotions become something else when Julien shoots Mme de Rênal and is confined to prison to await his execution. She sees herself as his wife, does everything she can to get him out of gaol, without any concern for appearances, for her rank or for the position of her father. Defending her name, one of the insipid young aristocrats she had rejected in favour of Julien is killed in a duel. 'This death made a strange and sickly impression on Julien's weakened soul' (*Rouge* 694). For Julien now, in prison, is reunited with Mme de Rênal, the woman he tried to kill. He has no time for Mathilde, he is 'tired of heroism' (*Rouge* 663). Mathilde is thus in a frenzy not only of despair for Julien's life but of jealousy—and in this condition a love of the head may indeed become a grand passion. Abandoned and forgotten, Mathilde is the most moving figure in the novel, as before she was the most lively and aggravating. She holds Julien's severed head after his death, but his head is all she holds. Her own love moves down to her heart, but Julien's love just moves away.

Stendhal continues the pun in his own review of the novel. Referring to the vignette, he says 'this head', Julien's head, had committed many follies before arriving, bodiless, in Mathilde's arms. These follies 'surprise without ceasing to be natural. That is the merit of M. de Stendhal' (*Rouge* 704—the review forms an appendix).

It is too. The eighteenth-century language, the echo of Fielding, should not mislead us. Stendhal is not interested in *either* nature *or* folly, he is interested in them both, and in both of them at once. To change the vocabulary, he is attracted by moments which are peculiar but true, moments where strangeness is not a writer's arbitrary invention but the expression of a major insight, the revelation of an instant where life's oddness is not simulated but seen. The most haunting episode in *Le Rouge et le Noir* combines precisely these qualities.

Julien's affair with Mme de Rênal is about to become public, the great scandal of all Verrières. Mme de Rênal herself and the abbé Chélan, Julien's mentor in the town, decide that a separation is necessary. Julien is to continue his studies at the seminary in Besançon. Having made this decision, Stendhal says, echoing an early simile of his own (*Amour* 328), Mme de Rênal is like a person who has taken poison, and who 'continues to function only by reflexes, as it were, and no longer cares about anything'. He refers to an anecdote about Louis XIV, who is supposed to have said on his deathbed: *When I was king.* 'Admirable phrase', Stendhal comments (*Rouge* 366).

Julien leaves Verrières. After three days, he comes back to see Mme de Rênal again. She knew he was coming back, she counted the hours, the minutes until his return, and in this way deceived herself about the finality of this meeting until it was actually upon her. From the moment Julien arrives, she sees the end, and only the end—'she had only one thought, this is the last time I shall see him' (*Rouge* 368). She says she loves him, but she sounds false, and Julien the suspicious momentarily imagines that he is already forgotten. The reverse is true. She will never forget him, but now all she can utter are blank and polite phrases, the mechanical sounds of regret. Dawn comes, she stops weeping, she says coldly that she is sorry that Julien will not be able to say goodbye to her youngest son. Julien leaves for Besançon unable to think of anything other than this 'living corpse' (*Rouge* 368). '. . . as long as he could see the belfry of the church of Verrières, he often turned round' (*Rouge* 369).

In one sense Mme de Rênal's behaviour is diametrically the opposite of what we would expect : she freezes when she ought to melt. And yet it is of course *true*, one of those odd truths which make us feel that life is both stranger and neater than it is.

Essentially, Stendhal is interested *only* in such truths, and the attempt to express them is a form of his wager with the novel. For if anything is likely to make the writing of fiction difficult, it is a commitment to what is incredible-but-true. Julien shoots the woman he loves, Vanina Vanini betrays her revolutionary hero because she loves him—she shops his group of guerrillas in order to have him to herself. Léonor, in the story 'Le Philtre', knows her man is no good, and yet also knows she will follow him to the ends of the earth. Perhaps, she says, he has given me a potion, for I can't hate him. 'Strange blindness,' the young man who loves *her* thinks, 'so young and so intelligent a woman, and she believes in spells' (*Romans* 84). Yet he too is under a spell. He loves her in spite of her avowed and irresistible passion for another man.

Julien in gaol says 'The person I tried to kill is the one person who will weep sincerely at my death' (*Rouge* 680–1). He is thinking of Mme de Rênal, of course, and being very unfair to Mathilde. He is carried away by the cleanness and perversity of his logic : 'Ah! this is an antithesis!' he thinks. Stendhal works precisely this way, but he is not simply making patterns.

Sophocles, in *Oedipus the King*, makes the gods, in effect, inhuman. It is a way of saying that they are non-human, beyond our comprehension. Tales of a Catholic God's cruelty serve the same purpose. Similarly, Stendhal's insistence on logical opposites is also an insight into a larger world of unpredictability. Having his characters do exactly what we think they won't or shouldn't do, is a way of saying his characters could do *anything*. The inverted geometry conjures up a life where there would be no geometry at all. Stendhal's subjects are always on the edge of escaping from both mathematics and reason.

We can see the dualism of Stendhal's title in this way: red and black, an attempt to get a binary grip on the flux of things. The two-part structure remains even in one of Stendhal's false titles for his book: *Seduction and Repentance*, suggesting a seamy and florid French Jane Austen. The joke here is typical of Stendhal. Julien does seduce and he does repent, in some sense. But as we shall see, his seductions were not really seductions, and his repentance was something else.

The red is the army and the black is the church. These are Julien Sorel's own strategic simplifications, his sense of the options of the Restoration. Or the red and the black is a roulette wheel, or the scarlet stain of blood on the priestly robe.[61] This may sound far-fetched—especially as Julien has no priestly robe—but it is true that Stendhal takes pains to create a rather elaborate symbolism involving the colour red. There are red curtains hanging in the church at Verrières—a reflection from them makes a pool of spilt holy water look like blood (*Rouge* 240). There are red damask drapes in the cathedral at Besançon, when Julien is helping with the trimmings for a festival, and is shaken to see Mme de Rênal praying there (*Rouge* 397). There is a crimson canopy at the entrance to the Duke de Retz' ball in Paris, attended by Julien (*Rouge* 486). The red curtains still hang in the church at Verrières when Julien arrives to shoot Mme de Rênal (*Rouge* 644). Hemmings speaks of a 'discreet' use of omens and portents here,[62] but the use seems to me downright elephantine.

During his early visit to the church in Verrières Julien comes across a scrap of paper on the Rênal pew. It refers to the execution in Besançon of a man whose name is an anagram of his own: Louis Jenrel (*Rouge* 240). Later, Mathilde has an accidentally prophetic thought about him. Only the death sentence really distinguishes a man, she thinks, it is the only thing which can't be bought (*Rouge* 489). Sure enough, Julien acquires this doomed distinction.

What happens, I suggest, is that Stendhal needs such heavy echoes when he thinks of his book in the abstract. Once he gets going, he forgets, or rightly neglects them. He is like Julien, who becomes one of the best-dressed men in Paris, but not one of their kind: 'once he was washed and combed and clothed, he no longer thought about his appearance' (*Rouge* 623). Stendhal expresses a similar appreciation of casual and unselfconscious elegance in *Rome, Naples et Florence* (*Rome* 137).

In their simpler and more immediate application, the red and the black dominate the whole book without any need of special rigging. Julien falls in love with the red, but decides that the times call for a change to the black—a translation, an adaptation. In fact, he is tossed between the two like a tennis ball between rackets.

He is first of all a juvenile Don Quixote, his ambition is a child's ambition, a quest for colour and adventure, a desire to get into the story-books. He sees the dragoons go by, and listens to his father's lodger, the old army-surgeon, telling tales of Napoleon's Italian campaigns (*Rouge* 238). Like Stendhal, the retired major clung to *that* Napoleon, the young general in Italy, and not the later one, the reactionary and short-tempered tyrant.[63]

But Julien's ambition is also something else, something meaner. When he was fourteen he saw the grand new church going up in Verrières, and began to think again about the army as a career. His mind is made up when he sees an old and worthy magistrate begin to give crooked decisions in order to please a young priest. Priests push people around, Julien wants to be a priest (*Rouge* 238).

Don Quixote was out to right the world's wrongs, Julien simply wants to 'make his fortune' (*Rouge* 239). He is vague about what making his fortune might mean, but for a start it means getting out of the place where he was born—'he hated his home town' (*Rouge* 239). From then on, it is a question of guessing at the right analogue for military glory, translating from the red to the black : a cardinal for a general, Mazarin for Marshal Ney. He dreams of a consummate hypocrisy, a Parisian, metropolitan ideal of deceit and roguery (*Rouge* 520–1). For where Don Quixote was a comic antique, rigged up in old armour and rattling out on the roads of Spain, Julien is alert enough to modernize his hopes, to paraphrase the Napoleonic legend to fit the times. The irony begins here, because the legend loses a lot in the paraphrase. What Julien loved most about the red was the colour, and at every step he takes towards success in the church, the army leaps up behind him like a crimson shadow, a mockery of his unnatural and unavailing cleverness.

On his arrival at the Rênals' to act as tutor to their children, Julien wonders whether he will have to eat with the servants or not—his anxiety on the subject is borrowed, Stendhal says, from Rousseau. He thinks of running away to join the army, rather than submit to such an indignity. But that would cut off his chances, he reflects—'but then no more promotion, no more ambition for me, no more of that fine trade of priest which leads to everything' (*Rouge* 235). When he gets to Besançon he is stirred by the idea of the regiments stationed in the town (*Rouge* 369). Soon after this, he finds himself exempted from a conscription because he is now a seminarist. He is moved. 'There then, gone now forever, is the moment at which, twenty years earlier, a heroic life would have begun for me!' (*Rouge* 404).

At Verrières, when a foreign king passes through, Mme de Rênal arranges for Julien to be a member of the king's guard of honour, and provides him with a bright new colonel's uniform. During the procession his horse rears, he feels he is a hero, an officer of Napoleon leading a charge (*Rouge* 312). Unfortunately for this daydream, Julien has to change hats very rapidly, for he is also a temporary sub-deacon for the further ceremonies connected with the pious king's visit to a local relic. He puts on a surplice and flattens out his hair. From the toytown red into the dreary but practical black. Or almost. Julien has 'forgotten' to take off his spurs, which show beneath his cassock (*Rouge* 313). It is a typical Stendhalian refinement, a sign of the fading times Julien lives in, that his uniform, when he gets a uniform, should be not red but sky-blue.

Furthermore, Julien's ultimate achievement in the novel is a confusion of the colours—a last mockery. He chose the black, but the colour of his final success is red. He is made a lieutenant of hussars, and given a title: M. le chevalier Julien Sorel de la Vernaye. It is true that he arrives here through his prowess in a black outfit—albeit a secretary's suit and not a priest's robe. But his prowess consists solely of getting Mathilde de la Mole pregnant. When he says: 'I know how to choose the uniform of my century' (*Rouge* 525), what is this would-be Mazarin talking about? A declaration of love from his protector's daughter. 'My novel is over,' he says later, 'and the merit is all mine' (*Rouge* 639).

There was merit in his conquering Mathilde, his taming her like a tiger, in Stendhal's image (*Rouge* 624). But he tamed her because he loved her, not because he thought she was a road to the top. Indeed he is so absorbed in his love for Mathilde, that he has forgotten his ambition—her father is about to become a minister, and Julien might well get a bishopric through this promotion (*Rouge* 600). His whole scheming life would then have been justified, he would have become a companion of the young bishop of Agde he so much admired during the ceremonies connected with the king's visit to

Verrières. But at this point, he can think only of Mathilde, and how to win her. The closer he gets to the top, the more he is distracted—he is like Kafka's heroes, falling asleep as the crucial message is due to be delivered.

And of course, if his achievement had been what he thought it was, if he had used Mathilde as a path to a commission and a title, then his behaviour would have been as shabby as Mme de Rênal's accusing letter made it seem. It is precisely this accusation, this stain on his honour, which is about to turn Julien into a would-be murderer. It confronts him with a view of his life which is false enough to be denied, but true enough to hurt. It confronts him with his own bewildered purposes, with the uncertain self he has been evading throughout the book, the unknown moral centre he has papered over with plans.

Julien's character is childish rather than complex. He has the child's fatuousness, selfishness, vanity, he likes the thought of the damage he can cause. With Mme de Rênal, he is 'madly in love', but his love is partly just 'joy at possessing, poor miserable and scorned creature that he is, so beautiful and so noble a woman' (*Rouge* 302). When her youngest child is ill, Mme de Rênal attributes this illness to Providence, which is thereby punishing her for her adultery. Julien thinks, 'Here is an exceptional woman reduced to extreme unhappiness because of me' (*Rouge* 323). He has similar moments with Mathilde. The poor peasant, he tells himself, has received a declaration of love from a great lady (*Rouge* 523). His egocentrism even gets into his syntax, and Stendhal's. Julien in Paris remembers Mme de Rênal's eyes as those which 'loved me the most' (*Rouge* 594). At the moment of shooting her, his arm shakes as he sees this woman who had 'loved him so' (*Rouge* 644).

He is easily moved, temperamental like a child, ready to weep at the slightest provocation. In his soul, Stendhal tells us, there was a storm almost every day (*Rouge* 277). He bears a strong if superficial resemblance to Jean-Jacques Rousseau, which is not surprising, since Rousseau is his model. The *Confessions*, we learn, were the only book Julien had to help him visualize the social world (*Rouge* 235). His *Koran* consisted of this work, a set of bulletins of the Grande Armée, and Las Cases' monument to Napoleon, the *Mémorial de Ste Hélène*. He has an 'extreme sensibility', as Castex says.[64]

Or has he? Stendhal sustains a running question on this score.

Certainly Julien frowns when dogs are run over (*Rouge* 252). But then we see him and Mme de Rênal, who was touched by his feelings for dogs, gleefully catching butterflies. In case we miss the point, Stendhal twice calls the butterflies *poor* creatures, and adds that the hunters stuck them *pitilessly* in their cardboard frame (*Rouge* 263).

Stendhal wants us to see Julien as sensitive, of course, and he wants us to see that sensibility is potentially fine. Julien is 'un homme de coeur', a man of feeling, and finally he proves it. But Stendhal is anxious that we should also see how erratic and morally dubious such a sensibility can be, and he is even anxious, at times, to cast serious doubts on the sensibility itself. Julien, we are told, is *almost* sensitive to a breath-taking landscape (*Rouge* 276). He is, again, ordinarily *insensitive* to this kind of beauty (*Rouge* 284). He is terrified on entering the seminary : 'A philosopher would have said,' Stendhal comments, 'but he might have been wrong, that this was the effect of a violent sense of the ugly on a soul meant to love the beautiful' (*Rouge* 377). The qualifying clause about the philosopher is not simply shiftiness on Stendhal's part, a refusal to put his cards on the table, nor is it an ironic means of saying how sensitive Julien really was. It is a way of holding us off from simple judgements. Julien is terrified. There may be many reasons. In fact, as we shall see, there are, and Stendhal needs this careful ambiguity.

The balance is not always perfectly sustained, though. When Stendhal suggests, indirectly but without visible irony, that Julien is a poor young man who is ambitious only because the 'delicacy of his heart' makes him want a few of the things money can buy (*Rouge* 252), we can only say that the whole novel cries out against this reading. That isn't the source of Julien's near-demonic drive, or his grinding class-hatred.

Julien is intelligent, he has an amazing memory. He has a sense of humour too. The worst thing about prisons, he says after a succession of visitors, is that you can't lock your door (*Rouge* 686). He dreams up a brilliant future for himself as he sits in gaol, based on what might have been. Colonel in war-time, ambassador in the ensuing peace, a grand existence in Vienna or London. Not exactly, monsieur, he then says. Guillotined in three days (*Rouge* 677).

His defining element is *fire* (*Rouge* 233, 260, 286, 494), energy, a fierce desire to succeed at any cost, and at whatever success would mean : 'he has the sacred flame, he may go a long way' (*Rouge*

417). A priest is talking here, but the usage is unashamedly secular: meaning insatiable ambition.

He is violent, he scares people, as Mme de Rênal's friend Mme Derville tells her: 'Your Julien is very violent, he frightens me' (*Rouge* 270). Mme de Rênal herself, in spite of her love, is uncertain about him. 'There are moments when I think I have never seen into the depths of your soul. The way you look frightens me. I am afraid of you' (*Rouge* 329). Later he intimidates Mathilde by a passionate political speech in her father's library—' "In a word, mademoiselle," he said, approaching her with a ferocious expression, "should the man who wishes to drive ignorance and crime from the face of the earth pass like a storm and destroy as if at random?" ' (*Rouge* 501). Mathilde runs off. Later still, offended by her, he grabs an ancient sword from the library wall and threatens her with it (*Rouge* 547). When she becomes pregnant by Julien, her feelings have a further element of fear, 'almost terror' (*Rouge* 640). Stendhal repeatedly reminds us of Julien's 'ugly look' (*Rouge* 233, 243, 641). When we first meet him he is animated by an expression of 'fiercest hatred' for his father (*Rouge* 233).

What are we to make of this childish, humorous, intelligent, ambitious, violent and intermittently sensitive boy? Can we say, with Castex, that he is 'fundamentally noble'?[65] That seems to miss the point. Can we speak, with Brombert, of the 'repressed and self-conscious candour of Julien's adolescent emotions'?[66] Certainly he is repressed, self-conscious and adolescent, there is no question about that. But candour? That surely is our romantic projection, not Stendhal's. Julien is above all an unknown quantity. Pirard, his Jansenist protector, tells him that there is something 'undefinable' about his character (*Rouge* 443), and the Marquis, his employer and an extremely shrewd man, tells himself 'I find something frightening at the bottom of this character. That is the impression he makes on everyone . . .' (*Rouge* 637). The Marquis writes to his daughter, 'I don't yet know what your Julien is, and you yourself know it less than I do' (*Rouge* 639). Mathilde is struck by this, thinks, '*I don't know Julien*', but then manages to convert Julien's moral opacity into yet another attraction (*Rouge* 639).

No one knows Julien, partly because Julien doesn't know himself, and partly because the character he presents is in any case an artifact, a composition, a montage of borrowed bits and pieces. The point about his using Rousseau as a model is not so much that the model should be Rousseau, although that does contribute a good deal to Julien's self-dramatizing style. The point is rather that he should be using a model at all, inventing himself by means of another person's reported life.

Stendhal has us guessing again, then. We can see that Julien really frightens people. Stendhal is careful to stress that this may be only a visual effect, Julien may just *look* scaring. And the resolution of this doubt is left hanging. We don't know the real Julien. Or rather we should not know the real Julien if he had not committed his crime. What we don't see in him, the zone of darkness in all his relations with other people, is the capacity, under special circumstances, to commit murder. His shooting of Mme de Rênal simultaneously answers all our questions about Julien and all his own questions about himself. Now we all know who he is.

The answer has to be violent and paradoxical because the repression is so profound. Julien wants to know who he is, but he is also afraid of knowing—above all of being known. He senses that the truth about himself may be ugly, and the two most disturbing moments in the book show us Julien confronted with a seriously intelligent gaze. First his father : 'Julien's great black and tear-filled eyes looked into the small mean grey eyes of the old carpenter, who seemed to want to peer down into the bottom of his soul' (*Rouge* 234). There is a curious sense of brooding threat here. Later, the abbé Pirard, head of the seminary in Besançon, fixes a 'terrible eye' on Julien during his first interview (*Rouge* 377). Julien faints. The ambiguity is complete. Shortly before this moment, Stendhal makes the remark I have already quoted about the effect of ugliness on a soul meant to appreciate beauty, so perhaps Julien passes out because he is so sensitive and Pirard is so scruffy and unappealing. Or perhaps he does it because he cannot bear this man to look at him in this way, because Pirard is a version of his father, the scrutinizing enemy eye. Sensibility, then, or a form of intuitive guilt, a refusal to acknowledge what Pirard might see in him. Stendhal, needless to say, is not going to tell us which.

We are close to the paradox which is at the heart of this shifting, delicate and yet curiously tight book. Julien Sorel, like most of us, wants to know who he is, but only on condition that he is who he wants to be. Otherwise he'd rather not know. As a result, the young Machiavelli of the Restoration, subtle and intriguing hero of the vestry and the bedroom, knows almost nothing either about himself or about his world. This is Stendhal's major irony in *Le Rouge et le Noir*, and he plays it essentially in two keys.

First, the moral key, Julien's fine feelings, decency. He has chosen a grubby path to the top, and he is aware of this. His friends warn him even more firmly. 'You will have to ill-treat the unfortunate,' the abbé Chélan tells him (*Rouge* 259), and indeed he does. He uses his influence with the Marquis de la Mole to give the lottery concession in Verrières to an idiot—for fun, to demonstrate to himself his progress in light-hearted cynicism. Afterwards he discovers that an honest and deserving man had applied for and had really needed the job (*Rouge* 483). But Julien is always able to silence his scruples. 'Everyone for himself,' he says, 'in this desert of selfishness they call life' (*Rouge* 524). The rhetoric here certainly betrays an uneasy mind, but it works. Julien doesn't give up his schemes and go home, or become a socialist.

He is too sensitive for the road he has chosen, too mean and too ambitious to quit. Nothing delights Stendhal more than to land his hero demonstrably in this fix. We see him at a dinner-party in the house of M. Valenod, the gross and shifty director of the Verrières workhouse. The place smells of 'stolen money', in Julien's phrase (*Rouge* 347). The inmates of the workhouse are separated from the director's dining-room only by a thin wall—a typical Stendhalian caricature of contemporary social relations. Perhaps, Julien thinks, they are hungry at this moment. Then one of them begins to sing a vulgar song. M. Valenod sends off a liveried servant to put a stop to this low-brow interruption, while his wife points out to Julien the cost of the expensive table wine he is drinking. Julien weeps. The guests then crash out a royalist anthem, and Julien communes with his conscience. So there, he broods, is the 'dirty fortune' you can make.

'While you stuff yourself with food you will have to stop the poor prisoner from singing. You will give dinner-parties with the money you have stolen from his wretched pittance, and during your dinner he will be even more miserable. Oh Napoleon! How sweet it was in your day to rise to fortune through the dangers of a battle . . .' (*Rouge* 348).

At this point Stendhal makes his famous 'attack' for Julien.

'I must confess that the weakness shown by Julien in this monologue gives me a poor opinion of him. He would be a worthy companion of those conspirators in kid gloves who want to change the whole way of life of a great country but don't want to have to reproach themselves with causing the slightest scratch' (*Rouge* 348-9).

We can't read this irony as a code—poor opinion equals good opinion—although critics have tried. Stendhal is not hiding his 'deepest meaning under a screen of deceptive transparency'[67]— whatever that would mean. It is true that Stendhal has a *better* opinion of Julien for his 'weakness' than he would have if he showed no weakness at all. But he would have a better opinion still if Julien were not involved in the contradictory game of trying to get to the top in a dirty world while keeping his own hands perfectly clean, and Stendhal's opinion here is in any case not the main point. Julien is sorry for the people in the poor-house, he has the grace to weep. But he himself chose his muddy road to fame and fortune, he is in no position to moan about the mud. We understand, and we sympathize with Julien's paraphrase of the brave Napoleonic legend, with his driving desire to make it—just as we can sympathize with his descendants, the angry heroes of the British fifties. But Julien's paraphrase is not *justified* by the society of the Restoration, any more than the British angries were simply right. Julien is not a sensitive lad born at the wrong time. That is *his* picture of him-self and the world, not Stendhal's.

This structural irony, this sense of Julien caught in a trap at least partly of his own making, qualifies all his liberal or philan-thropic outbursts. In Verrières, he feels hatred and horror for the high society into which he is admitted. But he is admitted, Stendhal adds, only at the bottom end of the table—'which perhaps explains his hatred and his horror' (*Rouge* 249). Sickened by the hypocrisy of Valenod's conversation in the salon of the Rênals, Julien rushes out into the garden. He is prepared to bet that the man even makes money on the parish's foundlings, 'those poor creatures whose mis-fortune is even more sacred than that of the others! Ah monsters! monsters!' Fine moral rage? A little inflated? We soon see in any case that Julien's sympathy for the orphans is only a version of his sympathy for himself, a metaphorical extension of his own dilemma : 'And I, too, am a kind of foundling . . .' (*Rouge* 249).

Julien is surveyed by Stendhal's logic, held in Stendhal's moral eyes as he is momentarily held in his father's and the abbé Pirard's. But his ambition is not only patchy and mean, it is also a mistake. There is something Julien wants even more than to get to the top. He wants to be a brave man, to prove that he is not a coward. When the old army surgeon told tales of the Italian campaigns, of painful operations performed in the field, Julien use to say to him-self, 'I wouldn't have flinched' (*Rouge* 256–7). He is in quest of analogues for this situation, of a chance to show his courage, not to flinch. The military metaphors which haunt Julien's language are thus not simply a personal characteristic which Stendhal has lent to his hero, and they are not simply verbal extensions of Julien's devotion to his model, Napoleon. They are a wistful bridge to the lost world where they belong, they are hints of action, readings of dull moments which will make them brighter.

Julien's plan is to succeed by willpower, energy and courage in a century which has outlawed just those things. He is constantly getting stranded between a romantic, active set of values and the pale, seedy scene of his worldly progress. Stendhal was fond of quoting an aphorism of Napoleon's to the effect that the one place a man cannot be a hypocrite is under enemy fire. In Julien's scheme the equivalent for courage under enemy fire *is* hypocrisy. The battlefield is the drawing-room and the seminary, and heroism is keeping your mouth shut, and your mind hidden.

This is the second main key in Stendhal's irony. The century is Julien's enemy not because of its nastiness, although it is nasty enough, but because of its refusal to be his enemy. Julien advances, and the world withdraws, leaving him with an empty triumph.

We see him on his way to his first night with Mme de Rênal, trembling with fear, inventing elaborate manœuvres and wishing he could just stay in bed and read. His knees give way as he leaves his room. He listens at the door of M. de Rênal, hoping to hear him awake, which would give him an excuse to call the confrontation off. No luck. M. de Rênal is snoring soundly. Finally, 'suffering a thousand times more than if he were going to his death,' he arrives in Mme de Rênal's room. She speaks sharply to him, he breaks into tears, which she in turn can't resist. A few hours later, he leaves her, having nothing further to desire, as Stendhal suggests we might put it, 'in the style of a novel' (*Rouge* 297–8). The first skirmish of Lieutenant Sorel is over.

Stendhal insists on the perfect authenticity of Julien's courage— 'Julien was right to congratulate himself on his courage' (*Rouge* 297)—because the dashing hero really was terrified, and yet managed to drive himself on to face the enemy. But he also insists on the comic context, and maliciously points out that Julien's success is due precisely to his failure to maintain his sang-froid, to stick to the scenario dreamed up by his 'so clumsy skill' (*Rouge* 298). Mme de Rênal would have been able to resist that.

This situation occurs again and again in the novel. It is an aesthetic or philosophical version of the the moral trap Stendhal is always setting for Julien. During the decoration of the cathedral of Besançon, in order to place a wreath on the canopy above the altar, someone has to run up a ladder and cross an old and possibly worm-eaten cornice, forty feet high. The professionals are hesitating down below, but Julien takes the wreath and bounds up fearlessly. Again, the courage is authentic, but presumably the irony is not meant to escape us. Such are the tests of courage available to a man of spirit in the nineteenth century. Oh Napoleon!

This view of Julien's career reaches its climax in his first night with Mathilde de La Mole. She invites him to appear in her bedroom at one in the morning. He is to take a ladder which is in the garden. Julien suspects all kinds of tricks, plots against him, imagines assassins lurking everywhere, scans the servants at dinner, wondering which ones have been detailed to kill him. He is afraid. 'Why not admit it? He was afraid' (*Rouge* 537). But again, courage is not how you feel, it is how you act, in spite of how you feel. 'Since he was determined to act, he gave himself up to this feeling without shame' (*Rouge* 537).

The night is calm and clear—'the weather was hopelessly serene' —the moon shines full on the façade Julien has to climb. 'Julien had never been so afraid in his life' (*Rouge* 538). Finally, after much meandering in the garden, he puts his ladder in position, and climbs up, pistol in hand. 'There you are, monsieur', Mathilde says as he surfaces, 'I've been watching you for an hour' (*Rouge* 539). There was no plot. Julien, still suspicious, checks the bedroom warily. Mathilde asks him what he has in his pockets—'I have all kinds of pistols and weapons' (*Rouge* 539). Both of them are pleased at having found something to say. Then they worry about what to do with the ladder, and decide to lower it down into the garden. How? 'I always have a supply of ropes in my room' (*Rouge* 539), Mathilde says, and Julien decides, wrongly, that he can't be the first caller here. Having got rid of the ladder, Julien asks how he is to leave, affecting a West Indian dialect. Mathilde, enchanted, answers in the same way, and thinks, 'Ah, how worthy this man is of all my love!' She grasps his arm, and Julien, thinking his enemies are finally upon him, whips out a dagger. He would like to look under the bed, to see whether an assassin might be hidden there but he can't bring himself to do it. At last, 'afraid of a future reproach against his prudence', he bends down and looks (*Rouge* 540).

Both lovers are desperately embarrassed, and Mathilde gets so worried about the informality of the occasion that she goes silent altogether. 'I have to talk to him,' she tells herself, 'it's one of the conventions, one talks to one's lover' (*Rouge* 542). And so they spend a night which seemed to Julien 'strange rather than happy' (*Rouge* 543), an imitation night of love, a stiff, social burlesque of all the best fairy tales. The prince remains a frog and the princess can't forget it.

There is a paradigm for this kind of comedy in *Don Quixote*, a book which delighted Stendhal as a child. The knight and Sancho meet a cart carrying two lions to the King of Spain, a present from Oran. Don Quixote insists that the cage of at least one of the lions be opened, so that he can engage the noble beast in combat. There is a good deal of resistance to this idea, on the part both of the lions' keeper and on Don Quixote's friends, but finally the cage is opened—Sancho and the knight's other companions having withdrawn to a safe distance. The lion, who is really big and really hungry, we are told, puts his head out, yawns, washes his face, and since he is 'courteous rather than arrogant', in Cervantes's words, and 'not interested in childish swagger', turns round and lies down again, showing his hindparts to Don Quixote.

Here, as with Julien, we can't deny the hero's courage, but we can't assert it either, because the threatened confrontation has not taken place. The proposition is that of an uncashed potentiality, a kind of joke recalling Aristotle's thoughts on virtue. Is a good man a good man when he is asleep? Well, not if he is always asleep.

The comedy carries the thrust of the whole novel, which is to present us with a flawed and in some sense unknowable hero—in a world which constantly refuses him his chance to define or redeem himself. We see then, or begin to see, behind this fallen, comic country, a place of Platonic wholeness, a moral and social Garden of Eden where potentialities would always be tested. Napoleon's France provides this mythical domain, the criterion by which the fallen world is judged. There, you rose to the top by merit, and you tested your courage on the way. If you deserved to rise, you did, if you didn't you didn't. In the real world, the reverse occurs. You can't rise by merit, and therefore there are no real tests—you will never know whether you deserved to rise or not. In *Don Quixote*, as the book progresses, the hero has less and less control of his life, less freedom even to make his own mistakes. He becomes the plaything of the duke and duchess, enters a totally structured world, a place of organized deception and error, a mocking mirror of his own initial attempt to reorder reality by means of the imagination.

Stendhal, however, rescues Julien from this world. And even within it, gives him a minor but significant success. Julien conquers Mathilde, with whom he is passionately in love, by pretending indifference. This costs him infinite pains, he has to remain cold as she becomes tender. How do I know, he says icily, that you will still love me eight days from now? Yet he thinks, 'Ah, let her love me for eight days, for just eight days, and I should die of happiness' (*Rouge* 621). Such self-control, Stendhal suggests in a note, proves that Julien has 'great character'—'This test is no doubt one of the most difficult to which the human heart can be put' (*Rouge* 712). There are several ironies lurking here, but they are not cancelling ironies. The test is a test. At one point in his planned domination of Mathilde, Julien slips, and tells her how much he loves her, how much he has suffered. 'His weakness was complete.' Then he realizes what he is doing, and thinks he already sees less love in Mathilde's eyes. He pretends he was lying, making phrases, churning out what he once made up for another woman. Mathilde weeps (*Rouge* 622-3).

This is a hard and sour vision, but at the centre of it Julien has found his moment, the analogue for the painful operation in the field. He isn't flinching. Yet, of course, Stendhal's relentless humour won't let go, the poor paraphrase still surrounds this achievement with mockery. The wounds of the Italian campaigns in the old lodger's stories have become Julien's hurt pride. The cure is not surgery but hypocrisy, pretending not to feel what you feel. The sign of courage has become its substance. This is a favourite idea with Stendhal.

But Stendhal does, as I suggested, finally rescue Julien from this world. Even his flimsy success with Mathilde is too much success, for it is success in hypocrisy. This is the besetting sin of Stendhal's theology, and he is romantic enough to help his heroes out of it. I wrote earlier that Julien is infected by his age, and that remains true, even to the end. But he is given a moment when his infection is erased—the moral ambiguity of that moment being precisely an index of its strange status in reality.

All kinds of people who should know better have suggested that Stendhal botched his climax, Julien's crime. We know he found his plot in a newspaper, the argument goes, and we can see that he is embarrassed by this twist in it. Therefore, to quote Frank O'Connor, he 'rattles through it at the rate of a mile a minute'.[68] Julien's act is clinically sound, Jean Prévost says, but artistically a mistake. Stendhal didn't take the trouble to make the crime look convincing, *because it was true*. 'This is the danger of truth in a novel . . .'[69]

Or it's the danger of novels as a standard of truth. When a writer like Stendhal is accused of being faithful to life but not to books, we seem to have come up against the limits of the professional literary view. Faguet was the first to voice this kind of objection to Julien's crime. He felt that an attempt at assassination was not in the logic either of the novel or of Julien's character—it was 'extremely strange, and, truly, slightly more false than is permitted' (*Rouge* 204, quoted in Martineau's preface). Permitted? Julien's decision is abrupt, and the shooting is described with an extreme terseness where Balzac or Dickens would have gone richly to town. The writing is not true to literature, in that sense, and the event is indeed 'extremely strange'. That was the point. Stendhal is not embarrassed by the violent ending to his story, because that was what attracted him to the incident in the first place. If he recounts it as a law-report would, it is not because he got it from a law-report and can't be bothered to fix it up. It is because the law-report had the tone he wanted.

Julien's crime is carefully prepared and beautifully narrated. Mathilde shows him the accusing letter which Mme de Rênal has written to the Marquis about him. Julien remarks on the Marquis' wisdom in refusing to marry his daughter to a man of the kind conjured up by the letter, says goodbye, and sets off for Verrières. During the journey he tries to write to Mathilde, but can't form the words on the paper. When he arrives in Verrières, he has difficulty in making himself understood by the local gunsmith, from whom he wants to buy a pair of pistols. Bells ring for mass, he enters the church. He sees Mme de Rênal and can't bring himself to shoot. She bows her head, he fires and misses. He fires again, and she falls.

Julien, then, who in Paris has learned to be a model, a monster even, of self-control, can't write legibly, can't talk clearly and can't shoot straight. He is an excellent shot, as Stendhal has taken the trouble to remind us only a page or two earlier (*Rouge* 641), and one of the best pupils of some of the best instructors in Paris (*Rouge* 469). He is plainly in the state of shock which Henri Martineau insists on (*Rouge* 209, preface). He has, after all, been in a similar state before : in a church, precisely, and at the sudden sight of Mme de Rênal. This was at Besançon, when he was helping to decorate the cathedral. It took him some days to recover, Stendhal suggests (*Rouge* 402). Mme de Rênal does this to him.

But is he in a state of shock when he shoots Mme de Rênal? Castex argues strongly against Martineau's case. If Julien can't write to Mathilde in the coach, it is not because he is disturbed, but because his coach is going so fast. If he can't make himself understood by the gunsmith, it is not because he is stammering with emotion, but because the gunsmith is a gossip, and has heard of Julien's good fortune, and won't shut up. Julien commits his crime not in Martineau's trance but in perfect lucidity, Castex suggests. It is an act of heroic vengeance, an expression of the lower-class energy which Stendhal so admired.

The fascinating thing here is that the text gives no help either to Castex or to Martineau. Stendhal does not say : Julien was so upset that he couldn't write to Mathilde. He does not say : the gunsmith was such a gabbler that Julien couldn't stop him talking. *Le Rouge et le Noir* is the '*novel of the motif*', as Proust says. 'Each action is followed by a part of the sentence indicating what is happening in the unconscious mind . . .'[70] But not here. We do not even know how long it took Julien to get from Paris to Verrières, and we are not given a single glimpse into his thoughts during that time. For good reason : he has no thoughts. His endless ratiocinations have made way for action.

More than this, Stendhal really means to leave us on our own here. At moments of crisis he simply will not tell us how his heroes feel, or how we are to respond. The Story 'Vanina Vanini' (1829) ends this way :

'Vanina was crushed. She returned to Rome; and the newspaper announces that she has just married Prince Livio Savelli ('Vanina' 772).

'Le Philtre' (1830), this way :

'—Ah ! Don't kill yourself, dear friend, she said.
No one has seen him since. Léonor has taken vows at the convent of the Ursulines' (*Romans* 85).

Either we understand these lines or we don't. There is a sense in which the whole of *Le Rouge et le Noir* depends on our feelings about Julien's crime. Either it completes the book, makes all its meanings clear, or the book collapses. 'The poor novelist,' Stendhal wrote to his friend M. Jules Gaulthier, 'must try to make people believe in *burning passion*, but never name it: it's immodest' (*Lucien* 736, quoted in Martineau's preface). At the highpoints of his novels, Stendhal follows this Jamesian rule with amazing firmness. This is all the more remarkable here, since Stendhal's 'source', the report of the trial of one Antoine Berthet, goes into details on just this point. The prosecuting counsel asks Berthet what he felt on the way to his crime—like Julien's, a shooting in a church. Berthet answers in a way that most novelists would find hard to resist: 'I didn't know where I was; the past and the present became confused for me: my existence itself seemed to be a dream . . .' (*Rouge* 719, the report forms an appendix). 'I erase, I don't add,' Stendhal wrote about his adaptation of a story by Scarron.[71] The words might have been his motto.

There is one clue to Julien's feelings, though. His arm shakes so much at the sight of Mme de Rênal that he can't shoot. 'I can't, he told himself, physically I can't' (*Rouge* 644). State of shock, then, after all (Martineau)? Moment of doubt (Castex)? It doesn't really matter. Martineau overplays his hand by suggesting that Julien has become a form of psychopath—'we are no longer dealing with a normal being, but with an authentically sick person' (*Rouge* 209, Martineau's preface). As Castex says, this reading takes all the interest away from Julien. He becomes a case, not a hero. But equally, he can be as lucid as Castex would have him, and we shall still not be much closer to understanding him. The condition of his conscious mind is not the point, and an act of vulgar vengeance will not serve as a climax to this rich and subtle novel. Julien is not 'for all the world like a Corsican cut-throat', in Hemmings' heavy-handed phrase.[72]

Hemmings' reading needs to be looked at, though, because like Castex, he does try to get us between the Charybdis and Scylla of Martineau and Faguet. Julien is not a maniac, Hemmings suggests, and Stendhal has not fluffed the ending of his novel. Mme de Rênal's letter, although untrue in all its emphasis, came close enough to the truth to ruin Julien in the estimation of the Marquis. 'It is by means of the most consummate hypocrisy, and by the seduction of a weak and unhappy woman, that this poor and avid man has tried to make a place for himself and to become something . . . I am forced to think that one of his methods of succeeding in a house, is to try to seduce the most influential woman there . . .' (*Rouge* 643–4). Julien *has* seduced women who could help him—although seduction is perhaps not the word either for his clumsy success with Mme de Rênal or for his anguished war of nerves with Mathilde. This is the one thing the Marquis cannot forgive : being vile, a calculating scoundrel. So, Hemmings' argument runs, 'with absolute logic', Julien commits the one action a real adventurer would never allow himself : murder in broad daylight, wrecking all his hope, all his ambition. His act is not an act of despair and it is not an act of vengeance. It is an act of self-justification.

There is some truth in this view, but not enough. Hemmings simply transfers Julien's calculation, as if *killing* in cold blood were a moral improvement on seducing in a similar if less lofty frame of mind. Attempting logically to kill a woman who loved him, in order to justify himself, might redeem Julien in the Marquis' eyes, but it would disgrace him in ours, and in Stendhal's. His act has to be an act of passion, or it is nothing.

Julien himself suggested to the Marquis that he should write to Mme de Rênal (*Rouge* 643)—presumably during their embarrassed interview after Mathilde had told her father she was pregnant. What did Julien expect? Was he being crass? Did he think of Mme de Rênal as a woman who had loved him, and would therefore write him a helpful letter of recommendation? Hardly. Was there some unconscious drive at work in him to destroy his own fine prospects, some sense that such success is not for him? Perhaps. More probably, he would just like Mme de Rênal's approval, her blessing on his oddly acquired fortune. She was, in a sense, his mother as well as his mistress—in a novel by Dickens she would have been called his good angel. He wants her to say yes to his future.

Now Mathilde shows him Mme de Rênal's letter to the Marquis. It is the reverse of a blessing. 'All I owe to the sacred cause of religion and morality obliges me, monsieur, to take the painful step I am taking here with you . . .' (*Rouge* 643), it begins, and the charge continues, sketching a portrait of Julien as the new Tartuffe, as if he had succeeded brilliantly in all the hypocrisies he stumbled through. Julien's response is many things. Amazement, pain at the thought that Mme de Rênal should turn against him. Fury at this blow to his ambition, to the future of his and Mathilde's child, of whom he is thinking more and more (*Rouge* 642). Desire for revenge. Quivering of a love which had never died, and which was reawakened by the letter, as a telephone call may bring back to you a person you thought you had forgotten. Surprise at the picture of himself drawn by Mme de Rênal—or rather by the young priest who dictated the letter to her—this was not how Julien saw his heroic doings in the bedroom. Jealousy, perhaps, at the tone of those religious phrases, remembering that if Napoleon was Mme de Rênal's rival, the church was his—so that those people who said Julien tried to kill her out of jealousy (*Rouge* 660, 667) were, like so many people in this novel, both right and wrong in their view. And perhaps above all Julien's decision—it *is* a decision, Julien is disturbed but he is not of unsound mind, no court would acquit him on those grounds—comes from the need to put an end to the turmoil created by this pious and cruel communication, to find some simple, violent act which will collect the confusion of the mind and the heart, and cut off his future, which is more than he can stand now. After the crime, in prison, Julien thinks insistently *I wanted to kill, I must be killed* (*Rouge* 650), as if the simplicity of the formula were his salvation. Which it is. It prevents him from thinking of anything but his remorse.

Stendhal rescues Julien from his success in the world for the sake not of his immortal soul but of his inalienable and inscrutable heart. He wanted to kill out of feelings of vengeance and violence and malice and love and jealousy and injured memories and injured pride and no doubt much else. His motivation is as complex as that, and more so. The point of his act for Stendhal is that it is a passionate act, rising from regions within Julien which the errors of his calculating mind could not touch. Julien is saved from the sins of his scheming ambition, but not by any upsurge of simple, generous sentiment. Stendhal, like Yeats, knows that the heart is a rag-and-bone shop, and the morality of *Le Rouge et le Noir* rests not on the nature of Julien's feelings but on their depth—the distance, as it were, that they have to travel to reach the surface.

There is more. There is another morality to Stendhal's novel. Julien's crime turns his life upside down, the death-sentence, which he expects and finally provokes, destroys his ambition (*Rouge* 647, 650).

'Ambition was dead in his heart, another passion had risen from its ashes; he called it remorse for having killed Mme de Rênal.
In fact, he was wildly in love with her . . .' (*Rouge* 664).

Another passion. We are reminded that Julien's ambition, which flawed his early love for Mme de Rênal, was a passion too.

Napoleon, the token of this ambition, evoked a language of love (*Rouge* 248, 265, 273, 439), was a serious rival for any mistress. There was even ambition in the love itself (*Rouge* 302), and there was of course a good deal more ambition in his love for Mathilde—which is perhaps why she *absorbs* Julien more than Mme de Rênal ever could (*Rouge* 589). During his affair with Mme de Rênal, Julien frequently felt he would rather read than sleep with her (*Rouge* 305), but when he tries to read to keep his mind off Mathilde, he doesn't take in a word (*Rouge* 620). What is he reading the second time? Napoleon's memoirs. Napoleon was not a rival for Mathilde.

But then this means that Mathilde cannot outlive Napoleon in Julien's affections, and when his ambition dies, his love for her dies too, extinguished like a moth by two pistol shots at another woman. *Le Rouge et le Noir* ends in a flurry of paradoxes. Julien remembers the days of his drastic suffering at Mathilde's indifference—'and to be able to say that I so passionately desired this perfect intimacy which today leaves me so cold . . .' (*Rouge* 667). His attempt to destroy Mme de Rênal returns her to him—for she didn't die, and comes to see Julien in prison. This is perhaps the most 'romantic' moment in the book. Julien imagines Mme de Rênal receiving the morning newspaper in her bedroom, and reading the news of his execution: '*At five minutes past ten he ceased to exist . . .*' (*Rouge* 680, Stendhal's italics). In his mind he traces the tracks of her tears down her 'charming face' (*Rouge* 681). An hour later he wakes from his sleep to find tears on his hand: Mme de Rênal fled from home and came to visit him. He forgives her her letter, she forgives him his attempt to kill her. Julien is 'wildly in love', we are told again (*Rouge* 685), and his speculations on death and the beyond are merely disguises for his distress at the sudden absence of Mme de Rênal, recalled by her husband. If there is a God, Julien thinks, I shall fall at his feet, and tell him that I deserve to die. 'But dear God, good God, kind God, give me back the woman I love!' (*Rouge* 693).

Julien's crime remains 'inexplicable', as two characters in the novel say (*Rouge* 655, 696). All the guesses about it in the book itself are clearly false, or too simple, and the same thing could be said about most guesses outside the book.[73] Revenge (*Rouge* 647, 656)? Jealousy (*Rouge* 660, 667, 697)? There is more than that. Julien shoots the woman he really loves, or in his terms the one person who will weep sincerely at *his* death (*Rouge* 681), and the odd, inverted logic of this proposition *contains* the complex resolution of Julien's life, aesthetically. But it doesn't explain it, and this is the great virtue of *Le Rouge et le Noir*. Julien's violent act stares out at us, clear, strong, final and beautifully fixed in its psychological and literary setting, part of Julien and part of the novel. But it is also irreducible, like most crimes in history, and like no other crime in fiction I can think of.

Julien did not, then, shoot Mme de Rênal just because he loved her. But his crime does in effect allow him to learn the truth about this love, it restores him, *by another road*, to Mme de Rênal and to himself—to the self he has been avoiding throughout the book. With Mme de Rênal, Julien comes closest to saying who he is— whoever he is. In the early days of their love, he almost told her of his passion for Napoleon, the hope and saviour of poor young men. He makes a fiery speech on the subject, and Mme de Rênal frowns, the charm is gone. She frowns because she doesn't like to hear him talk about money, but Julien doesn't know that, and sees in her only his class enemy again. He pretends he is repeating some remarks heard the other day, and Mme de Rênal tells him he shouldn't mix with people who talk like that (*Rouge* 304–5). That day, Stendhal tells us, Julien's happiness almost became a lasting thing: 'Our hero wasn't brave enough to be sincere' (*Rouge* 305). We now see him as 'calmer and less in love' (*Rouge* 305). His feelings for Mme de Rênal do pick up again, become extremely intense— especially when her child falls ill—and he is in a way *more* in love with her later. But he is less *well* in love, the damage is done, and the 'limitless confidence' (*Armance* 149) which for Stendhal is perfect affection, cannot be restored. Or could not be restored, if there were not those tender times beyond Julien's crime, those visits in the prison. Julien tells her everything now. He appeals against his sentence, which gives him two months' grace.

'Can we not spend two months together in a delightful way? Two months is a lot of days. I shall be happier than I have ever been, ever.
—You'll be happier than you've ever been!
—Ever, Julien said again, enchanted; and I am talking to you just as I talk to myself' (*Rouge* 683–4).

After Mme de Rênal has left, Julien even admits that he would, if she were there, tell her about his weeping and weakness in prison (*Rouge* 686). For Julien, there could be no greater gift. He would give her his pride. And this is the other morality of *Le Rouge et le*

Noir. It is not a question of Julien's being selflessly in love with Mme de Rênal, of his being saved by that—none of Stendhal's heroes is ever selflessly in love. Julien, to the end, is more like Mathilde, a play-actor, a worrier about appearances. But Mme de Rênal is perfect nature. Although she is intelligent and active, her head never rules her heart. Julien cannot share fully in such passionate innocence, yet something in him responds to it, and he left with Mme de Rênal the best of himself, as they both recognize in the prison. His crime, then, represents on one plane an amoral morality, a praise of passion for passion's sake. But the aftermath shows something else. The passion, dimly, confusedly, was on the right track, it takes Julien home to the only truth he will ever know.

Even then, Stendhal doesn't let up. Julien's main concern in gaol, apart from his restored love, is whether he will die well or not. Beyond passion and ambition, there is still vanity. Julien's preoccupation here is important, for the sense of discontinuity and non-climax it creates is a central perception with Stendhal. He resolves his heroes' lives, but he will not leave them simply resolved. He will not, in the end, use fiction to unmix things which are mixed in reality, and we must be careful not to unmix them for him. So Julien scrutinizes his courage, marks the ups and downs of his moods on a mental thermometer (*Rouge* 653). The day of his death dawns brightly, and Stendhal slyly remarks that Julien is in a 'courageous vein' (*Rouge* 697).

'Everything went off simply, properly, and without any affectation on his part' (*Rouge* 697).

It is the old dream, the old surgeon's painful operation back again, an ultimate chance to suffer and not to flinch.

We should, I think, see Julien's speech at his trial as a similarly mixed moment. On the one hand he is doing public penance for his deed—'Mme de Rênal was like a mother to me. My crime was atrocious, and it was *premeditated* . . .' (*Rouge* 674, Stendhal's italics). On the other hand, his supposedly dead ambition flickers again in retrospect as he sees the middle class jurors lined up in front of him. 'I see no peasants who have become rich on the jury bench, I see only indignant bourgeois . . .' (*Rouge* 675). He describes his crime as an act of class war : his crime was to get an education and want to rise in the world. There is no doubt that Julien is in a sense committing suicide here, as the sinister abbé de Frilair later suggests (*Rouge* 686). He is unlucky too, because the venal foreman of the jury is his old enemy Valenod, and Valenod has in his pocket a nomination to a prefecture. He can afford therefore not to do as he was told by Julien's powerful protectors, and to allow himself the pleasure of urging the death-sentence. But the chances are that he wouldn't have risked going against his orders if Julien had not provoked the whole jury by showing them that his death was in their political interest. And of course Julien cannot live now. He can't return to Mme de Rênal, he doesn't want Mathilde, he doesn't want his fine career in the hussards and the diplomatic service. He dies, then, like Octave de Malivert, in sight of a strange land. Only the instrument of his death is new, the perfect expression of Stendhal's mingling of society and the individual passion in the novel, of social ambition and re-emergent love in Julien. No ropes, no poison. He dies for his love, because he tried to kill Mme de Rênal, and because he can't live without her. But his weapon is an invocation of the class struggle, endorsed by a sunlit guillotine.

Part Two   The Soul's Toy

7. SELF

'Je sens cela souvent, quel oeil
peut se voir soi-meme?'
VIE DE HENRY BRULARD

Stendhal was dissatisfied with the style of *Le Rouge et le Noir*. He found it harsh, dry, 'choppy' (*Rouge* 1471, *Brulard* 194). Indeed, he was far from convinced of the book's literary merit on any terms, for some five years after it was published we find him writing :

'If there is another world I shall not fail to go and see Montesquieu, if he says, "My poor friend, you had no talent at all", I shall be annoyed but in no way surprised' (*Brulard* 7).

There is a touch of mock modesty there, of course, but the touch is faint. At the time of the remark—November 1835—Stendhal has been struggling with the unfinished *Lucien Leuwen* for a year and a half. He really is not sure he is a novelist, although he is sure he wants to be one—the animal's real vocation, he tells his friend Domenico Fiore, is writing a novel in an attic.

But he cannot have been in any doubt about the *truth* of *Le Rouge et le Noir*, its fidelity to France and the human heart as he saw them. The very harshness of the writing must have seemed a guarantee of that, since the motto of the first volume was Danton's 'truth, bitter truth'. Hard words for a hard world. And Stendhal's plan in Civita-Vecchia, once he was installed there as French consul, was to write another novel, to pursue stern truths again by means of fiction. But his consular work interrupted him too often,

95

froze his imagination, and he decided to look for truth elsewhere : in his own life, in his memory. 'Now above all I want to tell the truth. What a miracle it would be in this century of charades . . .' (*Souvenirs* 1428). He stumbles into autobiography, then, in order to keep his inquiry going, to keep himself busy, to sustain his vocation as a writer. The vessel of human life, he says pompously and improbably, needs ballasting with work (*Souvenirs* 1393).

We should not place too much faith in the seeming accidents in Stendhal's life. In reality he stumbles nowhere, and least of all into autobiography. He began a dense diary—'the history of my life day by day' (*Journal* 401)—when he was sixteen or seventeen, and was writing obituary notices for himself by the time he was thirty-nine. Ultimate dates and places, of course, were left blank.

'Henri Beyle, born in Grenoble in 1783, has died in . . . (October . . . , 1820) . . .' ('Autobiographies' 1487).

One such note ends :

'The Russian campaign left him subject to violent nervous attacks. He adored Shakespeare and had an unconquerable repugnance for Voltaire and Mme de Staël. The places he liked best in the world were Lake Como and Naples. He adored music and wrote a little book on Rossini, full of feelings which were true but perhaps ridiculous. He loved his sister Pauline tenderly and abhorred Grenoble, his birthplace, where he had been brought up atrociously. He cared for none of his relatives. He was in love with his mother, whom he lost at the age of seven' ('Autobiographies' 1490).

This is by a man who has not yet written any of his novels.

Stendhal's fiction is more autobiographical than most, a place haunted, like his own childhood, by the unloved father and the angelic mother. His heroes regularly ask themselves who they are, and both Octave de Malivert and Lucien Leuwen design full-length mirrors for their rooms (*Armance* 44, *Lucien* 805). So that when we come to the autobiographical works of Stendhal's time in Civita-Vecchia—*Souvenirs d'Egotisme* (1832) and *Vie de Henry Brulard* (1835–36)—we are prepared for something like a late version of Montaigne, an edgy, aphoristic Rousseau. Certainly Stendhal puts the correct questions. 'What kind of man am I?'(*Souvenirs* 1393). 'Am I kind, mean, clever, stupid?' (*Souvenirs* 1394). 'What have I been, what am I?' (*Brulard* 4). 'I said to myself : I should write my life, I shall know then, perhaps, in two or three years when it's finished, what I have been . . .' (*Brulard* 6). He explicitly compares himself with Rousseau (*Brulard* 214), calls his *Vie de Henry Brulard* his Confessions (*Brulard* 8); his answer to the great Delphic injunction to self-knowledge (*Brulard* 184).

Not that he cherished any false hopes about the enterprise, he has an extensive Athenian scepticism too. Indeed he is on occasion depressingly dogmatic on the subject, and one wonders why he goes on. 'One can know everything, except oneself' (*Souvenirs* 1448). 'It's something I often feel, what eye can see itself?' (*Brulard* 7). Even when he suggests that at least he knows his own life better than some lives he has written about—those of Mozart, Rossini, Michelangelo, Leonardo da Vinci, for example—he is careful to make clear that it is the *incidents* of this life that he knows better, its daily events ('Autobiographies' 1490). The heart of the matter, 'this character of Henry' (*Brulard* 65), remains virtually impenetrable. There are thus doubts at the very beginning of the programme : 'I do not know myself and that is what sometimes, at night when I think about it, distresses me' (*Souvenirs* 1394).

The casual parenthesis there, with its mocking glance at the urgency of the quest, practically sabotages the whole business. Montaigne and Rousseau were more serious than that. Stendhal too is certainly more serious than he pretends to be, but still not serious enough. He is too elusive and too frivolous for the job he has undertaken, and if we go to him for the scrutiny of self he seems to promise, we shall surely be disappointed. His consciousness, as Valéry elegantly put it, is a theatre : '. . . there is a good deal of the actor in this author. His work is full of remarks aimed at the audience'.[1]

The very questions he asks, turn out, on inspection, to be social and public, rather than private and probing. He wants to know not who he is, but what he has been. How has he performed in life? Has he taken his chances? Has he been 'lively or sad, witty or stupid, brave or timorous, in short generally happy or unhappy' (*Brulard* 6). 'Have I any common sense, have I common sense with any depth? Have I a remarkable mind?' (*Souvenirs* 1393). As he writes his life he repeatedly assures himself of the progress he is making in self-knowledge—'I know this character only since I have been studying it with my pen in my hand at the age of fifty-three' (*Brulard* 337)—but the actual fruits of this study remain surprisingly pale. Stendhal sees that his cousin Pierre Daru was not really an intelligent man (*Brulard* 343), he sees that his own lofty nonchalance about money comes to him from his great-aunt Elisabeth (*Brulard* 65). He discovers that although he doesn't know who he is, he knows what he likes and dislikes (*Brulard* 247).

Worse than this, from the point of view of Stendhal's projected confession, is his resolution not to tell us about the important things in his life. 'Throughout the whole course of my life I have never spoken about whatever I was most passionately interested in . . .' (*Brulard* 165). 'I have never been able to speak about what I loved, such a discourse would have seemed a blasphemy to me' (*Brulard* 151). There is of course a good deal of frankness in Stendhal's letting us know just this, but the barrier remains, the life, like the fiction, goes dark at its crucial moments.[2] Stendhal worries, at the beginning of *Souvenirs d'Egotisme*, about the possibility of destroying his memories by dissecting them, about 'deflowering the moments of happiness I have met with by describing them', but he brusquely resolves the issue. 'Well, that's what I won't do, I'll skip the happiness' (*Souvenirs* 1394). Which he does. *Vie de Henry Brulard* fades out in a flutter of expressions of helplessness as the story reaches Stendhal's seventeenth year and the beginning of his love for Italy and Angela Pietragrua. 'How can one give anything like a reasonable account of so many follies? Where does one start? How does one make it the least bit comprehensible?' (*Brulard* 393). 'How can I talk reasonably about those times? I prefer to put it off until another day' (*Brulard* 394). 'What does one do? How does one describe one's wildest happiness?' (*Brulard* 394). Stendhal stops the series with a terse, categorical goodbye : 'One spoils such tender feelings by recounting them in detail' (*Brulard* 395).

Certainly the interest and the talent are flickering here, as Stendhal himself knows (*Brulard* 389), and as the writing of the later parts of the book abundantly indicates. So that the impossibility of description may be temporary rather than fundamental. And Stendhal can of course be both precise and lyrical about tender feelings, about a servant of his grandfather's, for example :

'I once saw, in Italy, a figure of St John watching his friend and his God being crucified, which suddenly reminded me of what I had felt twenty-five years earlier at the death of *poor Lambert*, which was what the family called him after his death. I could fill another five or six pages with the *clear* memories I still have of this great sorrow. They nailed him in his coffin, they took him away . . .' (*Brulard* 129, Stendhal's italics).

He evokes his distress at his mother's death in a few words which could hardly be bettered, speaks of a 'dry, grey sadness, a sadness without tenderness, a sadness close to anger' (*Brulard* 35). Even happiness can be recreated. There is the sparkling start of *La Chartreuse de Parme*, the irruption, as Stendhal says, of the French into Lombardy in 1796, precisely the mood his pen fails him for at the end of *Vie de Henry Brulard*.

And yet all the gaps remain. What gets told is what is left over when the essential is gone. Stendhal's loves and his writing, the dream and the occupation of his life, are kept out of his autobiography, or merely alluded to. If he speaks more directly, it is stiffly, socially, like a man trapped in an enemy language. '. . . two of them were countesses, and one of them a baroness. The richest was Alexandrine Petit . . .' (*Brulard* 16). Or wryly, evasively. 'But once I had the art of comedy open on my table, I seriously stirred this great question : should I become a composer of operas, like Grétry? or a writer of comedies?' (*Brulard* 326). Stendhal's idea of sincerity, as Jean Prévost beautifully says, is a question of silences as well as of confessions.[3] His autobiographical work creates a remarkable impression of a life lived beyond language, of great events in the wings while time-killing banalities occupy the stage. But it is a negative sincerity at best, and its silences are oppressively loud.

Are we to conclude then with Valéry that Stendhal, for all his efforts and announcements, failed to tell us the truth because no one can tell the truth about himself, because sincerity is impossible, because the archives of the self, in Georges Blin's fine phrase[4] are always being tampered with?

'One writes the confessions of someone blacker, livelier, purer, more sensitive, more remarkable, even more *oneself* than one can be, for the self has its degrees . . . In short, Stendhal's own sincerity, like all intentional sincerities without exception, became indistinguishable from the show of sincerity which he staged for himself.'[5]

Of course—even if the formulation seems unnecessarily high and wide. We all lie about ourselves, but presumably some of us lie rather less than others, and we might well ask, in that case, where we are to place Stendhal. Further from the truth than many confessional writers, as I hope I have made clear. But only if we see the truth as a simple affair, a matter of admitting what really happened.

For there is a sincerity beyond lies, the pattern of a person which emerges from the hesitant untruths and half-truths of his story. Indeed such a sincerity may create a clearer, more intimate picture than the straighter, grander attempt, and Stendhal seems closer to us than say, Rousseau for just this reason. Valéry is wrong to present Stendhal's truth as somehow flawed by his self-consciousness, because his self-consciousness, precisely, permits him a major form of truth about himself.

It is a matter of correction first of all, of admitting not the truth but a lie. 'One can't win a school prize in rhetoric,' Stendhal wrote in a sketch for a story in 1831, 'without paying the price. I confess, I still love to lie sometimes. I am a poet at those moments, and a poet improvizing. But my sense of honour suffers from this pleasure and I try to lie as little as possible. I only lie in . . .' (*Romans* 162). The sketch breaks off there. Stendhal is constantly catching himself out in slightly too fancy a posture. Only his interest in politics, he tells us, kept him from a despairing suicide over Mathilde Viscontini, whom he called Métilde, his love left in Italy in 1821. Then he adds : Perhaps I was afraid of hurting myself too (*Souvenirs* 1396). Again, he lets us know that he lived with a charming actress in Marseille, and never gave her a *sou*. Mainly, his honesty reminds him, because he didn't have a *sou* to give her, his allowance from his father was far from princely, and was never very regularly paid (*Brulard* 11).

There is a striking image of this taste for dissimulation, of the profound and secret roots it can put down into a character, in *Le Rouge et le Noir*. Julien Sorel's protector at the seminary in Besançon, the abbé Pirard, has promoted him to a teaching position. Stendhal writes :

'Julien, in a fit of gratitude, did think of throwing himself on his knees and thanking God; but he yielded to a more genuine impulse. He went up to the abbé Pirard, took his hand and put it to his lips' (*Rouge* 402).

The genuine impulse as a second thought. The idea takes us a long way towards understanding Julien's crime and the novel's need for it, since the crime is a victory for the authentic response over a hypocrisy which has become almost more instinctive than Julien's instincts.

Stendhal recreates the movement in the opening chapter of *Vie de Henry Brulard.* He describes himself on a hill in Rome, in splendid sunshine, thinking about time and the past, about his life, his approaching fiftieth birthday. He drops a military reminiscence of the battle of Wagram in 1809, a memory of a friend who lost a leg there, then two or three pages later startles the reader with this exclamation: 'But how careful one has to be in order not to lie!' (*Brulard* 9). He was a civilian commissioner for supplies at Wagram, not a soldier (*Brulard* 10). In fact Stendhal was not at Wagram *at all*, even as a civilian. He was ill in Vienna, demonstrating again his extraordinary talent for narrowly missing history's great moments —as a young man he arrived in Paris the day after Napoleon's *coup d'état* of 18th Brumaire, as an older man he ignored the Hundred Days and Waterloo because he was in Italy and in love.

The person seen here is a man who lies, thinks better of it, and tells the truth but not the whole truth; who is stricken with conscience before his fictions are properly under weigh, yet who is keen enough on his fictions to smuggle something of them back even into their denial. Stendhal's heroes are allowed to escape from this unhappy oscillation by their actions—or at least Julien Sorel and Fabrice del Dongo are. They are put in a place where what they do cannot be a lie. They are in prison both literally and metaphorically, caught both by the world and by Stendhal's own hard logic, and they are in love in such a way that their last refuge from the truth is gone, they have lost even the chance to deceive themselves.

But Stendhal never arranges such a dispensation for his own life. Lies and truth simply alternate, zig-zag through the pages of his elusive, evasive autobiographical books. 'Shall I have the courage to recount humiliating things without redeeming them by infinite prefaces? I hope so' (*Souvenirs* 1394). The answer is yes, Stendhal tells us about his fiasco with the lovely Alexandrine, a failure to perform in a brothel, surely a painful moment to remember. There is no redeeming preface. But there is a redeeming *tone* which changes the whole story: 'Being in love, in 1821, gave me a distinctly comic virtue: chastity' (*Souvenirs* 1407). His love for Métilde is the cause of his flop with Alexandrine. 'I was surprised, that was all' (*Souvenirs* 1408). He helps the girl out with his hand, says a few poised words, and leaves. By association, he recalls another fiasco which is not only *not* a failure, but a triumph à la Talleyrand. 'Beyle,' a famous Milanese beauty remarks on a stairway, 'they say you are in love with me?' Stendhal, coolly, and without even kissing her hand, replies, 'They are wrong' (*Souvenirs* 1409). Again, Métilde is the cause of this refusal of a promising offer, and again, the arrangement of the material is flagrant. Stendhal's disasters are trophies, marks of a superior, sentimental heart.

Yet beneath all this, disclosed by the zig-zag itself, there is a confession which resists the arrangement, there are wounds which can be seen to hurt in spite of the bravery. Métilde loved him, Stendhal tells us in *Souvenirs d'Egotisme*. But did she? Three years later we find him returning to the unsettled question.

'Métilde absolutely occupied my life from 1818 to 1824. And I am still not cured, I added, having thought of her for perhaps a good quarter of an hour. Did she love me?' (*Brulard* 5).

Even after this the cherished hope returns, though, and Stendhal next conjures up a Métilde who 'refused to tell me she loved me' (*Brulard* 15). It is just the same old story, he tells himself in the margins of *Lucien Leuwen*, 'You're just a *naturalist*, you don't choose your models, you always take Métilde and Dominique as a pattern of love' (*Lucien* 745, Martineau's introduction). Dominique was a pet name of Stendhal's for himself.

The difficulty with catching Stendhal out in this way is that he has all too frequently caught himself out first, indeed often sets up such seeming slips deliberately. The early chapters of *Vie de Henry Brulard*, for example, show all the signs of careful composition, deceptively random associations bring Stendhal where he wants to be. The boastful half-truth about the battle of Wagram is planted on the first page ready for its correction a few pages later, a quick, casual sample of the uncertainty of good intentions.

For good first-hand reasons, Stendhal is one of the world's great painters of self-deception, he evokes incomparably the immediate surfaces of a shifting mind. Yet for him clearly, this mastery of the zig-zag, this endlessly wary self-consciousness, meant the death of his intended enterprise, and shut him off from the simpler sincerity which saves his major heroes.

We look in vain for the sadness that such an awareness ought surely to cause a man who has set out seriously to know himself. A note of boredom creeps occasionally into Stendhal's writing at this time, but that has to do with his job in Civita-Vecchia, his lack of amusing companions, with a slowing of the wit which diminishes his verve—it certainly doesn't look like distress at an important failure. And the reason for this, finally, is that Stendhal, like the unruly but faithful child of the Enlightenment that he is, aims at something wider than self-knowledge—or rather aims at self-knowledge only in the sense in which it would be indistinguishable from knowledge of man, the human animal, would further his pursuit of a 'theory of the human heart' (*Souvenirs* 1430). 'The two possible intentionalities of the study of self,' in the abstruse but intelligent words of Georges Blin, 'could not, in effect, in his view be desolidarized.'[6]

Stendhal writes about himself in the way that he wanted to write about Napoleon, or about the French Revolution, or the War of Spanish Succession. He wants to write history, which he sees as a mixture of botany and anecdote, a question of giving labels and giving examples—his own heart and head being simply the nearest laboratories to hand. His questions about himself are almost always asked in the past tense, they are inquests not explorations, he is after verdicts rather than insights. He looks at life from death's end, his autobiographical works are really extended forms of his obituary notices, teleological in the sense that they lay out the life as a configuration, a final shape. And although he apologizes to the reader for boring him with details of his shirts and his allergies (*Souvenirs* 1393, 1448), in reality he does very little of this. Here as in his novels, he seeks to find a type in the particular case—where *Le Rouge et le Noir* is set in the representative and final year of the Restoration, *Vie de Henry Brulard* begins with a round occasion in Stendhal's life, his fiftieth birthday. 'Ah, in three months I shall be fifty, can it be possible! 1783, 93, 1803, I count the whole score on my fingers . . . and 1833, fifty. Is it possible! Fifty! I am going to be fifty and I sang Grétry's tune :

When one is fifty . . .' (*Brulard* 4).

The line, from an opera called *False Magic* by Marmontel and Grétry, is actually *When one is sixty*, but it scans the same in French. More seriously, Stendhal is turned fifty-two at the time of writing, so the whole scene, with its careful dating and counting, is a fiction, a small novel. He breaks off, picks up his pen again, he says, after three years, on 23 November 1835. There was no break, the first chapter was all written in two days. Stendhal himself, in a series of notes addressed to the secret police of the future, explains that his book is indeed fiction, an imitation of Goldsmith's *Vicar of Wake-*

field, in which the hero, husband of the famous Charlotte Corday, becomes a priest at the end. The joke here is meant to be on posterity, if it is meant to be on anyone at all. But as Stendhal well knew, the joke was on him. He was more of a conventional novelist in his confessions than he ever managed to be in his novels.

8. *SOUVENIRS D'EGOTISME* (1832)

'... entre le chagrin et nous il faut
mettre des faits nouveaux ...'
VIE DE HENRY BRULARD

Stendhal began *Souvenirs d'Egotisme*, he tells us, as a record of 'what happened to me during my last trip to Paris, from 21 June 1821 to 6 November 1830. A space of nine and a half years' (*Souvenirs* 1393). A long trip, and the word in any case seems odd for a return to one's own country. Stendhal's nine and a half years in Paris were longer than he spent anywhere, except for the Grenoble of his childhood. He had been only seven years at a stretch in his loved Italy, from 1814 to 1821. Back there now, but in dowdy Civita-Vecchia instead of bright Milan, he lets his present thoughts take over his past. A trip to Paris is not what he made then, it is what he wants at the moment. '. . . my last trip to Paris . . .' A clear question practically cries through the phrase: And my next trip?

Yet that Stendhal could leave the word uncorrected as a description of a spell of nine and a half years in his native land is in itself an eloquent comment on his life: that succession of journeys, that exile which began when the schoolboy got away from home in 1799. Like the hero of his story 'Paul Sergar', abandoned a few months before he started writing *Souvenirs d'Egotisme*, Stendhal would rather die than go back (*Romans* 164).

It is a lonely life he has gone to. His friends, he tells us in *Vie de Henry Brulard*, would give a great deal to see a glass of dirty water thrown on him when he appears in a new suit. With a few exceptions, he adds 'I have had, all my life, hardly any friends except of this kind' (*Brulard* 17). An even stronger expression of this state of affairs appears in *Souvenirs d'Egotisme*, where Stendhal describes Mérimée as his best friend and then comments; 'I am not too sure of his heart, but I am sure of his talent' (*Souvenirs* 1467).

Stendhal himself doesn't really care for many people. His 'education in others', as he calls it (*Brulard* 333) began late and remained defective. 'Others' in his writing are always mere opinions, surfaces —they are what other people think of you (*Brulard* 30, *Lucien* 770, *Romans* 174). Even the syntax of the novels reflects this disturbingly subjective world : the impersonal *one* breaks in abruptly, converting a person in a dialogue into opaqueness, a voice or a gesture only, words or motion coming out of darkness (*Rouge* 278, *Lucien* 968).

How could he settle down? He thinks briefly of taking an English whore back with him from London, pale Miss Appleby who offers not to cost him much. Then he remembers his sister Pauline. He had asked her to join him in Italy in 1817, she had come and had stuck to him like an oyster, he says, expected him to provide for her future happiness. 'A terrible thing' (*Souvenirs* 1449).

Comfort, the happy home, is unthinkable for Stendhal—in spite of his attempt, some years after Miss Appleby, to marry an Italian girl, whose relatives providentially turned him down. He is a friendless, restless figure, a lone wolf in at least two senses of that sad phrase, immersed in the only serious human relation left, if friendship and domesticity are not to be his.

An attractive woman falls for him, taken with his fierce political talk in the salons, much as Mathilde de la Mole, in *Le Rouge et le Noir*, was stirred by Julien's. But he lets the chance go. 'The fact is that I didn't love her enough to forget that I am not handsome' (*Souvenirs* 1427). He adds, with characteristic irony, from a sudden aerial height which stands the subjective approach on its head : 'She had forgotten'. Beyond the joke here rises the perspective of the whole book, of *Souvenirs d'Egotisme* seen as a mass, indeed of Stendhal's whole life, or at least of one of his own favourite versions of his life. It is a life in which *loving enough* is everything, in which love of the right kind is a theological grace given or not given to unsteady mortal hearts. 'Love has always been for me the greatest of affairs, or rather the only one' (*Brulard* 212). Stendhal lists his attachments, beginning Virginie, Angela, Adèle, Mélanie, and ending 'imprudently, yesterday, Amalia' (*Brulard* 13). 'Most of these charming creatures,' he continues ruefully, 'did not honour me with their favours; but they have literally occupied my life' (*Brulard* 13).

' "When will you come back?' she said. 'Never, I hope." ' (*Souvenirs* 1396).

We know that Stendhal left Italy in 1821 for mixed reasons—his liberal friends thought he was a police-spy, the police thought he was a dangerous liberal. We know too the Métilde was impatient with her erratic suitor, and probably not in love with him at all. Here, however, in *Souvenirs d'Egotisme*, the story is pared resolutely to an essential line, all clouds of complicating factors are bravely swept aside. She loved him but wouldn't sleep with him. He left.

Her memory then pursues him. He corrects proofs of *De l'Amour* with tears in his eyes, thinking of her (*Souvenirs* 1428). He seeks out the Milanese in Paris, on the off-chance of having word of her (*Souvenirs* 1433). He changes colour when he sees her name, or its French equivalent, in a book (*Souvenirs* 1431). And finally the memory fades a little, blurred by a new mistress. 'She became like a tender ghost for me . . .' (*Souvenirs* 1404).

He confesses this ten years later, in a work intended for *us*, his readers of at least ten years later still. But at the time he confessed to no one. Indeed disguise, the reverse of confession was the 'guiding principle' of his life at this time (*Souvenirs* 1398).

'It would be the worst of misfortunes, I cried, if those dry men, my friends, with whom I have to live, were to learn of my passion, and for a woman I didn't have, at that' (*Souvenirs* 1398).

He must hide his heart, and does, in a movement soon to be echoed in *Lucien Leuwen*. Like Lucien, Stendhal becomes cynical, voluble, amusing, acquires a gaiety which frightens people (*Souvenirs* 1478). His wit, like Lucien's, is his soul's jester, a noisy clown for a moping king (*Lucien* 953).

It is perhaps worth commenting here on the temporary corruption of Stendhal's fiction by his autobiographical writing. The force of Julien Sorel's character, in *Le Rouge et le Noir*, comes largely from the fact that he is driven by a set of desires not formulated or perhaps even formulable, either in his mind or in Stendhal's prose. His ratiocinations, his long conversations with himself, as well as Stendhal's own sharp comments, pass over or alongside the real drift of Julien's actions. That is to say, Stendhal understands Julien intuitively, he knows what he must have Julien do. He understands Julien's crime in this way, for example. But he does not understand it discursively, he cannot explain Julien to us. Or if he can, he won't. Conversely, Lucien is given the quick and debilitating lucidity about the self which is generated in the autobiographies. This makes Lucien a much more engaging character than Julien but means that he is unable to sustain a novel around him. He is acute, good-humoured and funny, but what about the rage, the restlessness that creates action in a stagnant century? Julien's rage, or that of Balzac's more naïvely ambitious or vicious figures? More precisely, where is Lucien's *mistake*?

All Stendhal's major figures make profound mistakes, are caught in errors arising from an important flaw in their sense of themselves. They learn who they are in surprising and often painful ways. Julien Sorel chases happiness in the wrong places, tries to murder the woman he really loves but in some self-deceiving sense has forgotten. Gina Pietranera, in *La Chartreuse de Parme*, finds herself driven to the assassination of a prince by a love she will indulge but not face up to; Mosca, in the same novel, loses Gina because his character turns out to be more determined by his habits than he thought it was. Even Fabrice, again in *La Chartreuse de Parme*, a young man almost as clear-headed about himself as Lucien, and a good deal more languid about most things, acts out the paradigm. He is superstitiously afraid of prison, and convinced he is cold, incapable of the love that books and people are always talking about. Once in prison—he was right to worry about getting there—he is happy, falls blissfully, irredeemably in love in the best possible fashion, and goes back there voluntarily after a herioc escape.

I suggested earlier that tidy reversals of this kind were instances of structure, provided a form of logical hold, or at least an appearance of logical hold, on the scattered actions of the novels. 'Where the devil are the masses in these games of my pen?' (*Souvenirs* 1469). As far as I know, Stendhal never answered his question. But if he had, for the novels the answer would have been here: in a certain logical presence. But I want to suggest now that Stendhal's structures are more than structures, that they carry a major meaning as well as offer shape. They dramatize, formalize Stendhal's favourite insight, his sense of the distance between who you are and who you think you are, between the drive in the depths and the reasons you give yourself for doing what the drive makes you do.

For *heart* and *understanding* in Stendhal (*Journal* 448) we read zones of the mind, subconscious and conscious. I don't mean Stendhal invented the distinction, or was the first writer to pay any attention to the mind's underground activities—the perception itself is as old as the Greeks. But Stendhal was one of the first modern writers to make large capital out of such a view. So that if Fabrice's mistaken fear of prison is not really a slip in self-knowledge, because he couldn't know what he would find in prison, it still signifies, his life is still seen to be shaped into mocking symmetry by forces which know more about him than he does. The irony stands, says the same thing. The dominion of the subconscious in this case is attributed to the universe.

Without their mistakes, Stendhal's heroes are nothing. Lucien in love, or engaged in the greasy politics of the July monarchy, acquires the indispensable error, the necessary distance from the truth about himself, and Stendhal can then tell us, and show us, that Lucien doesn't know who he is (*Lucien* 962). The novel looks up at just these points. But for the rest of the time, Lucien does know who he is. He knows as well as Stendhal does, which is all too well.

Stendhal kept his great failed love from his friends—as he always did, he was 'unbelievably, insanely discreet' about such things (*Brulard* 16). 'To which of my friends have I ever said a word about my misfortunes in love?' (*Brulard* 5). But here, in 1821, or in Stendhal's hindsighted view of that time, it is not so much a matter of of discretion as of active, imperative disguise : anything rather than let them know.

There is delicacy here, of course. Why should he wear his love on his sleeve? But there is fear too. Stendhal did not sleep with Métilde, and can't forget this. His discretion is vanity as well as discretion; like the Frenchmen he regularly mocks, he doesn't want to seem ridiculous. There is after all a difference between a spectacular, unfortunate passion with all the trappings and a drooping love which never gets as far as the bedroom, and Stendhal, for all his insistence on the delights of sensibility—he is only twenty or twenty-one at heart he keeps reminding us, whatever the calendar may say (*Souvenirs* 1421, 1447, 1453)—is embarrassed, half-afraid that those dry men, his friends, will be right when they laugh. Presumably, although Stendhal does not say this, it was *because* he did not sleep with Métilde that the wound was so deep, marked him so profoundly, crept so slyly into his fiction.

Armance, for example, among other things, is plainly a version of this sad, extreme affair with Métilde. Octave's impotence is Stendhal's failure, Armance's stiffness is Métilde's reserve. In *Lucien Leuwen* a love affair very consciously modelled on Stendhal's shyness and misery in Milan—'You're just a *naturalist*, you don't choose your models, you always take Métilde and Dominique'—is not allowed physical consummation, although Stendhal has to go to extraordinary lengths to keep his lovers out of bed, turning his hero into an idiot and his heroine into a prude. There just aren't enough obstacles to keep them apart, which was exactly the case in Milan.

Of course, if Métilde didn't love Stendhal, that would explain everything. But Stendhal, in *Souvenirs d'Egotisme* and all his later fiction, is sticking to another story: a love perfectly requited but inexorably, mysteriously kept from fruition. If two lovers, like Fabrice and Clélia in *La Chartreuse de Parme*, are allowed a brief moment of physical contact, they are quickly taken apart, returned to towers or darkness; and when they steal together again, their child is killed off by Stendhal in the most gruesome and gratuitous way. On the other hand, if a love is settled sexually, as is Mosca's love for Gina, then it is not properly requited—Gina really loves Fabrice. We might postulate the same severely frustrated source for Stendhal's preoccupation, in the later years of his life, with convents, nuns and vows, reflected both in *La Chartreuse de Parme* and in his shorter Italian stories. The worry over Métilde, eclipsed by later affairs, appearing briefly and obliquely in *Armance*, seems to emerge as a full and unforgettable scar only after *Le Rouge et le Noir*, where sexual relations are easier, less problematic—it emerges, that is, only as Stendhal begins to write about it, about the period to which it belongs.

I want to point out that Stendhal's allowing his fiction to be haunted by Métilde, this intense fidelity to a particular failure of his own, this refusal to let his heroes enjoy what he himself missed, strikes a near-mortal blow at the 'imaginary revenge' view of his novels, whereby the fiction becomes a compensatory fantasy, a fairy-tale re-adjustment for the upsets of reality.

Stendhal does compensate, of course, patently. His heroes are slender, young and handsome where he is fat, old and ugly. He makes sure they are really loved—in duplicate, all of them, by the right girl and the wrong girl, as if to ensure that no flecks of starved vanity, no lees of failure will linger to raise doubts about their sentimental triumph. Julien has Mme de Rênal and Mathilde. Fabrice has Clélia and Gina. Lucien Leuwen, loved but as he thinks tricked by Mme de Chasteller, is proud of his conquest of Mme Grandet, because he *doesn't* love her, which turns his victory into a real achievement, not a prowess by infection, by *contagion* as he calls it—being loved while you yourself are in love. Here as elsewhere Lucien's novel suffers from his own and Stendhal's excessive lucidity. What is woven into the plots of *Le Rouge et le Noir* and *La Chartreuse de Parme* is revealed here and explicated as a form of fatuousness, a sexual timidity needing double assurance—or better, as a general timidity needing support in double sexual success. Stendhal is remarkably unkind to Mme Grandet. Stood up by Lucien one night, she falls genuinely in love with him in the most desperate and humiliating way—like Proust's Swann when he misses Odette one evening. The whole sequence *is* an imaginary revenge of a singularly unpleasant nature: Stendhal makes Mme Grandet grovel in Lucien's office, vigilantly checks his usual tenderness for anyone suffering. She is being made to pay for all the women who turned Stendhal down.

But mercifully such moments are rare; Stendhal's compensations are not often more than premises. His heroes are what he is not. They are loved as he might have been loved by Métilde, and they are loved by another exceptional creature for good measure. That sounds like a lot of compensation, which it may well be psychologically. But for the fiction it means little, it is the skeleton of fantasy to which Stendhal's truths cling, his personal legend, the place where he starts in the sense that Sophocles started with a foundling child and a riddle. Everything else about the novels remains to be said.

Souvenirs d'Egotisme itself calls for a similar comment. It rests on a rather intricate scaffolding of compensation which looks as if it ought to matter a great deal. Stendhal's failure to sleep with Métilde provokes, thematically, the story of the fiasco with Alexandrine in the brothel, which in turn calls for the story of his refusing two famous beauties in Milan (*Souvenirs* 1409). By association Stendhal then refers to his first meeting with Tracy, the philosopher, as a fiasco. 'I admired him so much that probably I flopped with him from an excess of love' (*Souvenirs* 1410). In each case a failure is turned inside out, given generous, distinguished ancestry: an excess of love, an odd, lofty loyalty to a woman you can't have. From the new viewpoint it looks like success.

And of course the whole book is offered to us as a tale of victory, of bravely sustained disguise, a triumph over the curiosity of a set of keen and cold friends. Stendhal's defeat disappears into the story of his success at hiding it.

But we should not stay too long with such games, fascinating as they are. They are only surfaces, strategies. Like the marvellous observations and anecdotes which fill out the pages of this brief book, they are mere temporizing matter, what Stendhal did then, what the book does now, while his main story pursues its subterranean course. We should see Stendhal's fine comments on Lafayette in this way—the face like an old family portrait (*Souvenirs* 1417), the great man's habit of pinching girls' bottoms as he waits for history to call on him (*Souvenirs* 1418)—as well as the remarks on Mme Pasta, the singer, and the beautifully reported trip to England. Afraid for their lives, Stendhal and his friend Lolot sleep with two girls in a house in Westminster Bridge Road—'a forgotten district' (*Souvenirs* 1445). Stendhal, like his own Julien, gets out his pistols and his dagger, puts them on a bedside table, and the description moves to his companion: 'She was charming, small, well-proportioned, pale'. Morning comes in the next paragraph with the laconic words: 'No one assassinated us' (*Souvenirs* 1447).

Beneath the funny and intelligent narrative of these years of his life, Stendhal is telling us, as he promised in the book's opening words, what happened to him. He was cured of his love for Métilde —partially or temporarily cured—and the cure is what is discreetly shown to us, turning a rambling and attractive memoir into something altogether more touching: an evocation of a heart mending. Stendhal gets drunk at Calais on the way to England, is lively, talks a lot. First infidelity, he says (*Souvenirs* 1438). In the house in Westminster Bridge Road he redeems his fiasco with Alexandrine, carefully alluded to in case we have not spotted the sequence of thought (*Souvenirs* 1445). 'It was the first real and intimate consolation for the sorrow which was poisoning all my moments of solitude' (*Souvenirs* 1447). Before this, and after this, mentions of a later mistress, Clémentine Curial, disguised as the Countess Du Long (*Souvenirs* 1395) and as Mme Bertois (*Souvenirs* 1477), hint at the coming end of the despair, the disappearance of the thoughts of suicide. 'It was only by chance, and in 1824, three years later, that I had a mistress. Only then was the memory of Métilde less rending . . .' (*Souvenirs* 1404). The image of Stendhal's next, and stormier, and certainly consummated love thus casts its shadow backwards and forwards through the text. And as Clémentine begins to move towards the centre of the narrative, as the story becomes her story, or threatens to, the narrative literally fades out. A few notes on a writer-friend masked beneath the name of M. de l'Etang, a remark or two about the heat in the margins of the manuscript—it is July, 1832—and the book stops. Stendhal's memories, if they are just memories, if they are not set in counterpoint to some half-suppressed theme, do not interest him. *Vie de Henry Brulard*, like *Souvenirs d'Egotisme*, dies as its secret subject is left behind.

There is a passage in *Souvenirs d'Egotisme* which breaks this perspective, looks away from Métilde. Stendhal remembers a conversation about suicide with Lord Brougham, who thought all the posthumous publicity might well put a man off killing himself. Stendhal suggested a discreet form of exit : you get into the habit of taking boat trips, and one stormy day you fall accidentally into the sea (*Souvenirs* 1434). With this chat in mind, along with his love of Shakespeare, Stendhal decides to cross the Channel to see Kean, in the hope, as he says, of putting a hill between himself and the sight of Milan cathedral (*Souvenirs* 1436).

We are on the edge of Stendhal's story here. The talk of suicide is in keeping with the theme, hints at a desperate dive into the waves as a means of ending it all. The overt reference to Kean and Milan suggests a simpler, less sinister design—Milan cathedral plainly means Métilde and nothing else. But the conversation Stendhal reports took place, as he himself says (*Souvenirs* 1433), before he had even met Métilde. He loved Shakespeare before he knew her too, indeed now asserts categorically that he has passionately loved in his life *only* Cimarosa, Mozart and Shakespeare (*Souvenirs* 1434). He goes on to evoke an Italy, a Milan from which Métilde is worse than absent, since she is only part of things, a woman, a sorrow, an element, not the place itself. Far from Milan representing her, as it does throughout the rest of the book, she herself is offered implicitly as just one of the charms of Milan.

'Fine places where my fine moments were set . . .' (*Souvenirs* 1440). Stendhal's spell in Italy in his thirties was the peak, the flower of his life, he tells us (*Brulard* 274, 330); he looks back on it from downward, barer slopes. He had his most extreme pains and pleasures there—a reference to Métilde, of course, but not only to her—it is where he wants to grow old and die (*Souvenirs* 1435).

Earlier, he had been initiated into sex at the same location, had discovered music, by which he means opera, had had his first grand passion for a spectacular lady, Angela Pietragrua. Milan, the first time around, had been just what Paris had failed to be for the escapee from Grenoble: the city of dreams, the scene and clear confirmation of his flight, the sign that it had been worth it. A characteristic sentence, jagged in sequence, but balanced like a tryptich in plan, says it all: 'I hate Grenoble, I arrived in Milan in May 1800, I love this town' (*Souvenirs* 1435).

Poor Métilde. A despairing suicide over her has been abruptly converted into a romantic love-death for the town she lived in. Milan is to be marked on Stendhal's tomb, he thinks of the inscription every day. Errico Beyle Milanese, who lived, wrote and loved, adored Cimarosa, Mozart and Shakespeare, and died ... (*Souvenirs* 1434). The great particular passion has dwindled to a small general verb in a graveyard: he loved. Within the book, of course, the tombstone is lying, the whole of *Souvenirs d'Egotisme* cries out against its pathetic, aesthetic posture. It is a new, sorry mask, a means of hiding even from posterity, or at least from that posterity which will not read or will not forgive a sentimental story, from people in cemeteries who expect distinction, exploits and clarity in the fallen lives they brood over. They are not to know about Métilde.

But the mask is not all mask. The light of this other Italy does briefly banish Métilde from her book, she wilts and looks pale in the face of this galloping prose from the land of operatic epitaphs. She recovers, Stendhal returns to his decorous, receding distress. But the lifted curtain has shown us, if nothing else, that she was not the whole story, that she was, among other things, a way of arranging a homecoming, a trip to Paris, in the mind. And we may have seen too that in the long run, for the life that goes on when *Souvenirs d'Egotisme* ends, the tombstone was probably right. Stendhal, that composite character we create from the voices we hear in his works, loved being in love, and Métilde was perhaps simply the finest and most memorable form of the despair he so tirelessly sought.

9. LUCIEN LEUWEN (1834-5)

'. . . ce qui tendrait à prouver que dans les
positions difficiles il faut agir.'
FÉDER

Stendhal was in the habit of destroying his written work as soon as
a printed form became available. The comments we have on *Le
Rouge et le Noir* and *La Chartreuse de Parme* are thus after-
thoughts, commentaries and apologies and accusations scribbled on
the margins or on the fly-leaves of the published novels. For *Lucien
Leuwen*, on the contrary, not finished by Stendhal and not published until after his death, we have more : the manuscript, the
whole business. Plans, drafts, notes, the novel, part of it even revised
by Stendhal himself. For once, we can see the master at work, as
Henri Martineau loyally suggests (*Lucien* 742, Martineau's preface).

Indeed we can, but not at his regular job, and *Lucien Leuwen*,
from this point of view, is a less precious bundle than it seems. It
is an attempt at something by Balzac, say, or Sue, or even George
Sand, a work unlike anything else Stendhal ever wrote. He is after
dense detail, proper narrative manners, a smoother, more flowing
prose. He wants thick, fully established supporting characters, people
with stories of their own, interesting in their own right; not simply
effigies strung out along the track of the hero, wheeled in when the
author needs them for a bit of plot-shifting. Above all he wants to
write a *novel*, a grand, full-bodied, slow-rolling affair, and not a
hasty, jerky tale of a young man's adventures on the way to the
guillotine; scenes of a social world and not just another imaginary
biography, inherited from the eighteenth century.

115

Stendhal was unjust to himself and to *Le Rouge et le Noir* in this plan—he had done well enough by the social world there, for all the thinness of his subsidiary characters. Even this thinness is an illusion, we should speak of their *smallness*. Stendhal's secondary characters, early and late, are sharply and finely drawn but distant, flung out to the margins of books dominated by the minds and perceptions of their principal figures. He probably knew too that he was following a false trail, that his talent lay elsewhere—'For none of my works' he wrote in the margins of his new novel, 'have I felt the modesty I feel about this one, May 14, '35' (*Lucien* 1492). Still, he went on.

We are given the friendly lancer Menuel, who finds Lucien almost unconscious after a duel, and whose life-story, like that of the captive in *Don Quixote*, follows hard on the heels of his appearance in the novel (*Lucien* 842–846). Then Dr Du Poirier, who is to be a major comic figure later in the book, the demonically witty provincial beleaguered by fear in Paris. He is compared with a pig, a fox, a hyena and a wild boar in the course of two pages (*Lucien* 846, 848); and more generically, twice called an animal (*Lucien* 848, 850). We blink a bit at this kind of characterization from a man who has just written one of the world's great novels, and when we are told, soon after, that Lucien in his desire to mix with the local gentry, has decided to 'howl with the wolves' (*Lucien* 855), it sounds like the last line of a very bad joke. But the intention, if horribly misplaced, is clear. Stendhal wants to create characters the way other novelists do, he wants to play with the rest of the children, to howl with the wolves himself.

Futhermore, responding to criticisms which had been made of *Le Rouge et le Noir*, he wants to introduce his characters soon enough, and then keep them in view, not let them slip out of sight as he had done the last time. Lucien's friend Coffe, who will have nothing to say until the second half of the book, is mentioned in the first chapter. Other names are dropped and left lying for future use: St Mégrin, Riquebourg, relatives of a later mistress and political associate respectively. Mme Grandet, destined for a significant part as the novel progresses, flickers pointlessly, mechanically, in and out of its earlier pages (*Lucien* 770, 911). Such comments look unfair because Stendhal didn't finish his book, and didn't correct much of it. But these are not things he could have corrected. He was not a symphonic writer, an orchestrator of rich plots and themes, he was a lover of opera, and pre-romantic opera at that : *belcanto* for the hero, with fireworks from the author at the piano. And of course there are other indications of his dogged determination, this time, to plod down the wrong road.

He hated descriptions, would sketch out a Roman scene, for example, this way :

'. . . the magnificent architecture of the neighbouring palazzi and the clusters of that savage, violent and easily moved people now inhabiting the land of the Gracchi and the Caesars.
(Ten lines of description)
He went up . . .
Lackeys in full livery on the stairway, holding flaming torches
(twenty lines) . . .
The announcements . . .
Finally, the salon . . .
Forty Roman ladies . . .
Several cardinals . . .' (*Romans* 168).

Again, this story is not finished, but the point holds. He cares only for moral descriptions, is bored by material places and faces (*Souvenirs* 1397, 1420), even goes so far as to suggest that Scott must have had a secretary to do his landscapes for him (*Souvenirs* 1472). He can be categoric : 'Writing anything other than the analysis of the human heart bores me. If chance had given me a secretary, I should have been another kind of writer' (*Souvenirs* 1473). Precisely, and a major perverseness of *Lucien Leuwen*, technically, is Stendhal's decision to double as his own secretary.

'My friend,' said Lucien's father, 'the thermometer is rising too quickly, would you kindly press the button of ventilator number two . . . there . . . behind the fireplace . . . Very good . . .'
Lucien, standing by the fireplace, looked gloomy, disturbed, tragic, looked in short just as the juvenile lead in a tragedy, crossed in love, ought to look . . .' (*Lucien* 1069–1070).

This is not all description but the combination of excessive 'scientific' detail with a heavy reference to literature—precisely the tricks which Balzac often exploits so successfully[7]—is embarrassing, grinding, injected rather than called for. We have only to look at descriptions in Stendhal's other manner to see what is wrong.

'Lost in a vague, gentle reverie so alien to his ordinary character, gently pressing this hand which seemed to him impeccably pretty, he half listened to the movement of the linden leaves stirred by the light night wind, and the dogs at the mill by the Doubs barking in the distance' (*Rouge* 279).

'The little road kept passing through copses whose trees sketched the dark contour of their foliage on a sky full of stars but veiled by a light mist. Lake and sky were profoundly calm; Fabrice couldn't resist this sublime beauty; he stopped, then sat down on a rock jutting out into the lake . . .' (*Chartreuse* 165–166).

These are applications, before Verlaine, of Verlaine's prescription for poems : landscapes as states of the soul. But there is no question of the soul's state being balanced or complemented by a correlative found in the world of material phenomena, the world is frankly converted into an allegory of a mood, an extension of feeling. Stendhal, who loved landscapes, who confesses to having travelled only for them, for the sight of fine views (*Brulard* 14), saw physical nature primarily as a source of metaphor :

'. . . the line of rocks coming up to Arbois, I think, and coming from Dôle by the main road was for me an obvious and perceptible image of the soul of Métilde . . .' (*Brulard* 14).

A courtship with the conventional contemporary novel is, again, clear here :

'. . . we beg permission to follow Lieutenant-General Count N for a moment, peer of the realm, and in charge, this year, of the inspection of the third military division . . .' (*Lucien* 784).

Stendhal's idea is to shift the focus of the narrative, to take us to a place where Lucien is not present; which with some slips, with one striking sudden reversion to Lucien's consciousness, he does. But even Dumas, who is not half so painstaking as Stendhal, is hardly clumsier. Similarly Stendhal slaves at flattening his prose, making it less *bumpy* (*Lucien* 1491), more numerous, as he has said a year or two before (*Romans* 456, 460), and manages to make it only anodine, a prose like all other contemporary proses. Balzac was later to say that Stendhal normally wrote like Diderot, 'who was not a writer'.[8] It was just because they were not writers, in the woolly, flowing, grandly professional way in which Balzac was a writer, that Diderot and Stendhal wrote so well.

We can see then why Harry Levin comes to speak of Stendhal in *Lucien Leuwen* as 'singularly ill at ease on the Balzacian terrain of contemporary France'[9] even if it is not the terrain that is the trouble. We can see too that beyond the reasons regularly rehearsed by critics for Stendhal's failure to finish the book—he had to work up his own plot and not, as in *Le Rouge et le Noir* and *La Chartreuse de Parme*, flesh out a skeleton already given to him; he couldn't realistically hope to publish his book as long as the present experiment, as he called the July Monarchy, was on—there are sound technical reasons for Stendhal's difficulties. He was turning his back on everything he knew and could do, on the forty years of subterranean training that had equipped him to write novels like *Le Rouge* and *La Chartreuse*. *Lucien Leuwen* is for Stendhal very much what *Mansfield Park* appears to have been for Jane Austen—an attempt to break out, to do something else, to widen horizons, to escape a set of limitations otherwise admirably recognized and respected—and the least we can say for such tries is that they help to show us how the other novels work. To be sure, for *Mansfield Park* and *Lucien Leuwen* we can say a great deal more too.

The uneasiness in *Lucien Leuwen* is not all Stendhal's. Most readers come to the novel, if they come to it at all, after *Le Rouge* and *La Chartreuse*, so that even Stendhal's achievements in the new vein, especially his achievements perhaps, tend to look like betrayals. His successes count against him with his failures.

There is for example, a cinematic fade-out on a physical detail which would not have disgraced Dickens. An old officer of the Revolution, broken, as Stendhal says by fifteen years of the Restoration (*Lucien* 778), weighs in his hand a silver-mounted meerschaum pipe, his first gift from Lucien, a rich man's son enrolled in his regiment, and thinks of all his future profits from this soft client. The chapter ends: '. . . hiding the pipe among his shirts, he took the key to his chest of drawers' (*Lucien* 779). There is this twist on a heavy narrative trick, very funny, and decently close to Fielding, Stendhal's model for much of the planning of *Lucien Leuwen* : 'We shall take the liberty of leaping boldly over the two months which followed. This will be all the easier as Leuwen, at the end of these two months, was not further advanced than he was on the first day' (*Lucien* 994). And the whole of the first chapter is a model of tidy, thorough exposition of character and theme. None of the jumps and bounces, the rough caricatural edges, the gleams of alarming ironies which mark the opening pages of *Le Rouge et le Noir*. Something steadier, less idiosyncratic, less amateurish.

Lucien Leuwen is expelled from the Paris Polytechnic for 'taking a badly timed walk'—'it was at the time of those famous days in June, April or February of 1832 or 1834' (*Lucien* 768). Stendhal meant to check the dates. The occasion, as Henri Martineau reminds us (*Lucien* 1489) was the funeral of Lamarque, an opposition general, attended by students in uniform, in spite of the fact that the whole school was confined to barracks for the day, but the text makes a perfectly clear meaning: a gesture of republican sympathy from the students, directed against the new middle-of-the-road monarchy. But Lucien is not a hard-line republican, has no social ambitions to spark his politics, And his main occupation, 'at the moment we meet him' (*Lucien* 768), is helping his worldly father to spend his money. There follows a quick portrait of the mother, of the company Lucien's parents keep, then a scolding of Lucien by his cousin Ernest for being simple, childish, happy, natural, insufficiently calculating, not solemn enough for the century. We then see Lucien in his favourite exotic nightwear, pacing the rich Turkish carpet in his room, glancing quickly and regularly at the sofa, where an officer's uniform is spread out. Happiness, Stendhal comments (*Lucien* 772).

It is nicely done, it is what Stendhal wants. Yet the scenes or constructions he botches in the novel often seem closer to what he ought to be doing. For example, Lucien, on arriving at his garrison in Nancy, falls from his horse in front of the window of a beautiful young woman, Mme de Chasteller, whom he is later to love and marry. This is clumsy enough comedy, but there is already a sharper irony lurking: riding a horse is virtually the only thing Lucien knows he does well, and yet precisely here he has to get thrown by the miserable nag the army has provided him with. Worse still, Lucien was on his guard for a difficult start in the regiment: scorn from his fellow-officers, a duel perhaps. No. A sprawl in the mud with a charming woman watching. Lucien then takes an apartment in Nancy, and is given, predictably, the apartment once occupied by a M. Busant de Sicile, whom local legend has firmly if quite wrongly cast in the role of lover to Mme de Chasteller. This again is heavy, too neat, a crying symbolic point recalling too strongly the red drapes in the church in *Le Rouge et le Noir*, the spilt holy water looking like blood, the anagram on Julien's name. But lumpish as the touch is, the music is now in the right key. Stendhal's affair is shapes, symmetries, logical snares, not the calm procession of the world as simulated by the more serious realists.

The touch is sometimes more lumpish still. At the end of the first part of the book, Stendhal has his hero and heroine on his hands. They are in love, have confessed their love, but he doesn't want them in bed, indeed needs to separate them so that the novel can get on to its next, wider parabola, a movement which will bring the hero back to his mistress only at the very end, after adventures in Paris and Rome. What is his idea? A trick played on Lucien's innocence. Lucien is to be made to believe that Mme de Chasteller is delivered of a child, clearly not his for very good reasons. Stunned, bewildered, broken-hearted, he is to leave for Paris. Stendhal does what he can to enliven this desperately poor and awkward idea— has the supposedly newborn child visibly a month or two old, yet Lucien failing to notice this—but he can't do much. There it is. Lucien in the closet, given a trumped-up rendez-vous, made to overhear an elucidating conversation created just for him, and finally shown the child. He gets out with what dignity he can, which is considerable, in the light of what Stendhal has put him through. The whole sequence is grotesque, lamentable.

Yet lamentable or not, it is, again, lamentable in Stendhal's manner, he was trying, out of his own invention, for the blend of weirdness and truth which he found, or was able to cultivate, in the ready-made stories of *Le Rouge et le Noir* and *La Chartreuse de Parme*. Life, his intuition insists, is an affair of erratic events in a slipping focus, ludicrous, angular, incredible, it is not the tight plot and firm *milieu* and fixed, complete vision of what was to become, in the hands of Balzac and Tolstoy and George Eliot, the classical novel. The world moves more than that, even Stendhal's errors seem to say.

And with this, we arrive at the major source of our uneasiness faced with *Lucien Leuwen*. The book is not finished. How do we know what Stendhal's mature talent might not have made of the episode of the transferred child? How do we know what he might not have done in the way of classical novels, if *Lucien Leuwen* had been a success for him? *War and Peace*, perhaps. *Middlemarch*. Not very likely. And all speculation aside, the problem remains. What are we to do with this incomplete subject? Treat it as the Romantics treated ruins, gloat on the standing arches among the fallen stones, perhaps even prefer the broken cloister to what it might have been whole? Collate all the plans, all the outlines, complete the novel in our head, and talk about that, our completion? In fact Stendhal himself gives us a lead here.

In *Vie de Henry Brulard* he speaks several times of his memory

121

as a fallen fresco (*Brulard* 102, 113–114, 157, 302), a set of wall paintings exceptionally vivid in some places, and completely erased in others, and a fallen fresco is exactly what *Lucien Leuwen* is for us: not a ruin but a set of scenes and stories with only their connections and their total context missing, fragments less spectral and and more self-contained than an isolated east façade or an edge of presbytery. That is to say, there are two separate senses in which the novel is not finished, one of which matters a good deal more than the other.

First, the story is not all told, and this doesn't matter at all. There is nothing that we need to know about Lucien or his world, or that he needs to know about it or himself, that is not shown in the novel we have. Whether the book was to end in his marriage or his death is simply a matter of management, sweeping up. In fact, Stendhal had a marriage planned. Lucien was to forgive Mme de Chasteller for having cuckolded him, for so he constantly thought of the matter, and they were to marry. Mme de Chasteller was then to give incontrovertible proof of her innocence to Lucien, who would thus have won all round: fine pardoning gesture rewarded by the news that there was nothing to pardon. Bliss. 'End of the novel' (*Lucien* 1527). We may feel that it was just as well that Stendhal did not get around to this. Indeed, the novel could end where it ends in its most complete modern version: with Lucien's departure for a diplomatic post abroad, his father dead, his mother installed and abandoned in genteel poverty in Paris. That Lucien should not return to Mme de Chasteller, that the full narrative circle should not close, in no way changes the quality of their love, beautifully rendered before Stendhal steps in with his lumbering device of the supposed childbirth. The portrait of this love is quite exquisite, one of the most authentically tender love stories in literature, I think. Or again, there is an even better ending for the novel within the work as we have it. Stendhal had designed a three-part structure: provinces, Paris, Rome (disguised sometimes as Madrid, sometimes as a place called Capel). In Rome he intended to pick up pieces from a novel begun in 1832, *Une Position Sociale*, where a self-doubting republican hero was to fence with the aristocratic wife of the ambassador, a lady in the late stages of religious panic. Stendhal then decided to leave off the third part, which meant, as Martineau astutely comments (*Lucien* 740), that the book was finished; all Stendhal now had to do was to revise what he had written. It also meant, as Martineau doesn't say, that Stendhal could dispense with Leuwen

122

senior's bankruptcy and death, and with Lucien's posting to Rome, and simply close his novel with the present chapter 67 : Lucien dashing off to Nancy and Mme de Chasteller, fleeing the attentions of his mother and father and Mme Grandet, the mistress his father has literally seduced for him. He could then add or not add the fairy-tale resolution mentioned above, forgiveness all round, the welcome in Nancy. The story would be over, what else would there be to say?

There would still be pieces of the plan missing, of course : Mme de Chasteller coming to Paris, her rivalry with Mme Grandet; the antics in Paris of the frightened Dr Du Poirier, malign agent of Lucien's departure from Nancy. This latter thought sounds interesting, but it only sounds so. Stendhal was always bad with characters he consciously planned as comic, his strength lay in surrounding characters he took seriously with comic perspectives.

But there is another, more important sense in which the novel is unfinished. It is too long and too thin. Stendhal had been obliged to 'make substance' (*Lucien* 1401) for *Le Rouge et le Noir*, to pad out the Parisian part of the novel, and he intends this time to work the other way round, to make *Lucien Leuwen* too long and then cut it. What we have is thus an uncut work. And at the same time, and more gravely, an undeveloped one. There are crucial passages in the book which are not good or bad but simply *not there*, novelistically—as imagined realities they simply do not exist. Thus Lucien's love-affair, incomparable in itself, has no beginning and no end. We see Lucien as paralysed in the presence of Mme de Chasteller, several times, as a good lover should be according to all the prescriptions of *De l'Amour*. What is then needed is some small, eloquent, activating event to turn things round, to give Lucien back his normal charm and to endow him with the special intimate intelligence he needs to make the conquest of this exceptional woman. Instead, there are just assertions. Lucien becomes 'another man', and Stendhal slips into one of his rare stretches of uncorrected sentimentality. Lucien is able to rustle up 'that nuance of delicate familiarity which befits two souls of the same quality, when they meet and recognize each other among the masks of the ignoble masked ball we call the world. Thus angels would speak if, sent from heaven on some mission, they were to meet, by chance, here below' (*Lucien* 923). Again later, after displaying a marvellous sequence of touching, painful and funny misunderstandings by letter, Stendhal finds he doesn't know what to do with his lovers, and just shuffles them from silliness to silliness. In the second part of the book, Lucien's father is elected to the Chamber of Deputies, and rocks the reigning government, which is a fine idea, but remains merely sketched. We are told about M. Leuwen's wit in the House, but never shown it.

We might say, as I have already said, that Stendhal's completed fiction looks like this too, slips off suddenly into darkness, is a metaphor for the abrupt tilts and vacancies of life; and we might say of the more fully realized parts of *Lucien Leuwen* that they would almost certainly not have been improved by Stendhal's re-working them—he had no talent for revision, and spent some time before he died at the thankless job of ruining *La Chartreuse de Parme* on the recommendations of Balzac. We might say, putting those two halves together, that the best parts of *Lucien Leuwen* are good enough, and that the total is not all that different from the irregular entireties of Stendhal's finished novels. But this won't do. The best parts of *Lucien Leuwen* are as good as anything Stendhal ever wrote—his desire to be Balzac softened into a willingness to be another version of himself, kinder, gentler with his hero, meaner and sourer with the political and social world around him. For all his mistakes and false starts and awkwardnesses here, Stendhal does find a new tone which is a perfect transition between the often hard notes of *Le Rouge et le Noir*, too Roman as Stendhal thought it (*Romans* 457) and the flighty lyricism of *La Chartreuse de Parme*. The sheer reporting of the later pages of *Lucien Leuwen* is impeccable, too, and to my taste, makes Flaubert's *Education sentimentale*, in its political aspects, look like a cardboard fantasy, society squinted at from the library window. But still, these are parts, pieces, not a whole, and there is the difficulty of dealing with them. What I have tried to do is pick up the moral slant of the successful patches, the vivid bands of the fresco, and this does form a unity of a kind. I am thinking of the following episodes : Lucien as a soldier in provincial society in Nancy; Lucien in love; Lucien supervising the death of the *agent provocateur* Kortis; and Lucien on his double electoral mission in the department of the Cher and in Normandy. I have of course referred to other things in the novel, but generally these sequences are what I now mean by *Lucien Leuwen*.

The moral slant. It is amazing how little, in his most overtly con-temporary novel, Stendhal appears to care about politics in the conventional sense : ideas, ideologies, parties, programmes. Politics in *Lucien Leuwen* is above all an art of treachery, a dirty if occasionally fascinating game, an exercise quite without honour and demanding small intelligence. 'All governments . . . lie all the time and about everything; when they can't lie about the substance, they lie about the details' (*Lucien* 1080). 'You must always treat a minister as if he were an imbecile, he doesn't have any time to think' (*Lucien* 1099). Lucien's father is rich in such advice, and nothing in the book gives us any grounds for supposing he is wrong. It is worth noting too how small a role politics plays in personal affairs in Stendhal's work generally. Julien Sorel and Mme de Rênal are kept apart by their difference of class, not by a difference in political opinions. Lucien and Mme de Chasteller seem set up for a pack of ironies playing all the way across the political spectrum, a game of hard tennis across the sticky court of the July monarchy—Stendhal even thought of calling his novel *The Red and the White*, 'to remind people of *The Red and the Black* and to give the journalists a phrase. *Red*, the republican Lucien, *White*, the young royalist de Chasteller' (*Lucien* 1489). But they simply give up their politics the moment they fall in love. 'Lucien had sacrificed his liberalism to her, and she her ultra-royalism to him; they had been perfectly in agreement on that for a long time' (*Lucien* 1027). As easily as that. And when Stendhal specifically manages a scene where politics appear to intrude, as the conservative Mme Grandet passes out in her passion for Lucien, and Lucien is said to be a party man in the middle of a love scene (*Lucien* 1375), Lucien's objection is not to Mme Grandet's party but to her meanness, he remembers her proud and nasty refusal to give anything to help clothe some political prisoners who were to be transferred from Lyon to Paris in the cold, and were likely to die from exposure in the process. The margin of the manuscript carries an eloquent comment on Stendhal's own comment on Lucien : 'For to be human is a party' (*Lucien* 1585). Stendhal's vision is always a moral vision, which is what edges his portraits towards caricature and means that the ugliness embodied in *Lucien Leuwen* by Louis Philippe was finally for Stendhal a moral rather than a political fact : perfidy, simply. Louis Philippe, in Stendhal's view, had betrayed the second Revolution of 1830, had let the people down, and *Lucien Leuwen* is about this king's country, invaded by the seeping consequences of his crime much as the land of Amfortas was laid waste by his wound. When the king is savagely lampooned in the later pages of the book, we are witnessing, obviously, the consul's revenge on a

125

master he despised; but the novelist may be at work too, moving intuitively to get the source and emblem and chief beneficiary of all the trouble into his pages, to let him be seen in action, seedily scheming, the summary of the shabbiness rife in France. There is another echo in the name of the book's comic villain, Du Poirier: *pear* was a code sign for the king, based on an unkind view of the shape of his face (*Lucien* 1495).

Stendhal occasionally set the beginning of the rot further back, in the early Empire notably. 'Happy the heroes dead before 1804', he cries at one point (*Lucien* 785). The career of Lucien's commanding officer in Nancy is an allegory of the moral rise and fall of France, from the heady days of the Marseillaise through the Empire and the Restoration down to his current cynical greed as he contemplates the expensive pipe Lucien has given him. But Stendhal's main focus is resolutely recent, four and five years back from the time of writing. The present régime is not only crooked, Lucien's friend Coffe remarks, it is 'essentially crooked', and more so than the Bourbons and Napoleon, 'for it constantly betrays its initial oath' (*Lucien* 1199). Stendhal is glowering over the current 'halt in the mud' (*Lucien* 773), an expression he borrows from General Lamarque, the man whose funeral cost Lucien his place at the Polytechnic. Stendhal later takes the phrase further, builds on it with a sardonic literalism. As Lucien begins work at the Ministry of the Interior he has the feeling of 'plunging himself into the mud' (*Lucien* 1102). Some time later, he and Coffe rattle into Blois in a coach piled high with pamphlets, charged with a doubtful government mission. They are pelted in the face with mud for their pains, and in case either we or Lucien fail to get the point, a metaphorician in the crowd cries: 'Look how dirty he is; you've brought his soul out on to his face!' (*Lucien* 1190). A stint of hard work staves off the memory of the mud at Blois, but Stendhal has no intention of letting Lucien off so lightly. His coach has been washed twice since the adventure, but when he puts his hand into a compartment to take out a book, he finds it still full of damp mud, and the book ruined (*Lucien* 1215). Last tricky touch: Lucien is decorated by the king for a wound received at Blois in the exercise of a mission (*Lucien* 1288). Literalization of the idea of dirty work, real mud on the face being then reinvested as metaphor. And of course Lucien and Coffe are up to no good. They are fixing elections, ensuring the return of nonentities, and in one case, actively trying to exclude an extraordinarily good man.

Lucien's role, then, is that of foil and victim of the immoral world of his time, and I want to insist on the harshness of Stendhal's view here. Lucien's world is not merely stupid, or flaccid, or boring, or corrupt, although it is all those things. It is rank, festering, and in this respect the worst of the worlds Stendhal portrays. In comparison, the Restoration of *Le Rouge et le Noir* looks almost like a golden age, full of the glamour of intrigue and of the high ridiculousness of extreme reaction—the régime was just too improbable to go on forever. This no doubt is why the royalists come off so well in *Lucien Leuwen*. They are hopeless in the grand manner, like the Italians of *La Chartreuse de Parme*, and at least they are faithful to an old idea, while the new men are faithful to nothing except their own avidity, and the old idea itself, seen from the swamps of the present, has a certain charm. Perhaps an early intuition of this went into Stendhal's ironic ignoring of the 1830 revolution in *Le Rouge et le Noir*: nostalgia for the known enemy as well as an attack on the pretended progressiveness of the incoming government.

Lucien's career is Julien's redrawn in crucial ways. For if *Lucien Leuwen* was intended technically as a new venture, a counter-novel, its subject is a continuation, a complement to *Le Rouge et le Noir*. Both young men face the same, initial, all-informing paradox: the desire to be a soldier in peace time, they are keen recruits born too late for the Napoleonic wars. Julien, as we have seen, thinks up a translation while still very young, he will get to the top by the cloth not by the knapsack, and if he finally gets a commission in the hussards as a result of his antics in a black suit, that is a piece of wit on the part of a seemingly haphazard fate. Lucien, on the other hand, is allowed the real thing for a start, with only a slight deviation from the simplest of paths: the lancers instead of the artillery, which is where his education at the Polytechnic would have taken him had he not been expelled. Of course the real thing is nothing like the real thing, nothing could be further from it. The chief combats in this army are battles of dignity with your fellow officers: 'the *order of the day* is to abstain, the *plan of campaign*, to do as little as possible' (*Lucien* 826, Stendhal's italics). Lucien laughs as he tells himself this. His first and only action in the army is a regimental visit to a nearby town to pacify some starving workers who have been imprudent enough to organize themselves into a union. Women and children of the workers howl at the regiment, shops close, and finally a mortal silence takes over. Everywhere, Stendhal

127

says, a vivid portrait of poverty, torn, grubby washing, windows patched up with old papers (*Lucien* 991). The regiment waits seven hours under an August sun, a shot is fired, hits no one. Lucien suspects immediately, and no doubt correctly, a put-up job, an attempt at provocation. At night they are relieved by the infantry. See the newspapers, Stendhal says, for the military, strategic, political etc. details of this great affair (*Lucien* 993). 'The regiment had covered itself with glory, and the workers had shown exceptional cowardice' (*Lucien* 993). There is a movement here towards Stendhal's final, all-quieting statement in this line : at Waterloo, in *La Chartreuse de Parme*, the only fighting Fabrice sees at close quarters is Frenchmen against Frenchmen. One could hardly spell out a defeat, the ruin of an army and a country, more clearly.

Lucien then, like Julien, needs a paraphrase which is more than verbal, something to bring the times just a little closer to the idea of glory; and he leaves the army, albeit for other reasons. Here is a major difference between his moral fortunes and those of Julien. Julien's paraphrase, black for red, is his own idea, and between this misplaced ingenuity and the inherent idiocy of the Restoration there arises a playful liberty, the novel has room to move. Lucien's paraphrase is his father's idea, and is in any case inevitable, no intelligence or agility was required to come across it. There is no war, therefore no battles. Since the July Revolution, the Church is as pointless a profession as the army. What remains? Of course, politics. And here, references to the military trade have none of the wistfulness they retain in *Le Rouge et le Noir*—Julien's commission may be a joke but it is a kind of reward. Lucien is greeted by his minister with a fulsome hint, an 'explosion of tenderness' : 'How happy I am to have such a captain in my regiment !' (*Lucien* 1116). The minister presumably means to be polite, to help Lucien metaphorically from his old job into the new, but the result is a mockery. Entrusted with his first difficult task, Lucien walks with the firm step of a man 'marching to the assault of a battery' (*Lucien* 1129), but where is he going? To a hospital, to make sure an unsavoury government agent doesn't squeal before he dies. His friend Coffe consoles him for the mud on his face at Blois by telling him it is the dust of the modern battlefield (*Lucien* 1192), but this in effect is sheer derision, compounded and completed by the absurd aptness of Lucien's receiving a decoration for a wound to his pride. The hollowness which keeps surfacing in *Le Rouge et le Noir*, the sense of a world which has slithered from substance to sign, which is in danger of becoming nothing more than a set of empty forms sustained only by the snobbery and poverty of imagination of the people in power, this hollowness along with the recurring mud defines the France of *Lucien Leuwen*.

There is nowhere for Lucien to go socially. He is a rich, stylish young bourgeois, aristocratic in taste and talent, he has neither the needs of the poor nor the crippling archaic status of the nobility. It goes without saying that neither he nor his father or mother have any of the vices of their own class. But before we decry this as rampant fantasy, wish-fulfilment, we must look more closely. Lucien's enviable social situation is in fact a trap, a plight. Like a later hero of Sartre's, he finds it hard to escape his father and therefore to be himself in any serious way. His father buys him into the regiment, his father gets him a job at the ministry, his father selects him a mistress and even makes sure she smiles on him. The result of all this is that the core of Julien's ambition, his need to test his courage and his character, a need blurred by his schemes for social mobility and his general wariness about anything that looks like a truth about himself, emerges in Lucien as a simple and fully conscious desire; as Lucien's only desire, in fact. He gets a second scolding from his cousin Ernest, who accuses him of having done nothing more in life than to have 'taken the trouble to be born' (*Lucien* 776), is upset and rushes off to see his father, tears in his eyes. Leuwen senior thinks his son needs some money, and offers it to him, thereby rubbing salt into the wound. Lucien is more moved still, grateful, stricken with an access of affection for his father, who tells him off for coming and loving him so 'furiously', and sends him to the Opera, where he is to pick up some light ladies and take them to dinner. Later, having acquited himself honourably of the evening's job, Lucien is worried by his sudden fit of sensibility, surprised by it in retrospect : '. . . really, I'm not sure of anything about myself . . . I need to act, and act a lot' (*Lucien* 778). The novel thus becomes Lucien's quest for action in this sense, for a test of the self. He wants to know who he is, to surprise himself less.

He is thus ready to run into a paradox after Stendhal's own heart. Here he is, about to be a peace-time soldier, fighting cabbage wars with starving workers, about to be killed perhaps, as he imagines, by a flying chamber pot hurled from a fifth floor by a toothless old dame (*Lucien* 774). He cooks up a conversation with Napoleon in the next world, subsequent to such a glorious death.

No doubt, he hears Napoleon saying, you were in that business because you were dying of hunger? No, general, Lucien answers, I thought I was following in your footsteps (*Lucien* 774). There is a severe, almost shocking version of the same exchange later in the book. It concerns Lucien's working for the government now, and takes place after the mud-throwing at Blois. Lucien answers Coffe's remark about the mud being the dust of the battlefield:

' "You mean that if you had an income of twelve hundred francs, you wouldn't be here."
"If I had an income of three hundred francs I shouldn't be serving a government which keeps thousands of poor devils in the horrible dungeons of Mont-Saint-Michel and Clairvaux" ' (*Lucien* 1192–1193).

Lucien is put cruelly in his place, poor little rich boy who doesn't need the money, and his high estimate of what Coffe would require to live on is itself a harsh comment on his inexperience, his isolation, his insulation.

But if he doesn't need the money, he nevertheless needs the job, for good reasons of his own. He wants to do something in the world, and the best the contemporary world can provide is this murky mission. It is surprising that with a paradox of this power in his hands, Stendhal should so often lose sight of it, and substitute similar but weaker forms so regularly. For this is what he does. 'Source of the comic,' he says, twice, in the margins of his manuscript, 'this absurdity: Lucien wants to combine the benefits of ministerial work with the fine sensibility of a man of honour' (*Lucien* 1559). Coffe is given almost word for word the same line within the text of the novel. And it is simply not true, it just looks true, tidy, neat. Lucien in fact is not after any benefits which are in opposition to the sensibility of a man of honour, and gambles all such benefits grandly, recklessly at a later stage in his electoral mission. Again, Stendhal repeatedly presents Lucien's political dilemma as a choice between a virtuous, boring America and a corrupt, decadent France with a few witty men left in it, and refuses to move the discussion beyond this level. Lucien is to choose between the only republic there is and the status quo in France. Plainly Stendhal is reproducing here a situation he felt to be his own, a man caught between a theoretical liberalism, and a practical distaste for proximity to the people, although he doesn't lend the problem to Lucien in quite those uncharitable terms. 'I care for the common people, I detest their oppressors, but it would be a torment for me to have to live with them all the time' (*Brulard* 139). 'My friends, or rather my so-called friends, raise doubts about the sincerity of my liberalism because of this' (*Brulard* 132). But Stendhal's friends, so-called or not, were wrong, and Stendhal was wrong insofar as he listened to them. Neither he nor Lucien was forced to emigrate or become a time-server; and neither of them did. They did something else, they kept faiths alive while doing drab jobs. And at least Stendhal, if not Lucien, saw the horror and the sentimentality of the need to *like* the oppressed before you will care for their case. Justice is not a question of taste.

Stendhal knows he needs a paradox, knows he has one in *Lucien Leuwen*, but nevertheless cannot keep it in focus. The result is a blur running right across the book. The traps which close so cleanly round Julien Sorel here click half-shut, hang open; symmetrical sentences reach out and then fail to hold the hero in any kind of logical grip. This is perhaps the hero's fault. He is kind, decent, modest, and except when he is in love, has a lot of logic of his own—he is, as I suggested earlier, too lucid for the novel's good. He refuses the silliness Stendhal seems to want to rush him into, and as Stendhal himself says in a note, the novelist is the hero's dog (*Lucien* 1537). If he won't shoot, the dog can't fetch. Lucien won't shoot, at least in this direction. He wants to be a man of honour in an honourless world, and as Stendhal well knows, this is not a paradox, and not much of an irony; it is not absurd, not comic, it is admirable, and virtue is always hard for fiction to bear.

Lucien's first step in his quest is backwards, for against all his intentions and severe manifestoes, he falls in love, awkwardly, stupidly, thoroughly in love, exactly as he had sworn not to. He had thought of love only as a 'dangerous and despised precipice' (*Lucien* 909), much as Mme de Rênal, before she met Julien, had seen the passions as a lottery, 'certain deception and a happiness sought by fools' (*Rouge* 262). Here as elsewhere, Stendhal's characters show distinct signs of having recently read *De l'Amour* —'Love is a delightful flower, but one must have the courage to gather it on the edges of a horrible precipice' (*Amour* 164)—while their author has moved on to a stormier, less aesthetic, less timid view of things. For the older Stendhal love is neither the precipice nor the flower, it is the dizzying, irreclaimable fall itself.

Certainly Lucien is interested in women, regrets his expulsion from the Polytechnic chiefly because he can no longer wear his sword, and Mme Grandet, one of the beauties of the new court, admired him in it (*Lucien* 770). Similarly, his first tumble in the mud at Nancy is a direct result of his trying to show off his horsemanship for a girl with ash-blonde hair at a window: Mme de Chasteller, although Lucien does not yet know her (*Lucien* 794). (Later, he falls again in the same place and for the same reason; another instance, as with Julien's recurring ladders, of a symbolism which mocks symbolism by its excessive transparency, redundancy almost). But women in such situations are mere mirrors for Lucien's vanity, his behaviour is simply part of his young man's style. Love, he thinks, is an old-fashioned amusement, a feature of the *ancien régime*, of a world where there was nothing better to do—he has yet to find out that his own world too offers nothing better, and a lot that is worse. 'Who bothers himself with women these days?' (*Lucien* 907). An old duke, who keeps a dancer the way other people keep canaries (*Lucien* 907).

Lucien scorns lovers like his other cousin Edgar, whose sense of their own value depends on a woman's judgement. He has a 'political heart' (*Lucien* 1008), feels that a man cannot love both his country and a woman (*Lucien* 947). All of which means, of course, that he is simply scared, that his thoughts on the subject are a rickety super-structure of self-deceit—as his nagging, unshakeable jealousy clearly shows. He is jealous of M. Busant de Sicile, erstwhile occupant of his apartment in Nancy, lieutenant-colonel, and rumoured lover of Mme de Chasteller, a man who in fact, the narrative tells us, was a kind of caricature of Stendhal himself, fat and forty and a nuisance, and treated as such by Mme de Chasteller. Not that Lucien knows this: gossip in Nancy is anxious to insist on flaws in any virtue, and is very firm about the Busant de Sicile legend. But in any case this past of Mme de Chasteller's ought to be a good sign for Lucien, if he wants, as he keeps pretending he wants, a light, undemanding provincial affair: she has a soft spot for the army, likes men in uniform. Instead he is tortured by self-doubt and envy, and nailed hard to the wall by Stendhal's insistent, unkind logic: he wants to succeed in love but is ready to despise his mistress because he sees a chance of success (*Lucien* 908). Lucien, who is rarely spared anything by his author, himself sees the ridiculousness of his position with a crippling clarity.

And the lady he loves is not much better off. She too is hard hit by the logic Stendhal lends her, behaves as she thinks immodestly, and finds herself desperately concerned about Lucien's opinion of her : 'If he didn't despise me, I should despise him' (*Lucien* 941). She is a person who is happy, light-hearted even, beneath an apparent solemnity. She is touched by odd small things, like Stendhal, and like Stendhal she loves Italian music. In many ways, she *is* Stendhal, much as Cathy Earnshaw, in *Wuthering Heights*, *is* Heathcliff. She is Stendhal's innocence, preserved in some safe region of the consul's withering heart, she is as surprised as Lucien by what is happening to her. She is in love before she knows it (*Lucien* 925), and not in the temporary, casual, fashionable way her friends would wish for her. 'There is a man' she says later, in deep shame, 'who must think I love him'. Lowering her head, she adds, 'And he is hardly wrong' (*Lucien* 1088).

In these parts of *Lucien Leuwen* Stendhal has written what he failed to write in *Armance* : a perfect fragment of his own version of *La Princesse de Clèves*, an extraordinarily delicate suite of scenes on the terror and occasional joy of loving for the first and only time. Lucien and Mme de Chasteller are bewildered children, caught up in something quite beyond them. Lucien, for example, almost confesses his jealousy to her, tells her he has a suspicion, and she, without thinking, asks : What suspicion? Of course he can't tell her, can only mumble about his respect for her preventing him from going on, which plainly makes things worse. She is flattered that he should care so, but anxious about the suspicion, and more anxious still about her own behaviour in allowing this kind of intimacy to a young man she hardly knows, and who may well be the cold-blooded Don Juan he sometimes seems. But she has to persist, asks Lucien whether his stiffness earlier in the evening—they are at a ball—was caused, then, by his suspicion. Lucien answers so simply and truthfully—he was shy, he says, he has never been in love before—that she all but tells him she loves him in return, indeed feels she probably has told him she loves him, mutely but clearly enough for other people at the ball to see. And a new worry thus surfaces : has she compromised herself in Lucien's eyes, thrown herself at him? (*Lucien* 928–932). Stendhal apologizes for Mme de Chasteller's childishness here (*Lucien* 932), but the apology is surrounded by none of his customary ironies. In spite of her marriage, he says, the only feelings she has experienced have been a timidity with princesses and an indignation with the Jacobins (*Lucien* 932–933).

Lucien does despise her, or tries to. 'All right, I shall love her and despise her, he told himself. And when she is in love with me, I shall say: Ah, if your soul had been purer I should have loved you all my life' (*Lucien* 948). Clumsy, pathetic fantasy. Mme de Chasteller behaves coldly to Lucien the next time she sees him, and all his tough resolutions die. His love now hurts so much that he throws himself into another existence, becomes a talker, a wit, a provincial comedian, with immense success. His mind, Stendhal says, was his soul's clown (*Lucien* 953). When his pain shows through, people take him to be imitating Byron (*Lucien* 954), staging a bout or two of romantic melancholy. He sees Mme de Chasteller again, even tells her how unhappy he is; but she holds firm. He then falls back feebly on the old Don Juan's standby: a correspondence, a form of fencing for which he could hardly be less well equipped. After three letters he gets an answer, but doesn't know how to interpret this first victory, indeed takes it to be a defeat, and composes a desolate response, which touches Mme de Chasteller, wins his battle for him after all. Unfortunately, he is dissatisfied with this troubled, immediate cry and follows it up at once with a fancier, worldlier composition of seven pages. Mme de Chasteller is annoyed, and writes, in effect, the terse note of dismissal that Lucien thought he had received the first time.

Stendhal is glancing here, as he does on several occasions in *Le Rouge et le Noir* (*Rouge* 531, 593–594, 603, 609, 613), at the eighteenth century's taste for letter-novels, paraphrasing what is virtually a parody of such a novel into his own running prose. But beyond the comedy we can see a sadness, the odour of loneliness borne on such misunderstandings, the disquieting isolation embodied in letters which cross, or even meet; in the very form of novels like *Clarissa* or *La Nouvelle Héloise* or *Les Liaisons Dangereuses*. All this is underlined for Lucien and Mme de Chasteller by the fact that they are able to see each other, that their letters go on corresponding without them. 'Don't believe the letter you will receive from me', she tells him (*Lucien* 967); but he does believe it.

They find each other first, though. They go out with a local family to a café in the woods, where a soulful orchestra plays slow music. It is one of those evenings, Stendhal says, which are among the greatest enemies of impassive hearts (*Lucien* 966). They talk, forget their doubts, pride, fear, false guesses about each other. 'It is for rare moments such as these that life is worth living' (*Lucien*

968). Later, after more misunderstandings, they go again to the café. Mozart. Life for Lucien has the beauty of a novel, a romance (*Lucien* 986).

It is strange, and oddly moving, to see Stendhal letting himself go in this way. His soft heart shows here as it does in no other work, even in *La Chartreuse de Parme*, generally regarded as his last lyrical word on the good things he has known or wanted. And the reason, or at least part of the reason, is that Lucien's bumpy, broken idyll, from the point of view of his quest, is a mistake, a lure, a side-track. Stendhal works by opposites, and he can release for Lucien every stored dream of Métilde because the whole adventure, in the alternating movement of his book, will be a profound irony, and therefore in some sense safe, not available for rough laughter.

Lucien's love, for all its tender triumph as love, is a series of moral set-backs, reveals alarming holes in his knowledge of himself. Mme de Chasteller enters a room where he is, and he can't move, can't talk intelligibly. He is as surprised as he would have been to find himself fleeing during a regimental attack on an enemy (*Lucien* 910), is humiliated to see how little he can rely on himself. 'What a lesson in modesty! What a need to act in order to be sure of oneself at last, in terms not of some empty probability, but of the facts!' (*Lucien* 910). He consoles himself somewhat with the thought of the extreme nature of his sudden disability. 'Since the physical effect is so strong, I can't be morally to blame! If I had a broken leg I wouldn't be able to march with my regiment either' (*Lucien* 910). But this doesn't help. Here, as originally with his startled father, his reactions have taken him completely unawares, and there is worse to come. At a later stage of his love, he manages to persuade Mme de Chasteller to let him call on her. She, fully conscious now of her love for Lucien, and afraid she may show it with a disgraceful, immodest clarity if left alone with him, engages as a companion Mlle Bérard, the nastiest gossip in town, a toadeater, Stendhal says using the English word ('the English, great portrayers of everything disagreeable') (*Lucien* 969). When Lucien arrives, his head full of elegant, intimate, charming ways of confessing his passion, the toadeater is installed with Mme de Chasteller in the salon, yellow and shining, golden glasses on her pointed nose. Lucien talks about the weather, manages a few veiled comments about the impossibility of saying anything under the prevailing circumstances, and leaves. There follows a remarkable insight, an anticipation of what Proust

135

was to call the intermittences of the heart. For Lucien is simply no longer in love. He is cured, and therefore of course full of self-reproach. Only yesterday she meant everything to him, and if he were to tell her so today he would be lying. 'Tomorrow I could be an assassin, a thief, anything. I'm not sure of anything about myself' (*Lucien* 975). He goes on to philosophize about the fickleness of men and the unhappiness of women who attach themselves to them. 'Great God, what is life? I'm going to have to be indulgent from now on' (*Lucien* 976). He details the qualities of Mme de Chasteller to himself, in the hope of stirring up a bit of the old feeling, and in the course of his brooding slips into a chilling past tense :

'Her nose is a bit aquiline; I don't like that in a woman, I didn't ever like it in her, even when I loved her . . . When I loved her!' (*Lucien* 977).

But then her harsh letter arrives, and his love comes flooding back. He has been throughout the affair completely at the mercy of his feelings, buffeted by the high winds of his adolescent heart. He has been, to borrow a phrase Stendhal uses of himself in *Vie de Henry Brulard*, his soul's toy rather than his soul's jester : '. . . what seemed true . . . one day seemed false the next' (*Brulard* 369). Clearly the quest has to be begun again.

The story of *Lucien Leuwen* is much the same as that of *Le Rouge et le Noir*. A young man finds love, wanders from it into a land which is not that of the heart, and returns, one way or another. It doesn't matter whether Lucien physically returns to Mme de Chasteller, whether he marries her or not, but the quality of his love for her, in relation to the political world he next enters, clearly demands that he realize where he should be. As he does. Once back in Paris, he finds it hard to believe that such creatures as Mme de Chasteller exist (*Lucien* 1175), which is a mark against Paris and a measure of her moral weight. As the book progresses the need to return to her keeps surfacing in Lucien's mind. I loved her madly, he thinks, remembering . . . 'as I still love her' (*Lucien* 1354). And when he begins to sort out his future, he decides almost unconsciously that he will do whatever she wants—is surprised to find this idea so profoundly rooted in his head (*Lucien* 1358).

Stendhal's central proposition has not changed, then. Lucien's passion, adolescent and intermittent as it is, is the novel's point of value, home. But *Le Rouge et le Noir*, by the force of its movement towards a violent crime, an image of passion breaking the bounds of calculation, is unable to do justice to the smaller truth that in passion's absence, temporary or otherwise, there are other things to do, achievements for the scheming intelligence, for the self-ruling will; for the head, not the heart. Certainly Julien has successes in this vein, but the novel beats them down firmly, and Stendhal's grudging admiration for the talented hypocrite, for the man who can hide or submerge his feelings, evident enough in his lifelong fascination with the subject but usually denied all the same, is, like his tenderness for lovers, allowed full-play only in *Lucien Leuwen*.

'What men' (*Romans* 198). The protagonist of *Une Position sociale* admires Italian clerics for their muscular control, for their ability not to bat an eyelid, not to show an ounce of what they are thinking. Beyond all paradox and irony, sidestepping Stendhal's cherished antinomy between just these elements, we can see that certain kinds of hypocrisy are indeed very close to favourite forms of courage in Stendhal: suffering in silence, not letting them know, Julien at the guillotine, Stendhal back in Paris after his fluffed affair with Métilde, Lucien Leuwen on two or three occasions in Nancy. And what *Lucien Leuwen* sets out to do is to paint a full picture of a success in this secondary region. Lucien's quest for self-knowledge is in truth a quest for self-mastery, and a remarkable self-mastery is what he learns he has.

'This is not like *Julien*,' Stendhal notes in a margin, meaning *Le Rouge et le Noir*, 'so much the better' (*Lucien* 1539). There were not enough details in *Le Rouge*, he felt, but on the other hand there was a grander manner, 'fresco compared with the miniature' (*Lucien* 1520). Another sense of fresco. *Le Rouge* describes the wide arc of passion, *Lucien Leuwen* gets down to the details, and we see now a better, profounder reason for the attempt at Balzac's method. Stendhal means to show us, not the ultimate and necessary triumph of feeling and hidden innocence, although he will embody that in his plot, but the daily skirmishes of innocence and decency with the mire and villainy of the contemporary world. And for even a small victory here not to look like pure assertion, like wild, noble fantasy, he has to reveal it to us piece by piece, he has to let us see exactly how it is won.

We see Lucien, then, working for the Ministry of the Interior, asked to supervise the death of an *agent provocateur*, Kortis. Kortis' job, along with dozens of others, doubtless, was to rough up relations between the workers and the military, to prevent those two threatening classes from seeing their common interest in toppling a régime which was doing very little for either of them. To this end, imitating a drunken worker, Kortis tries one night to disarm a young soldier. Unfortunately he has picked the wrong man, the soldier steps back two paces and shoots him in the stomach. Kortis is now dying, but not yet dead, and Lucien's minister is afraid he may talk. Lucien's job is to make sure he doesn't. Lucien dashes to the hospital, consults Kortis' doctors, one of whom quickly proposes opium to put the poor fellow out of his pain. Ah, Lucien thinks, a government man. The rest of the doctors disagree, however, and Lucien talks to Kortis, to the man's wife, in short manages the affair with tact and delicacy. No one helps Kortis on his way, Kortis talks to no one. Stendhal is careful to insist that Lucien, in spite of his horror for the whole operation, is happy. He had told himself uncertainly that courage was courage, even if the danger was murky (*Lucien* 1126), but is now, to his surprise, actively pleased with himself: ' "I am skirting death, and public scorn," he kept repeating to himself, "but I have navigated well" ' (*Lucien* 1139). He should have added, of course, that it wasn't his own death he was skirting. Nevertheless. He later tells his father that it was only with Kortis that he had managed to forget Mme de Chasteller to some degree (*Lucien* 1160).

The climax of Lucien's career with the ministry comes at Caen, where he and his friend Coffe have been sent to observe an election, above all to ensure that M. Mairobert, a rich, intelligent, incorruptible and thoroughly worthwhile opponent of the government, is not elected. Things look bad. The prefect of Caen has himself written an inept pamphlet against M. Mairobert, and thereby virtually given him the election. This is not, however, the way the prefect himself sees the matter, and he resents deeply the intrusion of two Parisian meddlers in his affairs. He quarrels with Lucien. The election of M. Mairobert seems inevitable, when Lucien has a dazzling idea. Suppose that, instead of trying to get the government man returned, they were to pool forces with the royalists, and hope to tilt the result against the left. After all, a royalist more or less in the Chamber of Deputies is no worry to anyone, while M. Mairobert . . . As Lucien's minister had said, with twelve or fifteen people like that, the House would be ungovernable. And so Lucien talks, bribes, intrigues, is charming, is brilliant. To no avail. The idea came too late, and the prefect was too stubborn. But Lucien, again, has performed well, with wit and courage. Part of him recognizes a 'perfect satisfaction' as he dashes about, dealing with the tricky clerics who run the right wing in Normandy. There is an element of nostalgia here, for the right wing reminds him of Mme de Chasteller in Nancy, and at the end of the adventure he thinks of writing to her. There is a nostalgia of Stendhal's own too in these fine chapters—devious Jesuits, to be resurrected in *La Chartreuse de Parme* as wily, unpredictable princes and intrigants, were much more his idea of the political life than the grubby, straightforward bribery of the age of Louis Philippe.

Success, then, for Lucien. The child in love, his soul's toy, has become a man in the world, master of his emotions and uncertain thoughts. The victory of course is clouded in irony. Lucien at Caen fails in what he was trying to do, and what he was trying to do in any case was worse than questionable. The price is high, too : mud in the face at Blois, close proximity to authentic, heart-sickening venality, the real crawling thing. The prefect at Lucien's other electoral port of call has spread a rumour of the opposition man's bankruptcy. But might this false rumour not effectively harm his business, Lucien asks. Innocence. So much the better, the prefect replies, he is not a man to worry about knocking a house down if that is the only way of saving the street from a fire. The Republic is pounding at the gates. 'As for me, gentlemen, when the interest of the king speaks . . .' 'Bravo,' Coffe says sardonically, '*sic itur ad astra*' (*Lucien* 1207).

Worse still, Lucien is rewarded for his passive performance at Blois, and reprimanded for his display of zeal, talent and intelligence at Caen. The world needs men with thick skins, it has no use for ingenuity. Lucien has accepted the rules of a dirty game, and if he has insisted on a couple of qualifications of his own—he will have nothing to do with assassinations, he sets a time-limit for his fidelity to the ministry—these are thin braveries, sad, negative assertions of an outlawed decency.

Yet for all that Lucien gets what he wants : he passes his test. In one sense he is the most heroic of Stendhals' heroes. His sensibility is finer than Julien's, and more constantly exposed, never repressed, and not ruined, or turned to cynicism. In spite of his social advantages, he has nothing like Fabrice's easy ride to fame. But there is something wrong, one irony too few or too many in the work around him. Julien's courage is quixotic, proven only in mockery, the lions lie down in front of him, while Lucien's courage is effectively tested, but at another level. The lions are not hungry, have no claws, no teeth, no strength, but they smell. Courage consists in driving their scented cart. In other words there is an imbalance here not found in Stendhal's other major novels, and not found in the work of his great near-contemporaries. In Balzac and in Flaubert, hero and world are worthy adversaries, equally rich and flawed and magical, or equally pathetic and banal and limp. Lucien's world reeks so highly that it is not able to create any comment on him, its failure to appreciate him is its failure, and in no way his. This is not to say that Lucien is pure or unreal or incredible; simply that the world is much worse than he is, while Julien and Fabrice are the world's men, saved from its faults by their passions, which is something else.

Consequently Lucien's moral success is lonely, and insignificant. No class stands behind him, not even a handful of representative young men, energetic peasants or attractive Italians. Lucien fights his way through the thorns like a prince, but the thorns close up behind him. His journey, his quest means nothing save what it means to him. And here we must return to the ambition with which this chapter began : Stendhal's desire to write like Balzac. He was wrong in thinking his talent lay that way, but he was right in thinking that *Lucien Leuwen*, if it was to work at all, needed Balzac's approach : the panorama, a sense of social forces, as Auerbach says,[10] not of individuals pitted against each other. Or rather, it needed either this, or another hero, a figure who would bear the corruptions of his time more radically within himself. For the human heart, where it is not an exemplary heart like Julien's, a place where psychology and sociology are one, or where it is not set in a context like that of *La Chartreuse*, its back turned frankly on the present age, will not bear the weight of a social novel. In pitting Lucien against Louis Philippe—for that, in the end, is what it comes down to—Stendhal is like Lucien himself at Blois. Having been hit in the face with mud, he wants to find the man who cried out the metaphor ('you've brought his soul out on to his face') and challenge him to a duel. Both are making archaic, attractive gestures, movements from an earlier time, they are taking on contemporary politics with the foils of an old-fashioned etiquette and psychology. For the offence represented by the reign of Louis Philippe, by the mud thrown at Blois, there is no individual redress, nothing a person on his own can do. It is a social fact, a part of the

140

new collective vision which Stendhal understood, even prophesied, but couldn't, finally, make his own. His failure, in any case, has rich compensations. 'In music, as in many other things, alas, I am a man of another century.'[11]

10. *VIE DE HENRY BRULARD* (1835–6)

'Le scélérat qui vous fait horreur
comme assassin, vous ferait pitié
comme père de famille.'
ROME, NAPLES ET FLORENCE EN 1817

For a man nominally so keen on self-knowledge, Stendhal never says much about the person he is at the time he is writing. In *Souvenirs d'Egotisme* he is eleven years younger; in *Vie de Henry Brulard*, begun at nearly fifty-three, he is a child. His obituaries, for obvious reasons, end when they reach the present. His heroes with the exception of Mosca, in *La Chartreuse de Parme*, are very young men; even Mosca is ten years younger than Stendhal. Only his diary reports on his current self, and he gave up the diary once his vocation as a writer was on its way down from dream into a developing reality.

There is one fairly close portrait, though. Roizand, the hero of *Une Position sociale* : a volatile character, easily moved, at other times hard, ironic for fear of his own sentimentality; a theoretical radical, over forty, mobile features; eloquent, witty on occasions, boring when the subject doesn't stir him; never speaks of the things he really cares about. More concretely, went with Napoleon to Moscow, fell with him in 1814, and is now, since the 1830 revolution, in the diplomatic service in Italy (*Romans* 166–167). The picture agrees with everything we know about Stendhal, from his own accounts, from the reports of contemporaries, from what we can guess at through his writings.

The self, then, emerges once almost naked, but in a story. Otherwise it appears only in the haze of memory, at a distance—Stendhal is the writer of the twilight hours he himself identifies in *De l'Amour*, moments of Proustian pleasures 'linked to the senses only by memory' (*Amour* 283–4). And this should warn us. Stendhal's truthfulness is not only qualified by his discretion about his loves, his work and his happiness, by his forgetfulness, it is also the victim of a displacing, censoring motion which apparently can be cheated only in fiction or in the thought of lost time. His confessed taste for lies, in other words, is a functioning defence, part of the armour.

Does this matter? I suggested earlier that we can build a form of cross-hatched truth from Stendhal's lies, reticences, half-sincerities, self-corrections, and so we can. But I want now to suggest something else. The large answer to Valéry's conclusion that no one can tell the truth in a confession is that at such pitches of generality, no one can lie either, since all our utterances reveal us, even our false ones, especially our false ones, perhaps. The virtue of this rather wild perspective is that it qualifies the idea of truthfulness as a standard for autobiography.

Let me be clear. There are all kinds of points of view from which truthfulness is important in an autobiography—or even, in a slightly shifted sense, in fiction. 'Lying,' Stendhal notes in the margins of *Lucien Leuwen*, 'bad in reality, worse in a novel' (*Lucien* 1528). But truth in literal, meticulous forms is not what an autobiography ultimately aims at, and Stendhal's hugest lies, or probable lies, his visions of his brutalized childhood, for example, offer more than a negative, patchwork sincerity. They really confess. It is not a question of a private, personal truth, as Bardèche proposes at the beginning of his *Stendhal romancier*, something we should care about because Stendhal cared. How can we verify a childhood memory, Bardèche asks, what calendar will show us 'the resonance in a human life of a well-spent summer's day'? It doesn't matter, he continues, whether Aunt Séraphie was as mean as Stendhal makes her, whether Stendhal's father was really the dry stick of *Vie de Henry Brulard*—'It is the distortion that counts and not the reality'[12] Not even the distortion counts, insofar as the idea of a distortion clings to an origin in the life, a source to be twisted. The force of an autobiography lies not in its subjective rendering of objective occasions but in its capacity to erase just that distinction, to make us attend to it as history, although we know much of it may be invented. Like history, it is the interpretation of the raw material of a chronology, and its truth is the truth of a good theory: its power to explain the stuff it started with.

We can't do much, then, with the thought of *Vie de Henry Brulard* as a source-book for the novels, although there are tempting moments. The young Henry, like Julien, hates his father and thinks himself a monster (*Brulard* 217), watches soldiers pass and considers enlisting (*Brulard* 176), adores religious ceremonies (*Brulard* 161–2, 169); his grandfather is an old army surgeon telling battle tales (*Brulard* 25); Stendhal himself indicates his model for M. Valenod, in *Le Rouge et le Noir* (*Brulard* 322). But it won't work. If anything, the debt is the other way round. The shadow of Julien is all over this life revisited, Julien's anger is a striking source for the fiery childhood Stendhal now claims to have had.

The theory that emerges, strongly if barely consciously, in *Vie de Henry Brulard*, is a theory of continuity, of the seamless life, the man found in the child, the child in the man. And if Stendhal sets a false date for the book's start—1832 instead of 1835—it is not only because he will be fifty in January 1833, and intends to arrange the music of his opening chapter round that thought, it is also because in 1832 he was writing *Souvenirs d'Egotisme*, his first mature attempt at self-portrayal, at self-scrutiny 'pen in hand', as he was fond of saying. The unbroken life is to be echoed in the illusion of an uninterrupted attention.

The Stendhal of *Vie de Henry Brulard* and *Souvenirs d'Egotisme* is above all a writer, a man whose vocation is very clear to him— his repeated remarks about writing autobiography because he doesn't feel up to fiction may be distinctly disingenuous, but they are not entirely false. He is, to some degree, writing to keep his hand in, to pacify the demon which, since *Le Rouge et le Noir*, has taken over from the easily distracted dilettante. He compares himself to a well-fed silk-worm. 'The ugly beast no longer wants to eat, it needs to climb somewhere and make its prison of silk. Such is the animal called a writer . . .' (*Souvenirs* 1472–1473). What Stendhal is saying in this rather forced image is merely that he now prefers writing to reading, but for him this is a dramatically new state of affairs. His literary tastes and ideals were and are those of a reader (*Brulard* 260), and the only talent he is sure he has is that of a sensitive, demanding critic. 'But to be able to perceive someone else's faults, does that mean one has talent? The worst painters are well able to see each other's faults . . .' (*Brulard* 7–8). But he knows now what he wants to do, there is no doubt left about that : live modestly in Paris, writing books or plays (*Brulard* 261), novels in fact, as he told his friend Fiore. We can add to the dream another cagey requirement, no prosecutions for his works (*Brulard* 359). His political ambitions were an error, he sees now (*Brulard* 13); he looks back with nostalgia on the lonely days of 1802 and 1803, when he was twenty, and studiously taking successful plays apart in order to put them together again. *Vie de Henry Brulard* roots this now flowering vocation firmly in childhood : Henry's mind is made up at seven, he wants to write comedies like Molière (*Brulard* 81), secretly drafts a first act at ten (*Brulard* 97), and throughout the book we hear of him writing, or thinking about writing—although he will not, ever, discuss *what* he writes. '. . . my compositions have always inspired me with the same kind of discretion and delicacy as my loves' (*Brulard* 97). This too, the mixed modesty and embarrassment, began early and stayed with him.

Similarly, certain forms of humour stay, a taste for neat, exaggerated and slightly gruesome mishaps : the leading actor in Corneille's *Cid* being carried away by his lines, waving his sword and stabbing himself in the eye (*Brulard* 37); a distinguished geometer awarded the Légion d'Honneur leaping for joy and stunning himself on a low ceiling (*Brulard* 206). The young Henry likes puns—a confusion between *ballet* and *balai* (*Brulard* 50–51), a scholar called Jean Bond (*Brulard* 89)—and if Stendhal doesn't swoop to such depths much later in life, he retains the acute linguistic awareness that often goes with a pleasure in the chance collisions of words, in the appearance of *other roads* in language. A potential extension of Julien's return to Mme de Rênal before leaving for Paris reads :

'. . . only a she-owl could be heard a quarter of a league away : the beauty of the evening moved Julien, and took something of his bravery from him. What bliss it would be to take her in his arms !'

Stendhal then adds, roughly :

'Who? the she-owl?' (*Rouge* 1469).

There are defining visions of happiness in *Vie de Henry Brulard*, days out hunting, time spent with friends, above all a visit to an uncle's country house which twice provokes a memory of Milan in 1800 and even makes Stendhal wonder whether he will go on with his book :

'I don't know whether I shan't give up this work. It seems to me I could only depict this fresh, pure, divine, enchanting happiness by an enumeration of the evils and the boredom of which it represented the complete absence. Now this must be a sad way of depicting happiness' (*Brulard* 114).

These are early forms of Stendhal's late joys, the way it would always be for him; and his young distresses too are prophetic. At the death of his grandfather's servant Lambert he feels sorrow 'as I have felt it for the rest of my life, a considered, dry sorrow, without tears, without consolation' (*Brulard* 127).

But the main, the insistent continuity of the book is political. The 'sad drama' of Henry's youth (*Brulard* 60), is played out on a wide stage, with leading roles for his father and aunt, expanded to truly incredible dimensions. The rest of the characters have small, attractive parts: the quiet, cultivated grandfather, the romantic great-aunt, the rakish uncle, two virtually invisible sisters. But the father and the aunt, an unholy alliance born of the boy's mother's death when he is seven—Stendhal would like to believe they became lovers—are constantly being whisked out of old Grenoble and thrown into world history. They are political oppressors, they love order, hate liberty; they are like contemporary kings (*Brulard* 176); worse, they are like the Russians putting down a Polish uprising in 1831 (*Brulard* 50). Henry's father is at one point literally identified with the Tsar, 'so much is it true that all tyrannies are alike' (*Brulard* 86). Their agent, the abbé Raillane, Henry's tutor, is an early version of the conservative rhetoricians of the July monarchy (*Brulard* 72)—Stendhal represents his distaste for the man as fading only before a graver reactionary horror: the Restoration (*Brulard* 90). Tyranny in fact is the recurring word (*Brulard* 110, 133, 158), and Henry, at the receiving end, is compared with the nations of Europe at the present time (*Brulard* 85), with the Italian city-states of the eighth century, gaining freedom as a result of their lords' slacknesses (*Brulard* 163), with the Milanese at the moment, ruled by Austria (*Brulard* 194). The occasions for these leaps into analogy are slender, to say the least. Henry is not allowed to play with other children, not allowed to leave home at the age of ten, is forced to go for walks with his father. Yet something saves the wild allusions from being ridiculous.

First, Stendhal is plainly not trying to dignify or escalate the contents of his childhood, the references are not there for that. If

146

anything the movement is the other way round. Stendhal's difficulty with politics, as we have seen, was to get some kind of purchase on the scattered and impersonal nature of history since the Revolution. He regularly thought in terms of signs, clues, single events which would summarize a whole complex and actions and reactions : the case of Colonel Caron, framed by the government and executed at Colmar in 1822; the riot in the rue Transnonain in Paris in 1834, savagely suppressed by the middle class now in power. And from this point of view it is less interesting to see your father as the Tsar, than to be able to see the Tsar as your father, a domestic, manageable ogre.

And secondly, the continuity that Stendhal argues for is really there, his political views, then and now, are the same, which gives a certain ease to the broad allusions. The process even works backwards, for if the child is surrounded, effectively, by the adult's world, by the unsettled Europe of the years after the Congress of Vienna, 'Europe as M. Metternich has arranged it' (*Rouge* 1473), the adult is also able to find himself in the child's behaviour. One might say that this merely means that the fifty-year-old Stendhal is projecting his opinions back on the child, as well as his sense of current affairs, but that isn't how it comes out. Stendhal may or may not in reality have been as delighted as he says he was by the execution of Louis XVI in 1793, but the boy in the book is completely convincing. He is *not* the man who is writing—although he may grow up into such a man.

Stendhal gives the boy Henry a thoroughly developed, although imperfectly understood, sense of justice, a 'filial, instinctive' love for the republic because it represents the opposite of oppression. He cares for his country in the same way, and sees the sentence of death against Louis XVI not as an expression of revolutionary wrath, still less of inhumanity, but as an act of 'national justice'. His family is in despair, but Henry is off-hand. Why shouldn't they execute him, he thinks, 'if he is a traitor' (*Brulard* 93). Similarly in an earlier draft of *Vie de Henry Brulard*, Stendhal reflects on his first notions of justice. 'It was not because they were disagreeable to me, but because they were *unjust*, that the verdicts of Aunt Séraphie, supported by the authority of my father, made me weep with rage' ('Autobiographies' 1494, Stendhal's italics).

But at the same time as Stendhal proposes these rational, or at least pre-rational grounds for his political choices, he also makes clear all the prejudices at work in his infant mind. Thus, he feels

147

a glee at the execution of the king which is in no way warranted by the thought of a just sentence, and confesses that even had he not been a young Jacobin and a patriot, he might well have desired the king's death simply because all the local priests, pals of his family, were so firmly against it (*Brulard* 94). Before that, he had suggested he became a republican primarily because the rest of his family saw themselves as aristocrats (*Brulard* 84), and we are thus given two conflicting pictures of the young man. He has an inherent, instinctive love of justice, an intuitive hatred of tyrants. He is simply perverse, a contradictor, he will be whatever is the opposite of what his disliked relatives are. 'Such I was at ten, and such I am at fifty-two' (*Brulard* 94). Stendhal is speaking here of his cruel joy at the news of Louis XVI's beheading, but the remark carries the burden of his book—indeed the death of the king and the reactions it provokes are in more ways than one the centre of gravity of the work. But what this means, more generally, is that the two pictures just remain, facing each other in the man as they did in the boy: poiltics as perverse reflex, politics as passionate choice. Well, which are they? Stendhal will not decide, he simply marks out the zone of discussion, sets up the poles with exemplary clarity and intelligence. He leaves room for talk of psychological determinations, and for authentic political concern.

Another aspect of *Vie de Henry Brulard*'s political continuity is less engaging. The boy's delight at the king's execution is not only evidence of an excited, irrational element in his political sympathies, it is part of a running plea for a hard line. 'The death of a guilty king is always useful *in terrorem*' (*Brulard* 95)—*pour encourager les autres*. And if we are upset by this severity, well that is a sign of the shredding of our souls and not, as we pretend, of civilization and generosity (*Brulard* 94). 'I may say that the approbation of people I regard as *weak* finds me absolutely indifferent' (*Brulard* 95). He is pleased by the guillotining of two priests in Grenoble during the revolutionary terror, and again adds: 'There is more, there is worse, I am still in 1835 the man of 1794' (*Brulard* 144). The slip there—Stendhal is writing in mixed French and English, literally calls a boy of eleven 'the man of 1794'—gives a large part of the game away. This rasping voice, so unlike the mocking but amply human voice of the novels, is also heard in *Souvenirs d'Egotisme* muttering about kings being the vermin of the human species (*Souvenirs* 1476), even thinking, in code, of employing his suicidal mood over Métilde in the national interest and assassinating Louis XVIII (*Souvenirs*

1398). Partly these are the boy's fantasies refusing to die—young Henry too made a list of famous assassins, was very keen on Charlotte Corday (*Brulard* 177)—and partly the harshness is in keeping with a certain violence which belongs to this childhood, and is evoked in several rough adventures, in the extreme nature of Henry's feelings for his mother, in the very name he chooses, perhaps. Father Brulard was Stendhal's grandfather's brother, a monk with a vast, bald head, known to have lived well and to have been a powerful influence in his monastery. Semantically the name suggests a set of thoughts along the lines of getting your fingers burnt, burning your bridges, etc. But more than this, the tough stand seems to reveal, in a particularly undiluted form, the celebrated imaginary revenge. Assisted by the ghost of Julien Sorel, Stendhal now creates an extreme political purity for himself, goes one better than Julien in that. In the secrecy of his office in Civita-Vecchia, the consul throws stones, makes the revolution. There is a confirmation of this reading in the fact that as soon as Stendhal was granted his requested leave, and could get out of the service of his despised monarch for a while, the hard political vision of *Souvenirs d'Egotisme*, *Lucien Leuwen* and *Vie de Henry Brulard* softens into the sad, accepting wisdom of *La Chartreuse de Parme*—and then returns as a form of anarchism in *Lamiel*, composed mainly in Civita-Vecchia.

'Such I was at ten, and such I am at fifty-two'. The disadvantage of this stout fidelity to yourself is that it suggests a remarkably limited, single-track life, and Stendhal knows this—a worry about the scarcity of the options he seems to have had keeps surfacing in the writing, on the edges of ostensible subjects. Certainly he believes that our lives are laid out for us early, draws a map at one point of the roads men take 'often without knowing', at the age of seven: towards public praise and fame, towards riches, towards literature, towards madness (*Brulard* 256). But then this means that he himself not only is faithful to his childhood, a complete, continuing character, but is circumscribed by it, the creature of his tyrants' whims. Very well, he can blame them all the more, they have made him what he is (*Brulard* 98), he is their handiwork (*Brulard* 200), they stunted his judgement (*Brulard* 296), their deputy Raillane scared him off swimming, gave him a fear of water (*Brulard* 72). Alternatively, perhaps, he is not their handiwork but his own man, resisting all baleful influences, in fact becoming just the opposite of what they want him to be, acquiring the character he has 'in spite of them' (*Brulard* 179). His grim education would then, like other things in his life, have been just what he needed (*Brulard* 181, 116), the source of a fine rebound. Stendhal will not stay with this thought because it lets his family off too lightly, and is in any case specious, to say the least.

The trouble is that Stendhal is pleased with his life, is claiming no redress—'I have had the rare pleasure of doing, all my life, more or less what I wanted to do' (*Brulard* 384). For all his many pseudonyms and frequently jumpy, frightened prose, he has a very secure sense of himself—he flirts with his uncertainties from a centre of barely shaken sureness. What then are we to make of his gloomy youth, which presumably formed him? How did he elude its worst effects? Stendhal's answer, untrue and not fully raised to consciousness but dazzling in its effect, is that he was lucky. He was lucky, and this means he escaped his family's projects for him, he read Rousseau and became honest (*Brulard* 168), met a brilliant mathematician and was saved from the scoundrelly career which his Jesuitical education had prepared him for (*Brulard* 301). He owes a small statue to Fortune, he says (*Brulard* 365); he even thinks at one point that it was by chance that he became a writer and not a composer (*Brulard* 330). At his most cautious Stendhal reserved his theory of chance for events in life, not people's characters—the result is an insinuating sense of the precariousness of seemingly solid, inevitable affairs. Gina, in *La Chartreuse de Parme*, is kind to Mosca, we are told, because she has just returned from the country and hasn't quite got back to her urban form. Eight days later she might not have had time for the count's slightly ridiculous advances, and almost every life in the novel would have been different. Similarly, Stendhal tells us that Gina, who is in love with her nephew Fabrice but disturbed at the thought, as if such a love were an incest, could have made him love her if she had tried—and the whole carefully wrought suggestion of a destined love between Fabrice and Clélia would have fallen like a house of cards. But here, in *Vie de Henry Brulard*, Stendhal needs chance to do still more, to carry his hero away from the villains of the tale, and to make his life look free, not doomed, not drawn up by the time he is seven. Better still, chance allows him now to *blame* his family for not dominating him, to berate the enemy for missing his chances. They could have made him a Jesuit if they had known how, if they had been more subtle (*Brulard* 124) they could have tamed him (*Brulard* 137, 179), converted him to conservatism (*Brulard* 139–140, 300).

Fantasies, of course, retrospective taunts. But Stendhal was perfectly capable of being well satisfied with the way things turned out while retaining a sturdy rancour for the people who could have made them turn out differently—a duality nowhere better illustrated than in the curious longing for advice which emerges again and again in *Vie de Henry Brulard*. The young man we see is a stubborn figure, plainly proud of having made his own way, not docile, not willing to listen, and yet he is constantly presented as being in desperate need of counsel, a little boy lost in the big world. Someone should have told him to write every day, not to wait for moments of inspiration, and he would have saved ten years that way (*Brulard* 166). Yet how could anyone tell him, since he talked about his writing to no one? He expects social tips from his cousins in Paris, hints on how best to pursue his ambition—that is what has been 'eternally lacking' (*Brulard* 343). And then he formulates clearly his divided notions on the subject: he regrets nothing much but *still* they were wrong not to tell him what to do (*Brulard* 367).

In fact, in this image of an abandoned, mismanaged, strangled life ultimately redeemed and made happy by a smiling fortune, fanciful as it doubtless is, we have what is perhaps Stendhal's best and most faithful portrait of himself. It is a picture of life lived on the nerves, unplanned, open to whatever happens, full of risks and yet always ready for them, able, by sheer alertness and energy, to convert every adversity into at least a moderate pleasure. This, in the end, is what a life dedicated to chance means. It is a tiring life, and fatigue begins to show in Stendhal's writing for the first time in *Vie de Henry Brulard*. For what else is that hunger for counsel, that returning rage at his family's failures, but a first stirring of the desire for someone else to take over? As someone else does, towards the end of the book. The young Brulard meets a mentor in Switzerland, travels to Italy with him; 'and he was for me, from Geneva to Milan, during a journey of four or five leagues a day, what an excellent tutor must be for a young prince' (*Brulard* 373). Oddly, the book which stands behind this book is not Rousseau's *Confessions*, which looks like an obvious model, so much as Rousseau's *Emile*, a manifesto for a young man's education.

'One day I said to myself . . . Might I not be the son of a great prince, and everything that I hear about the Revolution, and the little I see of it, a fable intended for my education, as in *Emile*?' (*Brulard* 224).

It is a grand and timid dream, and reported by Stendhal at the age of fifty-two, it takes on the colour of weariness. Its prospect is a life released from your own vigilance, cushioned in the attentions of someone else's mind, where even the French Revolution would have been tenderly arranged, with the best of intentions for your future.

It is tempting to trace the sequence of weariness in the novels, from hero to hero, as they succumb increasingly to good advice. Octave and Julien have a benign influence or two around them, but essentially they are on their own, they are the abandoned Henry Brulard. Then things change in a story called 'Philibert Lescale', which has not been satisfactorily dated but plainly belongs to the climate of *Lucien Leuwen* and the years in Civita-Vecchia. Philibert is the natural son of a rich merchant, now dead. His mentor is the narrator of the story, who looks almost like a projection of Stendhal himself, dryness, fear of showing feeling and all, into the role of father. Young Philibert is told not to spend too much money, to join the legitimist opposition to the government (does this place the story after July 1830?), not to read any books and to keep a singer at the Opera as a mistress—this last as a protection against a serious passion. A note added to the story supposedly two years later brings this wry twist : the narrator was wrong, he feels, to have insisted on the singer, Philibert has just had a duel over her with a fake Russian prince ('neither a prince nor a Russian') and is dead (*Romans* 104). Lucien Leuwen receives very similar advice from his father, worldly, competent, anti-romantic counsel, and he does well with it. But he realizes too that he has to leave it behind, that his father, as he says, 'is like all fathers . . . ; wittier and indeed more compassionate than others, but he nevertheless wants to make me happy *in his way* and not in mine' (*Lucien* 1355, Stendhal's italics). Lucien rejects his father's way, ditches the mistress found for him as a defence against love, and returns to Mme de Chasteller and a world of emotions his father would not understand.

At this point in the sequence comes *Vie de Henry Brulard*, with its belated begging for help. And sure enough Stendhal's next major hero in Fabrice, in *La Chartreuse de Parme*, a young man who apart from a few upper-class pranks, does exactly as he is told, and finds fame, fortune and love. *Lamiel* offers a return to a more independent character, but in this, as in other respects, it fails—as if to say that after Fabrice there is no way back to Julien.

All this is true enough, plainly happens in the fiction; but it looks thin because it merely scratches at a larger and I think ultimately unmanageable subject. In *Vie de Henry Brulard* Stendhal announces flamboyantly that he was in love with his mother, who died when he was seven, exactly as he was later in love at the age of forty-five—physically rather poorly equipped for the moment, as he says, but he would have learned (*Brulard* 26). His love was 'as criminal as possible' (*Brulard* 27). Correspondingly he detests his father, is jealous of him in retrospect, after his mother's death (*Brulard* 110), and sets about finding a new, more acceptable progenitor. His grandfather, for example, was his 'true father' (*Brulard* 41–42); but then his grandfather was too peaceful, and Henry invents a composite figure, made up of his grandfather and the father of one of his friends, at once learned and jolly, calm and sociable (*Brulard* 239). The comparison with his own father here is explicit. Advice to a young man, then, is a part of this subject, something the father should have provided but couldn't, or wasn't allowed to. Stendhal is occasionally tolerant in *Vie de Henry Brulard*, he sees that his father cannot have been all he exaggerated him into. But more often he is simply stubborn still, proud at his victories over a stiff, pathetic parent. 'What I am about to say is not handsome' he writes, and describes his departure for Paris, his father weeping slightly, himself not touched but merely struck by his father's ugliness (*Brulard* 310).

It is all too good to be true, too clean a case of loving the mother and hating the father. There are still more than sixty years to go to *The Interpretation of Dreams*. Yet it is too close to the fiction to be left alone, it would be absurd to ignore a sizeable recurring theme in the novels because it looks too tidy, or too clinical. In what follows, then, I wish to describe, with due caution, what is there. It is not usually a good idea to think in terms of the Stendhalian (or Balzacian or Cornelian or Dickensian or Calderonian) hero; meanings rarely carry from one fully realized context to another, and in Stendhal's case, for example, Fabrice is the hero of *La Chartreuse de Parme* only in a technical, accessory sense— effectively he is the juvenile lead. What I have in mind here, though, is a story which concerns neither Julien nor Lucien nor Fabrice (nor Octave nor Lamiel), or rather concerns them all in a certain light : a life scattered across succeeding novels.

The story tells of a growing rivalry between a mother and a young mistress; of the dispersal of a father into several incarnations, and a late tenderness for him in one of these roles. It begins with a boy who is impotent and ends with a girl who is an orphan.

In *Armance* mother and mistress are in league, friends, allies, which could be taken to mean that they are the joint enemy, the bogey of some regressive sexual stage—in any case there is no conflict between them. In a distant typological sense, they are able to be allies no doubt *because* the hero is impotent, because the sexual dimensions of their roles are not invoked. In *Le Rouge et le Noir* sexual dimensions are invoked but again, there is no conflict. Julien's mother is dead, and we hear nothing of her. Her place is taken by Mme de Rênal, who is both mother resurrected and perfect mistress found, and although a young girl, Mathilde, appears as a rival, she is not a real rival. Julien loves her, but only with his head, not with his heart—those old psychological anatomies were firm favourites with Stendhal—and he has only to fall through to the forgotten level of true passion to recover himself and Mme de Rênal. Rivalry then becomes literal, although not explicitly sexual, in *Lucien Leuwen*. Lucien, betrayed as he believes by Mme de Chasteller, rushes home to his mother : 'I was in love, and I have been deceived' (*Lucien* 1064). But he is wary with his mother about his love and later decides intuitively that she must learn as little as possible about it. '. . . my mother must neither love nor hate Mme de Chasteller; she must not *know she exists*' (*Lucien* 1360, Stendhal's italics). His mother becomes caught up with his father into a single, over-protective parent, he runs from their 'paternal, maternal, sempiternal care' (*Lucien* 1359), lights out for Nancy, 'regretting nothing in Paris' (*Lucien* 1377), neither father nor mother. *La Chartreuse de Parme* picks up the conflict thus clearly spelled out, and returns to it its sexual connotations. Fabrice's mother fades before the energies of her sister-in-law Gina, who takes over her role completely. Gina worries about the incestuous quality of her love for Fabrice, although she is not in fact related to him at all. She is not even his aunt, she is the sister of Fabrice's nominal father, a dreary old Italian reactionary whose cuckoldry brought Fabrice into the world. But her habitual behaviour with him is too motherly for her comfort, and for his, she is Mme de Rênal seen losing, seen as too old, too maternal, rejected for a young girl. The situation of *Le Rouge et le Noir* has progressed to its inversion : the young mistress is the true love, the mother a hindrance, a tie to be cut away, left behind. An allegory of a boy's maturing, no less.

The story of the father's avatars is more complex. He is banished from the heart, replaced in the imagination, and found in two forms in reality for good measure. He is first hated : Julien's real father, Fabrice's nominal one, Lucien's too to the extent that he is ultimately the enemy of his son's freedom. *Lucien Leuwen* is generally more open about the situation under discussion, and correspondingly short on figures of myth—poor M. Leuwen has to do several jobs.

The father is then recreated as an absent, powerful, romantic character : M. Leuwen in his role as genie, able to work wonders for his son, whom he calls a prince (*Lucien* 1069); Fabrice's real father, the stern Napoleonic general; and most curious of all, the father invented for Julien not only by his friends, the abbé Pirard and the Marquis de la Mole (*Rouge* 417, 477, 480), but also by an enemy, an aristocrat he has a duel with (*Rouge* 475). Even Mathilde has a hand in the mystification, in the attribution of a secret, noble ancestry to Julien (*Rouge* 516), and Julien himself begins to wonder whether it may not all be true (*Rouge* 641). The peasant turns out to be a prince, not in fantasy but in other people's thoughts of him, so there must be something in it. There remain two closer fathers, a symmetrical pair echoing the two loves of *Le Rouge et le Noir* : a father for the heart, for moments of tenderness, the priests Chélan and Blanès in *Le Rouge* and *La Chartreuse* respectively, the decent, distinguished old General Fari in *Lucien Leuwen*; and a father for the head, dry, distant, witty, a man you can respect but not, somehow, love—the abbé Pirard, the Marquis de la Mole, Lucien's father most of the time, Gina's ministerial lover Count Mosca. This last father is the person whose absence is most cryingly felt in *Vie de Henry Brulard*, whose advice is taken in *La Chartreuse de Parme*. And to repeat, for once, a quite gratuitous speculation, we see here perhaps not only a sign of wear and tear on Stendhal's heavily exercised nerves, but also an image of the childless Stendhal riding out into paternity. He is the ironic, reluctantly loving father of his fictional young men, and his voice, quite often, is indistinguishable from that of Mosca or the brittle M. Leuwen.

'Who thinks of them now except me . . . ?' '. . . who doesn't like to be remembered?' (*Brulard* 56). *Vie de Henry Brulard* counts also on a longer continuity than the one I described earlier. Throughout the book Stendhal is thinking of his readers of 1880, he is very firm about the date. There is a hope of immortality in it, and Stendhal means to take the people he has loved with him, this work will be their memorial.

'. . . who remembers Alexandrine, who died in January 1815, twenty years ago?

Who remembers Métilde, who died in 1825?

Are they not mine, left to me who love them better than anyone else in the world?' (*Brulard* 132).

It is a delicate attention, but as Stendhal well knows, slightly misplaced, too modest. For if Métilde and Alexandrine are indeed remembered when Stendhal is read, it is not primarily because they are enshrined in *Vie de Henry Brulard*. It is because Stendhal wrote novels which lead us to believe, correctly as it happens, that *Vie de Henry Brulard* may be interesting. We should not, therefore, regret too keenly the delight with which Stendhal received the news of his leave in 1836, and abandoned his book on the spot. 'The imagination flies elsewhere', he wrote on his manuscript (*Brulard* 389). He was off to Paris, and once there, would dedicate himself, as Martineau has put it, to sunlit thoughts of his other Italy.

Part Three   The Last Romance

11. *LA CHARTREUSE DE PARME* (1839)

'. . . que tous les souvenirs détrônés,
tous les grands malheurs, finissent
par la bataille . . .'
MARGINALIA

'Toute vengeance coûte à qui se venge . . .'
LUCIEN LEUWEN

There is a temptation towards the fairy-tale, towards a vision of
La Chartreuse de Parme as a late, magical blessing on an awkward,
haphazard career. It is Stendhal's own book in a way in which very
few books are quite their author's own. Only Proust affords some
kind of comparison. Not Balzac, not Dickens, not Flaubert. Not
Tolstoy. *La Chartreuse de Parme* is both more limited and more
luminous than that, a work remembered rather than imagined. It
is less a set of occasions and characters represented with talent,
with genius even, than it is Stendhal's life set to Mozartian music,
the opera of his lively, well-stocked mind; personal but never private,
a confession fully realized in fiction. My images here are not original,
they are common currency in Stendhal criticism, what the book
calls for, simply.[1] One can't say less. And at first sight, it looks as if
one can't say much more.

There are too many successes; or rather the single success jubi-
lantly ties too many threads. First the childhood dream, sustained
through life, fed by light opera, of a delicate, kind laughter, a world
of smiles from which sneers and satire would be banished, a forest
of Arden, as Stendhal himself says (*Brulard* 337). He is still in sym-

pathy, 'as I was at ten when I was reading Ariosto, with everything to do with tales of love, forests (woods and their vast silence), generosity' (*Brulard* 180). In *La Chartreuse de Parme* he returns from the rough regions of his earlier novels, he is his own Cimarosa, makes his own *As You Like It*. He is a Frenchman who has escaped the vanity and nastiness of the French as he saw them. Or again, he wanted to be Molière, devoted years of his life to painful mechanical preparations for fame as a writer of comedies, and now it all comes home, he is Molière *by another road*, the failed, unfinished sketches were not a waste, they were a secret apprenticeship.[2] Best of all, we see the man strangled by his discretion, the man who suppressed all the essential parts of his autobiography, finally breaking the bonds, revealing himself as the poet of Napoleon's entry to Italy, for example, as a lordly extrovert letting his happiness loose into every sentence of his excited, hurrying prose.

None of this is false, but it tends to be dazzling, and it tends to make *La Chartreuse de Parme* look less like a masterpiece in its own right, which it is, and more like a literary reward, marriage with the princess, first prize in the lottery Stendhal regularly talked about (*Amour* 85, *Souvenirs* 1436). It is also seriously misleading, for it leaves us quite unprepared for at least three key features of the novel : its remarkable sadness, its sense of decline and loss and leave-taking perfectly embodied in the progress of Gina Pietranera's passion for her nephew Fabrice; its refusal of political reality, the turning of its face towards romance; and the patchy, unequal quality of the book as a whole—Stendhal's talent for cloak-and-dagger melodrama, for example, is visible only to someone who hasn't read much in the genre, and Fabrice's escape, a highpoint of the novel's physical action, is cannily converted into a reported escape, an adventure talked about but not told. In this respect Stendhal falls well behind Mérimée and Dumas, whom he kept, mistakenly but regularly, trying to overtake.

We need to retrace our steps. If *Le Rouge et le Noir* was more or less the invention of an instant, the result of an inspired night in Marseille when Stendhal thought of the book, and if hindsight has to squint to perceive its incubation in *Armance*, the reverse is true for *La Chartreuse de Parme*. Stendhal, back in Paris for a leave of three months, mysteriously stretched to three years, did not recover the sunlit Italy of his mind as easily as he had hoped. It all looked propitious : he was among lively friends, had no administrative duties, and the two chief drawbacks of Civita-Vecchia, business and boredom, were thus erased. He knew what he wanted to do. But he groped almost until the end of his leave before finding a way to do it; and this time, we see him groping.

Paris must have disappointed Stendhal a lot. Old mistresses had other things to do, old friends refused to become new mistresses, and he himself seemed incapable of finding fresh consolations or energies. His writing of this period is an uneasy nostalgia, a rummaging among old books, old ideas, old angers. He takes up his life of Napoleon again, for example, abandoned in 1818, and tries to remobilize some of his fury at the great man's detractors, yes-saying Restoration dwarfs, as he saw them, dancing on the giant's body, denying the good he did along with the bad. One can't imagine Stendhal as a Bonapartist—he disapproved of Napoleon's dynastic ambitions—but he was not a man to refuse a stick to beat the Bourbons and Louis Philippe with. He esteems Napoleon, then, in the measure of his scorn for what came after him.[3] And carried away by his attempt to stir up past time, he writes, like a mistaken Julien Sorel in old age: 'Love for Napoleon is the only passion which remains to me . . .'[4] Not true. But the murmur of an elegy in the verb is. *Remains* . . . He is feeling tired, feeling his fifty-three years.

Some of his projects look desperate. He begins a romantic tale called 'Le Conspirateur' in an assize court in the Auvergne. A countess leaving crosses glances with a prisoner arriving in a coach. The prisoner drops a bundle of letters, she picks it up, and of course reads through it avidly when she gets home. She wonders whether the prisoner still loves the lady they are addressed to. What was she doing at court? She was attending the trial of a young man who had tried to shoot a woman who loved him. All the best people in town had been there. The young man's name was Berthet, alias, as in well known in literary history, Julien Sorel. Stendhal is attempting a form of oblique sequel, trying for a chain-reaction of sentiment, from Julien and Mme de Rênal to his new characters. There is worse. A lady poisons her husband and children in Paris and plans to join her reluctant lover in Brazil, and Stendhal sketches out the opening of a grim, sensational novel about her. Later, in August 1838, that is, after two years of his leave are up, he starts a story called 'A.—Imagination' about a character with no imagination. 'Use my imagination to depict the absence of imagination. Say to myself: What should I feel in his place and make him feel the

159

opposite' (*Romans* 493). What he means, of course, is that there must be a way of putting the empty spaces of his own bleached mind to use. A *cri de coeur* reaches us from the manuscript : 'I don't know where I'm going' (*Romans* 494).

Stendhal wrote one long, attractive fragment in these years, and a fine travel book : *Le Rose et le Vert* and *Mémoires d'un Touriste*. He published three Italian stories adapted from old chronicles— soon he was to publish a fourth, and to make *La Chartreuse de Parme* out of a fifth. But only the travel book was new—was about a region new for Stendhal, France.

Le Rose et le Vert began as a reworking of a story called 'Mina de Vanghel', written immediately after *Le Rouge et le Noir*, a rather arch affair about a German girl in France, full of symmetrical chunks of national character. It went well beyond this, developed into a narrative of real wit and charm, but then struck another difficulty : the book was turning into the abandoned *Lucien Leuwen*. 'I see my young duke', Stendhal says of his hero at one point. 'But perhaps I have already said that somewhere. Yes, Mme de Chasteller's lover' (*Romans* 474). Worse, as he must have realized himself, his hero and heroine by the force of a pressure plainly coming from Lucien's unquiet ghost, are beginning to merge into each other, into a single, distinguished, lonely creature, lost in a forest of incomprehension. What after all is the difference between Lucien who wants to be loved for himself and not for his father's machination, and Mina, who wants not to be married for her mercantile millions, and Léon de Montenotte, who doesn't like people to know he is a duke. Léon, in fact, is the perfect expression of Stendhal's trouble at this period : an engaging fellow trapped in worries about politics, seeing nothing to do, except visit the brightly lit past. He is the son of one of Napoleon's most dashing generals, and his idea of action is to go to Egypt to see the sites of his father's battles. In *La Chartreuse de Parme* Stendhal converts a similar thought on Fabrice's part—his life is over, he thinks, at twenty-three, he would just like to see the fields of Waterloo again before he dies—into an evocation of a whole weary, dying climate, a place where only love can breathe a little life.

The violence of Stendhal's Italian stories presumably serves a similar purpose. His documents, in effect, were the sensational journalism of the past, full of pious commentary but hot from the press, or pretending to be. The gibbets are still up at the end of 'Vittoria Accoramboni', the executions not yet over. Béatrix Cenci, in 'Les

Cenci', died only four days before the supposed writing of the chronicle, and Stendhal himself notes, 'What I like in this account is that it is as contemporary as possible. The poor girl was killed on 11 September 1599, and the account was completely written by 15 September' ('Cenci' 1454). The stories as we have them in Stendhal's versions are full of agonies and nasty death : a dagger twisted in a girl's heart, nails through an old man's head, a neck sawn through with a knife. They are full of courage too, pain bravely suffered—Béatrix Cenci, by a nice collision across the centuries, is able to bear torture which we can't bear to read about—and in their terseness and lack of literary shape they represent well enough Stendhal's dislike for rhetoric and emphasis, for condescending or elegant arrangements of material. One of his Renaissance villains, dying, is given a remarkable epitaph. He shows more greatness of his soul than his brother because he says less : 'words are always a strength one looks for outside oneself' ('Palliano' 732). Stendhal's heroes, at their best, always have Stendhal's style—or better, Stendhal, doomed as he is to words, being a mere writer, does what he can stylistically to approach the behaviour of his heroes and heroines, who are firm and silent when action is called for, never waste themselves in speech. There is a model for a certain kind of sincerity in such moments, an embattled, distrustful kind, very much Stendhal's own : if you don't talk, you can't lie.

Stendhal bought the right to copy some old Italian manuscripts in 1833, and at his death fourteen ample volumes were found to be in his possession : one original, probably seventeenth-century, and thirteen taken from originals either by Stendhal or by a secretary. His renderings of these stories, published between 1837 and 1839, look like literary hackwork, means of making money and keeping in touch with editors and publishers. He translates, arranges; in only one case, 'L'Abbesse de Castro', appears to have invented extensively; and then adds a casual introduction—his remarks on the figure of Don Juan prefacing 'Les Cenci', for example, are acute but remarkably disordered and irrelevant. The tale is hardly at all about the old rogue Francois Cenci and almost entirely centred on his daughter Béatrix. Stendhal published two of the stories anonymously, and two under a pseudonym. Later, after *La Chartreuse de Parme* had appeared, three of the four previously printed tales were brought together in a volume under the name Stendhal, and just before he died Stendhal contracted to deliver another large and non-anonymous bundle.

But he did not intend his work on the old chronicles to be merely a way of passing his time while he thought of something for a novel. As early as 1834 he had written to Sainte-Beuve from Civita-Vecchia to tell him about the material he had acquired; his 'perfectly true anecdotes, written by contemporaries in a semi-jargon'. 'When I'm a poor devil again', he continues, 'living on a fourth floor, I shall translate them *faithfully* . . .'⁵ The mixture of violence and documentary flavour attracts him seriously. There is more than this, too, although modern editions of the tales tend to blur what was clearly Stendhal's project.

Chroniques Italiennes. Perhaps, Martineau remarks hopefully, Stendhal had indicated the title somewhere in his papers. We don't know. Standard texts now contain eight stories : 'L'Abbesse de Castro', 'Vittoria Accoramboni', 'Les Cenci', 'La Duchesse de Palliano', 'San Francesco a Ripa', 'Vanina Vanini', 'Trop de faveur tue', 'Suora Scolastica'. Of the eight, two were written before Stendhal acquired his old chronicles, and one is, like *La Chartreuse de Parme*, a transposition from a chronicle into another period. In other words, only five stories reflect old sources directly, and more important, only five are set in the sixteenth century : L'Abbesse de Castro', 'Vittoria Accoramboni', 'Les Cenci', 'La Duchesse de Palliano', 'Trop de faveur tue'. The others are set in 1726, 1740 and the 1820s. The particular setting was essential for Stendhal, he was not writing picturesque tales about Italy as the land of eternal song and sunshine and bandits, he was writing about a specific moment in the imagination's history, a stormy country when the world was young, as he says (*Chartreuse* 505). Taking one of his anecdotes for another, shifted story was something else, a different enterprise. What we have, in fact, in the main tales, is a form of coarse, unsystematic sociology of art. This is the Italy of the great painters, of Benvenuto Cellini, or better, it is the Italy which comes just after them, the end of a strong, violent age, the last moment of the world's youth. Leonardo, Raphael, Michelangelo, Cellini, died in 1519, 1520, 1564, 1571 respectively, and Stendhal's tales pick up and move among the shredded remains of this glory. He is careless, occasionally suggests he is writing about the fifteenth and not the sixteenth century, and the seeming precision of his dates is, no doubt, a fraud, part of the mock-documentary tone. But the intention, nevertheless, is very clear. 1600 is the deadline, the day it was over.

Plainly it doesn't matter whether the stories were authentic or not, and Stendhal can't really have thought they were. What we are to look for, he says, is not historical certainty but the habits and customs of the home of Ariosto, Machiavelli, Raphael, Michelangelo, Correggio, Titian, 'and so many others' (Chartreuse 504–505). In this perspective, even the probable untruths and exaggerations of the chronicles become a virtue, because they show the popular imagination at work, show certain facts of feeling hidden from graver and more scrupulous history. Like the sensational newspapers of his own day that Stendhal so enjoyed, they show a race of men chasing happiness, in Stendhal's favourite phrase, making legends, arranging myths which will brighten and in some sense legitimize their lives. This, I think, is what we should take Stendhal's rather stiff promises of special light on the 'depths of the human heart'[6] to mean, since it can't mean psychology—that, as Stendhal himself remarks, is just what is missing from the chronicles.

He intends something a little more strenuous than romantic local colour then, although he does, as a good friend of Mérimée, enjoy the element of pastiche, and sets up each of his narratives with a stretch of faintly archaic prose at the beginning.[7] But nevertheless, to retrieve, by a commodius vicus, 'the lost thread of my argument, this too is old stuff, goes back to the years of Histoire de la Peinture en Italie. Stendhal is now offering borrowed illustrations for his earlier borrowed book, and the theories of art and society dispersed among his Italian tales are his old theories: an age gets the art it deserves, art is conditioned by climate, political repression is bad for civil life but good for art, and in spite of/because of our progress towards democracy we have fallen upon sad, effeminate days. I suggested earlier that Stendhal saw the need to make connections between the life of an individual and the life of the world around him. He saw art as a meeting ground. But the connections he himself made, apart from the radical and exemplary infection of Julien Sorel by the France of the Restoration, are erratic at best, never get beyond a bright thought or two. As he said in Souvenirs d'Egotisme, 'My judgements are just insights' (Souvenirs 1393).

His gropings. A good deal of Stendhal's activity in these years appears plainly in La Chartreuse de Parme. His passion for Napoleon colours the marvellous opening pages, full of the joy of a military victory in a good cause, of the liberation of an oppressed people by a young army, Napoleon's army, in Italy, in 1796. His return to the age of the great painters takes him back to the time

163

when he was writing about them, to his spell in Milan after Waterloo, the flower of his life, as he said. The memory surfaces everywhere in his novel, in landscapes, characters, dialogue, feeling.

A certain taste for intrigue, or rather for the sight of intrigue followed by its downfall, can be seen re-emerging. A priest in *Le Rose et le Vert* is anxious to convert the heroine and her money to the service of the Catholic Church. He is astute, canny, tactful, but he is baffled, trapped into errors, by the sheer innocence of Mina and her mother, their nice German openness mingled with their considerable intelligence. In a more extravagant vein, there are ladies in the Italian stories whose excessive guile brings death and disaster all round. Looking back, we can see an echo of 'Philibert Lescale' here, of the young man killed for following crafty advice, and looking forward we can see the shadow cast by Fabrice's mild acquiescence in other people's plans for his future. The wicked witch, the outwitted priest are Stendhal's secret, ongoing doubts about all the counsel he was longing for in *Vie de Henry Brulard*. But more than this, of course, intrigue becomes the very soul of *La Chartreuse de Parme*, that extraordinary portrait of court politics which Balzac described as a new version of Machiavelli's *Prince*.

These things show, then, but only to hindsight, and they show in the way in which fragments of last night's conversations show in early morning dreams. They are what is there, what was on Stendhal's mind. He was groping more anxiously than this, though. The urgent question was not what to put into a novel, but how to write a novel of any kind at all.

'I need a passion', he wrote on the manuscript of *Le Rose et le Vert*. He reaches out for violence, crimes, prisons, and in one or two happily abandoned plans, a secret maternity for his heroine, or at least rumours of such dire trespass, to be cleared up when the obstacle was no longer needed. In effect, *Le Rose et le Vert*, for all its charm and delicacy, is a wilting, dwindling affair, and the Italian stories, for all their gore and action, are curiously lifeless. Stendhal needed more than a passion, he needed a passion spoiled, squandered, cut off like Julien's by the guillotine or heaped on an unworthy or unheeding object like Gina's. Prison was a half-glimpsed metaphor for this, an intuitively understood sign of the closing off of a world of feeling, and if Stendhal's interest in the sensational crimes of his period was probably much akin to that of the calamity-consuming public of any age, he also had other impulses. He knew, dimly, what he wanted, but the peculiar unity of *Le Rouge et le*

Noir made it difficult to go back or to go on. Passion and the prison there were everything, they provided plot and structure, the necessary paradox : a boy who shot the woman he loved, a hero who escaped from illusion in gaol. A passion, that is, *was* the structure, offered all the symmetries Stendhal needed, and a prison was where it ended. We see him trying again in *La Chartreuse*, and he does manage to make a kind of structure out of an expectation of a prison—but a flimsy, evasive structure, as we shall see. What is clear to us from a reading of *Le Rouge et le Noir*, even without a knowledge of *La Chartreuse de Parme*, could hardly be clear to him : that passion and structure are two elements, that he needs both, and that he is not likely to be lucky enough to stumble again on a subject where they are mingled.

If anything, he needs structure more than he needs passion. He needs it not only to hold his scattered perspectives together but also to block off the vistas, to enable him to finish a book at all. His writing is full of points of view invading other points of view before they are fully established, and when he is making judgements on himself or on his work, this can be irritating. But the uncertainty gives the fiction an extraordinary, compelling restlessness, a sense of life caught in its quickest movements, of a language shifting as fast as passing reality. The prince, in *La Chartreuse de Parme*, is rattled by Gina, ready to sign anything she wants him to sign. His minister Mosca omits a compromising sentence from the letter she drafts, the prince thanks Mosca with a glance, and is immediately planning his way out of the trap, the trick by which he will placate Gina and yet get his revenge. From defeat to a prospect of wily victory, in a moment. Similarly, affections are placed, passionately, but never allowed to settle completely, never allowed any purity or peace. Gina loves Fabrice but Fabrice loves Clélia. Gina is broken by this, severely aged, and yet at the news of a gallant action performed by Mosca she is able to feel for him something 'which strongly resembled love' (*Chartreuse* 407). Then Fabrice is in prison again, and her feelings fly back. Later they return, in a mild form, to Mosca. In *Le Rouge et le Noir* the resolution is, to a small degree, unresolved again, as I suggested. In *La Chartreuse de Parme* Fabrice's case, his killing of an actor in self-defence, is literally reopened, Fabrice having escaped has to return to gaol so that a new trial can take place : an exaggerated image of a life that refuses conclusions. If the ending of *La Chartreuse* is jerky and hurried, it is not, as Stendhal suggests, because his editor would not let him fill it out, it is because he had already started, within the last chapters, on another novel, and his editor would have none of it. He introduces a new character, Gonzo, a court gossip, with great circumstantiality, and we see a whole further book begin to take shape. Clélia is married, and faithful to a vow she has made, meets Fabrice only in the dark. They have a child. Fabrice wants the child to be with him, insists. We see his torment as he harries Clélia, knowing he is hurting her but unable to stop, because he wants his son. It is a new novel. It is true, as Blackmur says, that Stendhal envisages no fate for his heroes other than truncation, but perhaps that was the only way he could get their stories to stop : kill them off. In other words, we may have run into another reason for Stendhal's finishing so little of what he wrote : his personal and philosophical difficulty in seeing anything, books, loves, discussions, hopes, sentences, as finished. There is a tribute to the force with which Stendhal rendered his vision of incompleteness in what has become almost a tradition in writing about him : a confession of failure, the throwing up of critical hands, the admission that there is all too much more to say.[8]

One last direction of Stendhal's groping. On his copy of his source for 'Vittoria Accoramboni' he noted that he had thought, in 1833, of turning the story into a novel like *Le Rouge et le Noir*, but couldn't imagine where anyone who was not an antiquarian would get enough details. The idea, then, of a historical novel had crossed his mind. In *Le Rose et le Vert*, he has his hero worry about his privileged social status, and offer himself the obvious coarse consolation : you didn't create the inequality, it was there before you were, why not profit from it. Stendhal comments : 'But he was too honest or too thoughtful, or, if you like, too gloomy, to let himself sleep on that pillow' (*Romans* 265). Stendhal himself was too honest or thoughtful or gloomy to settle for contemporary realities, yet it hurt to look at them. If we add to this worry the thought of the historical novel a new line appears. Stendhal needed to write a romance, an escape not a confrontation. He was older than he knew. Like Lucien perhaps, giving himself eighteen months to play the ministry's game before returning to his own strict, aloof morality, Stendhal gave himself, finally, one novel to let the world go, to accept it as it was. *La Chartreuse de Parme*, born the day Stendhal thought of combining an old chronicle with an account of the battle of Waterloo he was working on, was to be a short rest in what many temperaments call wisdom. It was too long a rest. Stendhal was never again to recover his anger or his demanding ideals—although he never stopped looking for them either, raking the embers of his old rage.

There is no better measure of the mood of *La Chartreuse de Parme* than Balzac's remark at the end of his famous and generous review : M. Beyle used to be a liberal, but the 'profound meaning' of his new novel is 'certainly not opposed to monarchy'.[9] Balzac is right. Stendhal was cagey all his life, never stuck his neck out extravagantly. Writers are the hussars of liberty, he once said, but he was a fairly cautious hussar. Yet he was not dishonest or scared, and Balzac would not have been able to make this remark about *Le Rouge et le Noir* which, significantly, he disliked, or about *Lucien Leuwen*, had it been possible for him to read it. The stern Jacobin child of *Vie de Henry Brulard*, the man who called kings the vermin of the human species, has now written a novel that a monarchist can feel happy with. Of course Balzac, from another extreme position, disliked the July régime as much as Stendhal did, and there would be nothing strange in a royalist and a republican agreeing there. But that is not what happens in *La Chartreuse de Parme*.

What attracted Balzac was a certain kind of lucid conservatism, and if the book was not about Metternich, as he thought, it was about Metternich's world and Metternich's philosophy, based, as Namier wrote, like all conservatisms, on a 'proper recognition of human limitations'. A character in the story 'L'Abbesse de Castro', part of which was written immediately after *La Chartreuse de Parme*, prefaces the launching of an elaborate piece of simony by these words, which might well have been Stendhal's motto for his novel :

'Eminence, she said, we are both very old; there is no reason for us to try to deceive ourselves by giving beautiful names to things which are not beautiful . . .' ('Abbesse' 635).

The ironies of *La Chartreuse* regularly run this weary way. Mosca, jealous of Fabrice's effect on Gina, sees that Fabrice might well be killed in a light adventure he is conducting but nevertheless arranges for his life to be saved. 'If the reader is very young,' Stendhal comments, he won't see what is so virtuous in this action (*Chartreuse* 162). A new prince, towards the end of the book, has 'among other infantile ideas', the hope of having a '*moral* ministry' (*Chartreuse* 416–417, Stendhal's italics), and Stendhal gets a lot of good comedy out of this dream of innocence. It is impossible, for example, to explain to the prince how crooked most of his administrators are, he would believe you were crooked yourself—how else would you have perceived such things.

But the conservatism of *La Chartreuse de Parme* is not primarily a view, it is a premise, a climate, an assumption enclosing the book. The image of the game hangs over the novel : whist, chess, figures for the play of politics and power (*Chartreuse* 111, 119, 137). Who complains about the rules of such games? What this means, in the light of Stendhal's known passions and opinions, is not that he has come round but that he has given up—temporarily, as he thinks. Where Julien Sorel goaded himself on through his sticky paths by thoughts of Napoleon's rising star, of the young general who couldn't lose, *La Chartreuse de Parme* is set in the shadow of Waterloo, emblem of the death of a huge vision.[10]

Stendhal is careful to portray the exact quality of this decline. It is a slip from politics to personalities, from unities to pieces, and when Balzac suggests that not even a republican could be stirred to regicide by Gina's having the prince of Parma assassinated, he is, again, right : 'It is a play of private passions, that is all'.[11] It is all, and it is a far cry from the meeting of politics and the individual in Julien. Napoleon's Italy, at the beginning of the novel, is a society; what happens to one man happens to many : 'Lieutenant Robert's story was more or less that of all Frenchmen . . .' (*Chartreuse* 30). But Waterloo is a breaking, a chipping into fragments, marvellously reflected in Fabrice's piecemeal perceptions of the battle, scattered sensations merely, stills from an early newsreel, a dead man's dirty feet, an open eye, smoke rising beyond a patch of willows, trees clipped by gunfire, a ploughed field plucked by bullets. Other things die at Waterloo too, and it is worth noting that the lyricism of *La Chartreuse de Parme* is released largely by the hopelessness of the case it represents. If Stendhal is able to become his own Tasso or Ariosto—'tales of love, forests (woods and their vast silence), generosity'—it is because the original is discredited, because chivalry has gone from the world. Fabrice's horse is stolen by the comrades in arms he was romantically warming to, and he weeps.

'He shed one by one all his grand dreams of sublime and chivalrous friendship, like that of the heroes of *Jerusalem Delivered*. To see the approach of death was nothing if you were surrounded by heroic and tender souls, by noble friends who would take your hand at the moment of the last sigh. But to sustain your enthusiasm while surrounded by vile rogues!' (*Chartreuse* 69).

The failure we saw in *Lucien Leuwen*, a novelist's incapacity to render the movement of social forces, is here presented as the failure of history: time has slithered back, it is the eighteenth century again, the old régime, an age of rule by the mistress and the confessor (*Chartreuse* 411). There are new, post-Napoleonic fantasies, of course: the prince of Parma, a confirmed despot if ever there was one, a man who is imitating Joseph II when he is not imitating Louis XIV, sees himself as the constitutional king of all Lombardy. But the old repression is really in control. There is a revolt towards the end of *La Chartreuse*, put down gallantly but foolishly by Mosca at the head of a couple of battalions—foolishly because he believes as little in what he is defending as in the ideology of the attackers. What would have happened? Two months of a republic, perhaps, before neighbouring powers stepped in (*Chartreuse* 411). Or a fortnight of looting, before the foreign troops arrived (*Chartreuse* 413). In any case, nothing durable. People who keep talking about a republic, Mosca says ironically, prevent us from enjoying the best of monarchies (*Chartreuse* 412), and the novel's republican leader says what amounts to the same thing, sets the seal on all hopeful radical thoughts: 'Anyway, how can you make a republic without republicans?' (*Chartreuse* 419). All Lucien Leuwen's nagging doubts are endorsed, enthroned.

These are sad ideas for some people, Stendhal among them, and my use of the word romance perhaps calls for an explanation. I am not thinking of the shape of *La Chartreuse* or of the characters in it, but rather of what I may call its weather, its flight from the 'tangled, exposed state' which Henry James sees as the proper preoccupation of novelists. James, in fact, in his preface to *The American*, offers the perfect definition:

'The only *general* attribute of projected romance that I can see, the only one that fits all its cases, is the fact of the kind of experience with which it deals—experience liberated, so to speak; experience disengaged, disembroiled, disencumbered, exempt from the conditions that we usually know to attach to it and, if we wish so to put the matter, drag upon it, and operating in a medium which relieves it, in a particular interest, of the inconvenience of a *related*, a measurable state, a state subject to all our vulgar communities . . .'

169

Not true for the private experiences represented in *La Chartreuse de Parme*—old age, for example, drags sadly on Gina and Mosca—and personal relations in the novel are as complex as they are anywhere in fiction. But it is true for the political and social conditions of the book, the *medium*, as James says. *La Chartreuse de Parme*, alone among Stendhal's works, asks no questions of the world.

Two heroes. Ferrante Palla, the doctor-poet-revolutionary who assassinates the prince and is momentarily loved by Gina, a character for whom Stendhal himself plainly feels a good deal of misplaced affection, is perhaps the least successfully drawn of all Stendhal's figures. The climate of the book will not allow him to appear as anything other than a stiff, gesturing buffoon. And then Fabrice. Fabrice is charming and delicate and intelligent but he is also off-hand and arrogant, and incurably selfish and irresponsible. He kills an actor, admittedly in self-defence, but nobody in the novel seems to worry much about what actually happened—the cheerful assumption is that Fabrice has a right to bump off a member of the lower classes if he feels like it. Similarly, he wants to stay in prison when his friends are trying desperately to get him out; he doesn't think of his aunt's anguish, he thinks only of staying where Clélia is. He never quite forfeits our sympathy for any of this, and the reason, I think, is that Stendhal sees him as embodying everything that was fine about the *ancien régime*. Stendhal's Jacobinism never blinded him to the good times that were had in the old days, and we occasionally even find him wishing he lived before 1789. Fabrice is the perfect aristocrat, unconscious of the extent of his privilege and therefore able to bask in it with authentic, untroubled grace. Along with his regret at the collapse of comedy, because the new public is too coarse for fine feeling and wit, Fabrice is one of Stendhal's few reservations about the Revolution.

I am inclined to see a certain kind of innuendo in the book, a hint of sexual good fortunes for Fabrice and around him, in the same way. First, there is his birth. We are never told conclusively that he is a son of a visiting French officer, but we are given hints we can hardly ignore, suggestions of his mother's affection for Lieutenant Robert, and slightly strained narrative lines remarking that Fabrice 'found himself, by the chance of his birth, to be the second son of this so lordly Marquis del Dongo . . .' (*Chartreuse* 33). Later, when he is arrested as a spy on his way to Waterloo, Fabrice escapes with the aid of his gaoler's wife, a 'handsome Flemish woman of thirty-six', and Stendhal twice tells us unnecessarily that he left her bedroom at the break of day (*Chartreuse* 54, 55). Later still, a pretty maidservant brings Fabrice a message from la Fausta, a singer he is courting, and when she leaves him, again at dawn, she is 'extremely happy' with his manners (*Chartreuse* 237). I confess I don't really know what to make of this. It seems gratuitously dark and surreptitious. We know Fabrice is an attractive fellow, has not been short of mistresses in his exile. Perhaps Stendhal wants us to imagine hidden depths in Fabrice's life, secrets. Or perhaps he means us to see such behaviour as just another aristocrat's advantage : look what falls into his lap, look what he can get away with.

But surely *La Chartreuse de Parme* is a contemporary political novel : Stendhal took the trouble to modernize his old chronicle. How then can it be a romance, in any sense? In fact, the mere possibility of a modernization simply continues and strengthens the argument. Julien Sorel was not able to translate over a period of less than twenty years, the Napoleonic model ran him into all kinds of difficulties in the Restoration. Here Stendhal shifts a whole story, with pope, cardinals and a dazzling courtesan, two hundred years at a blow, and without any effort. For Rome read Parma, for pope read prince, for cardinal read minister. Only Gina is a sparkling anachronism, a restless, brilliant woman from another age. There are changes to be made, of course. The violent vendettas of the Renaissance have given way to the small politics of the Congress of Vienna. The prince of Parma, far from assassinating his enemies wholesale, has once had two liberals hanged, and now goes in mortal fear for his life—Mosca's chief credit with his sovereign being his ability to make the prince's panic look less emasculating than it is. It is Mosca who suggests they look under the bed at night and even in the cases of the bass fiddles (*Chartreuse* 114). But the general result of the switch from the sixteenth century is not to bring things up to date but to suggest that nothing has changed. Fabrice on his way back from Waterloo is insulted, he thinks, in a café, and promptly forgets all the modern etiquette he has learned. He doesn't consider a duel, he draws his dagger and leaps on his enemy— 'Fabrice's first movement was right out of the sixteenth century' (*Chartreuse* 95).

Italy has progressed only towards pettiness. Otherwise it is the same backward, quarrelling, ungovernable place it always was. Stendhal's portrait is affectionate, but not complimentary.

His novel becomes timeless, then, as ultimately all historical novels are. It is released from contemporary contingencies, a romance. But it is tired romance, an ironic idyll, the world it offers is not better or brighter than the real one, it is simply safer, a world with familiar pitfalls and antagonists, a shelter from the new and unexpected. The retreat is not into fantasy but into chess or mathematics, into a place where the rules of the game are known and if you can keep your scruples quiet—for why should you air them, if they can have no possible effect—the game can be fun. 'Games, in Stendhal', as Blackmur remarkably said, 'are how you handle the incomprehensible.'[12]

There is one grim, dizzying sense, though, in which *La Chartreuse de Parme* does speak to its age. Suppose its pictures are literally faithful to a present reality, suppose that small states in Italy in the early nineteenth century are just like the fictional Parma—and we have no reason to believe many of them were very different—then the whole of Europe, by extension, a place of divided and oppressed countries, some more progressive than others but all of them reactionary by Stendhal's standards, would itself be trapped in the sad romance, in the absurd, insulated story, the archaic daydream, the fond thought that the French Revolution, and with it Napoleon, could be put away and forgotten. Romance as fiction and romance as a ludicrous but inescapable contemporary truth are distinctly different things. Even as he turns from France and his own day, Stendhal is able to let loose a handful of polemical shot over his shoulder. Metternich, Namier wrote, 'annotated the margins of the great book of human insufficiency and inertia'. Fabrice's Parma, for all its slightly febrile charm, could well have given him a page or two.

One of the indications in Stendhal's source was magic. 'The author', he notes, meaning his Neapolitan chronicler, 'explains a lot of facts by magic . . .' (*Chartreuse* 504). His ingenious translation for his predecessor's credulity is to give his hero a generous provision of fine old Italian superstition. Fabrice has a mentor, the abbé Blanès, an astrologer, who succeeds in lending his pupil very little of his arcane science, but leaves him with a 'limitless confidence in signs predicting the future' (*Chartreuse* 40). Fabrice interprets the flight of birds, (*Chartreuse* 49) and zealously watches an oak-tree which he regards as an oracle: it puts forth leaves in early spring to let him know that his plan to join Napoleon during the Hundred Days is sound (*Chartreuse* 50); a branch is broken in a storm or by a neighbour's malice to represent a coming mutilation of his young life—a small one though, for the tree itself is sturdy and still growing (*Chartreuse* 180).

The novel is full of minor predictions, most of them registered by Fabrice, but some left for the alert reader to gloat over. They are there to surround a major prophecy, a theme sounded literally more than a dozen times: Fabrice's irrational fear of prison, perfectly justified, although justified with surprisingly pleasant results.

Fabrice's visible enthusiasm on the way to Waterloo, along with his Italian accent and his unmilitary appearance, causes him to be arrested as a spy as soon as he sets out for the front. Prison, then, instead of glory. He bribes his way out, is given the clothes and the documents of a dead miscreant, which worries him no end. 'I have inherited his being, as it were . . . The presage is clear, I shall suffer much from a prison . . .' (*Chartreuse* 55). He even thinks that his own imprisonment will bear a relation to his dead benefactor's crime: stealing some silver and a cow, and beating up a peasant (*Chartreuse* 55, 82). There is a rather ugly joke on Stendhal's part here: Fabrice is later gaoled for killing an actor and running off with the actor's girl.

The theme now shifts key. Various prisons threaten Fabrice on his return from Waterloo, or rather the same prison, the renowned Austrian Spielberg, threatens him for various reasons—for having been to Waterloo at all, for returning to the territory of Milan when he should be in cautious exile, and finally for killing Giletti, the actor. He had to cross into the Austrian states to escape pursuit— what's more, he is once again carrying a dead man's papers, the unfortunate Giletti's passport.

But the Spielberg is not his destined prison. Prison awaits him in Parma, where he ought to be safe, because he has powerful friends in his aunt and her lover Mosca, the prince's minister. In fact, it is their power that lands him in prison, since his crime, committed in self-defence and generally allowed to be insignificant anyway, as only a mountebank was involved, is played up by the political opposition to Mosca, and a severe sentence is delivered against Fabrice as a result of intrigues at court. However, by another too-tidy reversal, Fabrice is not distressed by the much-feared prison, for love and happiness await him there, indeed when he escapes he can't wait to go back, and when he is released again drags out his life in mournful splendour, with one interlude of bliss which Stendhal refuses to describe for us. 'Here, we beg permission to pass, without a single word, over a space of three years' (*Chartreuse* 488). From there he retreats towards death in his charterhouse. The charterhouse really existed, Martineau tells us, north-east of Parma, but the information is not only naïve, it is misleading. Certainly Fabrice had been to another monastery on two different occasions, and Stendhal, we are told, used the word charterhouse loosely— meaning any kind of convent or monastery with *clausura*.[13] But then the force of the title surely becomes all the clearer. Prison is where Fabrice finds himself, writes religious sonnets, and scribbles in the margins of St Jerome. Secular studies, a means of paying court to Clélia, but then that suits Stendhal's theology well enough. The charterhouse of Parma, the one securely closed, contemplative place in a city of pride and ambition and rancour, is the prison on a high tower where Fabrice is kept.

What are we to make of this rather rickety machinery? Stendhal had used similar devices in *Le Rouge et le Noir*, with a remarkable lack of success. There we were faced with two elementary choices. Julien Sorel, in the church at Verrières, finds an oblique prophecy on a scrap of paper, news of the execution of a man whose name is an anagram of his own. We can assume Stendhal is serious about this, that such meaningful coincidences are a part of the picture of life he is offering—but then not much else in the novel confirms this view. Stendhal certainly thought life was capable of tricks just as fantastic, but he also saw life as more elegant and discreet than that in its echoes and bad jokes. Alternatively, we can assume that the anagram and its accompaniments—spilt holy water, crimson curtains—are simply heavy-handed juggling by a beginning novelist, attempts to ensure the visibility of a theme, to lay tracks for its return later in the book. I find this more likely.

Perhaps Fabrice's fulfilled superstitions represent the same thing, done with slightly more art. Stendhal attributes his own compositional needs to his character's education and temperament, and thereby acquires the freedom to set up his themes as he likes. No. That sounds right, but it wouldn't really be much of an improvement on the lame technique rejected in *Le Rouge et le Noir*, and in any case that isn't how the theme reads in *La Chartreuse de Parme*. Fabrice's prison doesn't suggest bad or even competent orchestration of a motif, it suggests mystery, creates a sense of fate for a sceptical author and his no doubt even more sceptical public.

First, Stendhal himself mocks Fabrice's credulity, tells us that his superstition is in fact his religion (*Chartreuse* 168), a shaky science converted into a dreamer's happiness. But then, changing hats, becoming creator as well as narrator, he makes Fabrice absolutely right, since everything prophesied for him comes true. Not only for him. The abbé Blanès predicted a prison for Fabrice, but he also predicted a great crime to be connected with his imprisonment: Gina's having the prince assassinated, her revenge, her supreme and impossible gift to the unfeeling Fabrice. The movement created by these denials and endorsements is close to that set up in *Tom Jones*, where Fielding explicitly rules out the happy end as any kind of realistic prospect in life and then winds up his book in a grand, improbable way, the just rewarded, the evil punished and sent to the North. He thereby asserts the genre of his work in a flamboyant way: comedy, a universe of happy ends where life is imitated in various ways but not in its outcomes. Similarly Stendhal proclaims his intentions, announces his world of romance, a place where fantastic prophecies come true.

Do they? Stendhal, like a good rationalist, sketches in a doubt, suggests that Fabrice's sense of things is partial, that he only counts presages that work and forgets the failures of his omens (*Chartreuse* 168). All right. But then the novel itself forgets the failures too, supports Fabrice, since his anxious readings of his destiny all turn out to be correct, we never see him wrong. In fact, what happens here is what happens later in works like James' 'Turn of the Screw' or *The Sacred Fount*. Stories are suspended between rival impossibilities, between two sets of explanations for a puzzling event, neither of which will do. We can't and Stendhal can't, accept Fabrice's view of the future as minutely predictable. But we can't see all his prisons as merely coincidences either. As in James, the fiction tips the scale towards the more orderly but more fantastic of the options: true prophecy here, ghosts in 'Turn of the Screw', a magical theory of the transferability of youth and wit in *The Sacred Fount*. In every case the story escapes towards mystery, into a dimension all of its own.

Still, there is something strained about Stendhal's insistence on Fabrice's prison. It comes not from the handling of the theme or from its more far-reaching implications but from its moral meaning, or lack of moral meaning, within the immediate context of the book's action. Prison is at the heart of all the paradoxes of *La Chartreuse* and it is not, finally, the prison's fault if the paradoxes are hollow. It is the fault of paradox as a structural principle, of the weakness of paradox in a world where logic itself, or at least Stendhal's logic, looks helpless, stranded, superannuated.

There is a marvellous moment of symmetry towards the middle of the novel. Fabrice, having killed Giletti, reaches the Austrian frontier bearing Giletti's passport. He is nevertheless afraid that he will be arrested as Fabrice del Dongo, wanted for his wanderings on the eve of Waterloo. The passport official has a different worry. He is a friend of Giletti's, and can't decide what to do with this young spark bearing Giletti's passport. If he arrests him, he'll get his friend into trouble, because Giletti has probably sold his papers. On the other hand, what happens if his superiors find out that he has stamped the passport knowing it was carried by someone who was not Giletti. He leaves the room, lets a colleague deal with the matter.

Conflicting errors stare at each other, the perfection of the discord makes a new harmony, a balanced dance of contraries. It happens again and again in the book. Gina, in her early days at the court of Parma, pleads for the pardon of a prisoner she has met in the citadel. Her plea is granted, evidence of her extreme favour with the prince. But the man she has freed is a squealer, whose confession brought about the death sentence of the poet-revolutionary Ferrante Palla. Fabrice's gaoler, Clélia's father, reports that his client is alone and in despair when his client's affair with Clélia, conducted by signs, is at its height. After Fabrice's escape Gina, irritated by his gloom, sarcastically suggests he ought to write to Clélia's father and apologize for breaking gaol. Fabrice in fact has done just that. These are small forms, echoes, splinters of the main irony built on the prison, which has several faces, or epochs. Fabrice fears his prison but finds happiness there. The boy who is unable to love when he is at liberty, finds a destined love waiting for him in gaol. He wants passionately to stay in prison while his friends want passionately to get him out. Having escaped from prison, he goes back of his own accord.

There is no way of knowing where Stendhal's idea started, but one of his sources offers what is clearly the logical core of his paradox: a prison with a view (*Chartreuse* 510). When Fabrice's fine view is blocked out, it is replaced by Clélia. The trouble with all this apart from its considerable heaviness, is that it is empty; neat but meaningless, a natty but slender joke, and one cannot sling a large novel on such things.

Except that Stendhal can. It is an extraordinary gamble, and one that just comes off. We have seen him failing with a wider, harder canvas in *Lucien Leuwen* and yet not squaring up his traps, the logical snares that might have held Lucien as those of *Le Rouge et le Noir* held its hero. Passion was a first course in logic for one of the characters of *De l'Amour* (*Amour* 116), and that, precisely, was what it was for Julien. His love for Mme de Rênal, released by his attempt to kill her, brought down the whole illogical edifice of his ambition, of his attempt to replace the red by the black without losing any of the brighter colouring. The paradox of his self-deception held the book together, and his revealed love broke the paradox and allowed the book to end.

Fabrice is caught in similar straights, shown to be a hypocrite when he is being as sincere as he can (*Chartreuse* 212); and his prison in one sense saves him, leaves him with no distractions from his love. But the logic of the narrative of *La Chartreuse*, whenever it appears, appears as an intrusion, a visitor from another, stiffer country. Stendhal's logic, as Jean Prévost points out,[14] is design, not sequence, geometry not arithmetic; and the subject of *La Chartreuse*, and to some extent *Lucien Leuwen*, is sequence itself, growing up, growing old, the slow death of hearts and affections. There is no proposition to encompass such realities, no closed form for them except our ultimate mortality.

Paradox will not do then, and yet paradox is Stendhal's oldest habit, the most familiar mode of his mind. Effectively, *La Chartreuse de Parme* rests on a false frame, on a set of ironies which look solid but are in truth extremely fragile. This, perhaps, is the key to a riddle which reading the novel often presents. Why does one go on, what keeps one wanting to know what happens next in this scattered work? It is really little more than six or seven unforgettable *bravura* scenes sustained by a functional narrative, lonely peaks in loosely connected valleys : the French in Italy; Fabrice at Waterloo; Gina at the court of Parma; her duel with the prince; her distress; her revenge; her isolation. One answer is the sheer charm and verve and intelligence of the writing. and it is a good answer. That, above all, is why one keeps reading *Vie de Henry Brulard*, for example, which is even more scattered. But one reads *La Chartreuse* rather more eagerly than that all the same, one is held more firmly. The reason, I think, is that Stendhal's repeating symmetries, the constant suggestion of paradox and tidy irony, make up a mirage of control, of a central, presiding meaning, of a direction which the novel simply doesn't have. But then it has it while we read it. We are shuffled from one expectation to another, waiting for the ironies to meet or unfold into a major action or emotion, and by the time we have realized, if we realize, that they won't, it is too late, the book is over. This is Stendhal's best magic, a culminating piece of sorcery: the place of an absent structure is supplied by an illusion of structure.

It wouldn't work, of course, if the book were not about something else too. *La Chartreuse de Parme*, as Balzac saw, is not really about Fabrice at all, and therefore still less about his prison. Much as the interest of *Ulysses* shifts from Stephen to Bloom, the interest of *La Chartreuse*, beginning with Fabrice, moves towards age, to his aunt, who comes to dominate the book, in terms both of her effect on its actions and of her impact on us. The force of her presence is such that it is often hard even to see Fabrice and harder to believe he deserves such splendid expenses of energy and devotion. The structure and the passion of *La Chartreuse de Parme*, the false structure of paradox and the authentic passion of Gina, are blurred by Stendhal's sleight of hand; we think, briefly, that the two elements are one, as they were in *Le Rouge et le Noir*. Then the haze lifts, and we see how separate they are. Two books, one fairly thin and the other superb. One lends shape to the other's feeling.

Balzac compared *La Chartreuse de Parme* to Racine's *Phèdre*, and he knew what he was doing. Gina's love for Fabrice rejoins the famous forbidden loves of legend, adds to their stock, borrows from their colour. Fabrice, faced with his recognition of his aunt's feelings for him, thinks of Joseph and Potiphar's wife. He knows Gina is not fully conscious of the extent of her love, she would be horrified, would see it as an incest (*Chartreuse* 158). Stendhal himself, later, adds another loaded allusion: a crown prince who 'unlike Hippolytus son of Theseus, had not rejected the advances of a young step-mother' (*Chartreuse* 308). And yet there is nothing incestuous or ungrateful about Gina's love for Fabrice. She is probably not related to him, and if she is, she is his aunt. She is not married to Mosca, she knew Fabrice before she met him, and indeed began her affair with Mosca during Fabrice's flight to Waterloo— almost as if to protect herself against the possibility of his not returning. Mosca is, or becomes, Fabrice's benefactor, so there is a comparison with Potiphar there, and perhaps, in a metaphorical sense, with Theseus. As a giver of advice, Mosca is partly Fabrice's father. Still, Mosca is not really the difficulty.

The difficulty, for both Fabrice and Gina, is the delicate one of shifting key within an old relationship. Gina can't bring herself to do it, and Fabrice is not sure how to stop it happening, one day or another. Sure enough Gina, struck suddenly by Fabrice's grave, adult demeanour, by the sight of the serious young man he has become, flings herself into his arms, and he, moved and in spite of all his good resolutions, covers her with kisses (*Chartreuse* 190). But then Mosca appears. Two days later Fabrice has his scuffle with Giletti, and is reunited with Gina only when, for her, it is too late. He is already in love with Clélia.

Mosca's chance arrival saves the novel then, keeps it going. Stendhal likes to suggest such things, a life and a literature thrown recklessly open to small hazards. He is also careful to suggest that in spite of the horror she would feel if she were to see the full range of her affection for Fabrice (*Chartreuse* 109), *does* feel when she realizes it (*Chartreuse* 163), Gina would nevertheless have given herself to him if he had made the right moves. Stendhal even adds that she could have made the conquest of Fabrice—since at that time he loved no one else—by a little coquetry, by giving him a rival, for example (*Chartreuse* 164). She doesn't though, and this first indecision on the part of a remarkably determined woman, this first holding back from something she wants, is the beginning of a decline for her, a step towards her later desperation, when she will have a murder committed primarily in an attempt to reassert, vainly, her active presence in the world, her continuing ability to affect events.

Fabrice is infinitely fond of Gina, she is still his charming, youthful aunt, the person he loves best in the world. But that is because he is not in love. He is concerned about this, wonders, as Stendhal's heroes always do at some point in their career, whether the famous feeling is perhaps not a myth, merely something people talk about, and resolves, *because* he cares so much for Gina, never to tell her he loves her (*Chartreuse* 166). There is a marvellous mixture of genuine affection and wary, childish calculation in his later deliberations on the same subject. His friendship for Gina is his life, he tells himself, he can't ruin it by turning it into a banal, hysterical affair full of recriminations. And in any case, Gina is a powerful person in the world, she provides him with money and horses and a coach and a position. He doesn't want to lose that (*Chartreuse* 225, 226). In prison he comes to love Clélia, and looks back on his tenderness for Gina with surprise. He can't see how he came as close as he did to loving her. She is effaced, aged, by the freshness and calm of Clélia. She is fifty years old for him (*Chartreuse* 322).

The echoes of Hippolytus and Potiphar, of a young man pursued by the warm attentions of someone too closely connected to him, are in effect an accompaniment, not the main subject. They are there to fire certain associations, to make us think of terse triangles, for example. Mosca, Gina, Fabrice. The names flicker in a series of strange little jokes, as if to indicate both the relationships and the complexities and confusions among them. Fabrice and Gina are briefly mistaken for General Fabio Conti and his daughter Clélia. This would make Fabrice Gina's father, as Gina is quick to point out. Everyone laughs. Then she straightens out the matter by explaining that Fabrice is in fact her son. Later the Paris newspapers get hold of a story about Fabrice's probable succession to the archbishopric of Parma, only they get the names wrong: Gina's nephew Count Mosca is to be the new prelate. By a last irony, when Gina has escaped from Parma with Fabrice, her servant Ludovic tells inquisitive observers that Fabrice is Mosca's son.

There are two triangles. Mosca loves Gina who loves Fabrice. Gina loves Fabrice who loves Clélia. Mosca's love is timid, passionate, silly, beautifully drawn, and the love between Fabrice and Clélia is nicely rendered. They are the basic young lovers of the sentimental imagination, the love-interest. But ultimately only the link between the triangle matters much to us. Gina loves Fabrice who doesn't love her. Which is a way of saying that only Gina matters.

The stages of Gina's passion are very clear, make a progression which looks oddly, deeply inevitable in a novel caught between Fabrice's superstitions and Stendhal's dogged reliance on the idea of chance. She loves Fabrice as a child, watches him grow up. As Balzac says, she has no children of her own—although the Gina which emerges in Balzac's lyrical review of *La Chartreuse de Parme* is in fact rather too maternal, too grand and noble and lofty, one of Balzac's own slightly overblown women. There is, of course, something motherly in Gina's feelings for Fabrice, but she doesn't make a motherly impression, she is too clearly competitive, too young for that. Then Fabrice returns from Waterloo and she falls thoroughly in love with him. The love has a later, reinforcing moment when he comes back, solemn and manly, from the theological college in Naples where he was supposed to be preparing his bright clerical future.

There are rumours of her affair with Fabrice everywhere in Parma. Clélia has heard of it (*Chartreuse* 267), the prince makes a malicious reference (*Chartreuse* 254). At one stage almost everyone except Gina herself knows about it. Mosca sees it in her eyes when she is talking to Fabrice, and falls cruelly into envy and a sense of his age. 'Ah! however careful I am, the look in my eyes must be old! Isn't my gaiety always close to irony? . . . I'll say more, I must be sincere here, doesn't my gaiety give a glimpse, as of something very near, of absolute power . . . and meanness?' (*Chartreuse* 154). Fabrice knows. An old rival knows. In a softer novel these rumours and inferences would be wrong, a fine purity would be left to Gina and Fabrice. But for Stendhal, and for Gina, the purity of the affair is an unhappy accident, an absence of physical consequences for a passion that can swell and proliferate without them. When the intrigues of the court have finally thrown Fabrice in prison for his murder of Giletti, she dismisses Mosca, tells him it is all over, and makes an eloquent confession, a declaration of love for an absent hero comparable to Cathy Earnshaw's speech to Nelly in *Wuthering Heights*:

'I swear to you before God and on the life of Fabrice that there has not passed between him and me the smallest thing that a third person couldn't have witnessed. But I shall not tell you that I love him as if I were his sister; I love him by instinct, as it were. I love in him his perfect and simple courage . . . In short, if he is not happy I can't be happy. There, that's a phrase which well describes the state of my heart; if it's not the truth, it is at least as much of it as I can see' (*Chartreuse* 289).

She is in fact saying almost as much as she knows about her love. But she is saying it in the large shadow of all she doesn't know. She doesn't know how jealous she can be, she can't know that she will later hasten Clélia's marriage with a kind of eager rancour, in the faintest of hopes of getting Fabrice back. Her remark about his happiness is perhaps true but it is pathetically partial. If Fabrice is happy without her, she will be in despair.

The heart of the matter, the fissure in Gina's life through which all her distresses will come flooding in, is her own doubt, a shyness, a failure of nerve. Her anxiety about a possible sense of incest is trivial compared with her terror at the thought of being too old

181

for Fabrice—she is fifteen years older than he is. We have seen that she was right to be afraid. Faced with Clélia, Fabrice thought of Gina as fifty. Fabrice *is* her threatened youth, if he could love her she would still be young. His imprisonment thus means a form of death for Gina, fully displayed in the narrative—to her maids, seeing her virtually unconscious on her bed in sorrow, fully clothed, in her diamonds, pale, her eyes closed, she seems to be lying in state (*Chartreuse* 287). To Mosca she seems to have aged overnight : '. . . and yesterday so brilliant, so young !' (*Chartreuse* 288). Prison is a place where time passes. Fabrice has plenty of time, Gina hasn't.

But her despair at Fabrice's capture has other components too. She is an active woman, in love with movement. She is attracted to Parma partly by the thought of Mosca's power—'The memory of the count became mingled with the idea of his great power' (*Chartreuse* 118)—and embraces Ferrante Palla when she sees him ready to assassinate the prince. 'There is the only man who has understood me', she murmurs (*Chartreuse* 371). Her heart returns to Mosca when she has heard of his suppressing the revolt in Parma. Her love for Fabrice itself is connected with Fabrice's expedition to Waterloo, his 'perfect and simple', if mercilessly thwarted courage, and there is a moving echo, or rather a moving absence of echo, late in the book, when he has escaped from prison in best swashbuckling manner and has nothing to tell her, no story. There is no going back to the endless, charming discussions after Waterloo when they weren't sure whether Fabrice had been at a battle at all and if he had, whether it was the right battle. Those childish days, by now, are gone for Fabrice too. He can think only of Parma and getting back to Clélia.

With Fabrice's imprisonment, therefore, there rises in Gina a fierce, suffocating, debilitating rage, because there is nothing she can do. When a sentence was given against Fabrice with him safely out of the country she marched in to see the prince and simply threatened to leave Parma, to withdraw all the light and joy she was shedding. She was happy to be active—as all Stendhal's women are, they are invariably superior to his men in this. Mathilde de la Mole, Mme de Rênal, Gina, Clélia, they are all enlivened by danger, quickened into extraordinary acts of intelligence and courage. The men are brave enough but in a willed, strained and usually comic way, their imaginations exalt their perils, paint dragons on every wall. But now, with Fabrice in the prince's hands, ready and waiting for the first poisoner who is sent along to deal with him, Gina can't leave and she can't do much if she stays. She has been betrayed by the prince, who had promised not to sign Fabrice's sentence and significantly, the order of her fury runs from that to Fabrice, from her sense of humiliation and outrage to a concern for his life. His life is more important to her, but it surfaces second in her anger. And here, in the pit of her impotence, she vows vengeance on the prince. 'You can kill me this way, so be it, you have the power to do it; but afterwards I shall have your life' (*Chartreuse* 281).

Her vengeance is the moral climax of the novel, as Julien's crime was for *Le Rouge et le Noir*, but with a difference which could hardly be greater. Julien's shooting of Mme de Rênal was his redemption, what he had to do. In spite of all appearances, it was *right*. Gina's crime, equally clearly, and yet for reasons just as hard to bring to the surface and to formulate, is wrong. It doesn't save her, it stains the rest of her life.

Needless to say, it is not a question of Christian sin, although the climate of *La Chartreuse de Parme* is less favourable to violence than it looks, for all Stendhal's frequent talk of poison and vengeance in southern latitudes. Mosca has not had a single person killed during his term as minister, and describes himself as 'so squeamish about such things' (*Chartreuse* 432). He sometimes thinks, he says, when the day ends, of the two spies he had ordered to be shot, perhaps a little hastily, during the Peninsular War. He invents an improbable reactionary newspaper for Parma because he prefers the idea of a hundred atrocious absurdities to the thought of one hanged man. Certainly there is a touch of prudence in his humanity, he doesn't want the hanged man's family hunting him down (*Chartreuse* 139), and he appears, at the end, to have forgotten the sixty people he caused to be killed in the revolt. He also rebukes Fabrice sternly for not having slaughtered a servant he stole a horse from—sentimental and careless behaviour—but nevertheless he is Stendhal's picture of a man in power who remains decent, and not a butcher. He offers a striking contrast to the bloodthirsty child of *Vie de Henry Brulard* and to the even bloodthirstier consul writing that book, and he offers a clear contrast to Gina too. His idea of old age is to be incapable of acting childishly (*Chartreuse* 115). Hers is the stirring of her conscience at the memory of an assassination (*Chartreuse* 391).

The setting is wrong for Gina's vengeance, then, it belongs in another, older age. But even there, perhaps, it would have seemed excessive. It is too late, Fabrice is free when she orders the signal to be made to Ferrante Palla, who is to poison the prince. Water from a reservoir in her palace is to flood the streets of Parma, and Ferrante will know the time has come. She will give wine, she says, to the inhabitants of her country village, and water to the citizens of Parma, because they would have loved to see Fabrice die. She is hiding her uncertainty about the killing here, perhaps, rejoicing in the sign as if the sign had a meaning of its own. There is something too small for vengeance in her scheme, it is not much better than a resentment, and it is her own half-awareness of this which weakens Gina. In the Renaissance world to which she belongs people were killed for adultery or for having killed others, and even in Stendhal's France the crimes that attracted him were committed for love. Gina has the prince assassinated out of hatred, worse, out of the festering memory of her helplessness on the day Fabrice was put in gaol. It is a crime of the head, the work of slighted self-regard; it is a harsh act without dignity.

But all this could have been overcome if Fabrice had loved Gina. She intended the prince's death as her welcoming gift to him, they were to have exulted over it together. As it is, she can't even tell him. 'I did that for him,' she thinks darkly (*Chartreuse* 403). She didn't. But without him it has no meaning. Julien was sustained by an intuitively held morality of his own, which was strong enough to batter back all assaults from conventional views of what he had done. Without Fabrice, Gina has no inner mine of energy and defiance, she cannot set up her values against the world's because they have been revealed as barren, as the mere waving of a small fist not, ultimately, at the prince or at Parma, although they were to suffer, but at middle age and death, at the lines on her face, the fading of her pulse and the thought that Fabrice may never love her. The way is open, then, for the world's values to come seeping in, she has no defences. A half-remorse sets up house in her mind (*Chartreuse* 391), and when Mosca suggests killing an enemy in order to get Fabrice out of prison for a second time, she says no. She doesn't want him to have black ideas in the evenings (*Chartreuse* 433). The enemy concerned, she adds, owes his life to the fact that she now loves Mosca better than she loves Fabrice (*Chartreuse* 418). If the tone of the book were different we might see a gentle resolution out of classical comedy here : the old folks together, leaving the young folks alone. But this is Gina's defeat, gracefully acknowledged, for she hardly knows how not to be graceful, but ghastly for a woman whose glory it was never to repent, never to look back, never to think again about something once decided on. What saves the enemy's life and leaves her quietly married to Mosca in the end is not only age but the worst kind of scar brought with her from her youth : shame for a senseless, violent and irrevocable gesture of malice. Stendhal's remarks about the unsullied joys of vengeance in Italy (*Chartreuse* 372, 397, 439) are a smoke-screen, a materialization of Gina's discomfort in the narrative; a way of holding us off from what she herself would rather not know.

Two last life-long themes, admirably caught up and rescued in *La Chartreuse de Parme* : distinction, and doomed love.

Stendhal often gives his heroes and heroines rather awkward, silly snobberies, especially about money. They are regularly surrounded by gross buffoons, stooges strung out along a single caricatural dimension. I am not thinking of the minor characters, they are often remarkably done. I am thinking of the enemies, the husbands, the fathers, the suitors who keep trying to invade or tear down the carefully guarded castle of the protagonist's superiority, and who fail miserably at the first moat, fall back with typical coarseness and cowardice. Julien Sorel's essential difference from the people around him is masked by his social difference, he is in the territory of another class, but we are not meant to miss it. He would have been different anywhere. And when Stendhal begins to rail on the roughness and incomprehension of the world, you can be sure he is about to pat the exquisite sensibility of his hero, of Octave or Lucien or Léon, on the back.

It doesn't look promising, but it has a fine moment in *La Chartreuse*, the fruit of work on the Italian chronicles and a well-placed memory of Shakespeare. The novel, like most of the chronicles, ends in a scuffle of deaths. Fabrice and Clélia have a son who dies. A few months later Clélia dies. Fabrice retreats to a charterhouse and dies after a year. Gina survives him by very little. The romance suddenly takes on the configuration of an accomplished tragedy. Everyone who counts is dead, and the stage is left to the competent and the well-meaning, the Edgars, the Horatios, the Fortinbrases, people who can keep the world going but who do not breathe the icy air of the tragic heights, of the upper slopes of a privileged but terminal experience. Stendhal's favourite characters don't breathe all that much icy air either, but he manages to make the division of levels into the metaphor that had escaped him for years, an image of a moral distinction which would be a form of grand but ambiguous blessing.

What about Mosca? He is left alive, and 'immensely rich' (*Chartreuse* 493). Precisely. Mosca commits a *courtisan's* fault in this book, he is embarrassed by the situation Gina has impetuously created by threatening to leave Parma and omits a crucial sentence from the prince's signed promise to her. It is true that the prince would probably have tricked Gina anyway, even without Mosca's unwitting assistance, but neither Mosca nor Gina nor the reader is allowed to forget his slip, the moment when a habit of subservience was stronger than either his quick intelligence or his loyalty to Gina. Mosca, for all his virtues, is a prisoner of the world, and that is just what Stendhal's chosen characters are not. The distinction which he often clumsily, and in *La Chartreuse de Parme* broadly and splendidly gave to them is in the end neither a fantasy nor a literal truth. It is a speculation on freedom, on a purity which, one way or another, might resist all blandishments, never give in. Lukács speaks of a 'final refusal to accept a compromise'.[15] Gina was lucky, then, to be allowed to die in this company; and immediately upon finishing *La Chartreuse de Parme*, Stendhal wrote the later part of 'L'Abbesse de Castro', where a brave and touching heroine gives in gradually to the worst and most demeaning temptations, and dies by her own hand, driven by her own scorn for herself. It looks like a new, sad reign, but Stendhal quickly turns his fiction back towards innocence.

'She dismisses Léon whom she adores' (*Romans* 479). This line from a plan for *Le Rose et le Vert* echoes not only Stendhal's favourite version of his affair with Métilde—'Model: Métilde loving Dominique', he notes (*Romans* 479)—but also Racine's *Bérénice*, and less directly, half a dozen of the world's great loves, crossed by civic duty or quarrelling families or a husband's sword. In all these stories we may, if we wish, see the obstacles to the love as in some sense allegorical, emblems of love's own impossibility, but they are, nevertheless, there. Stendhal mumbles a bit about the need for external pressures on his heroes' lives (*Romans* 462), but in fact he is simply not interested in such things, which leaves him with almost impossible requirements for a love story. The love must be returned, the lovers will preferably be kept out of bed, the necessary obstacles will come from the lovers themselves, and not from some alien agency. *Armance*, *Lucien Leuwen*, *Le Rose et le Vert* and *Féder*, a novel started soon after *La Chartreuse*, all founder, wholly or in part, on these demands. In *La Chartreuse* Stendhal makes a small concession, allows Fabrice and Clélia to sleep together, once in prison under direst stresses, and often later, but in darkness then, and surrounded by guilt and foreboding. As if in return, he is given a huge and probably unrecognized reward, the more or less accidental result of his insistence on Fabrice's fate and on the oafishness of nominal impediments like Clélia's father and later, her husband.

Fabrice's fated prison gives a history to his love before it starts, since Clélia was what prison was to give him. She in turn feels guilty about her love since her father is the governor of the gaol. She helps Fabrice to escape but vows to the madonna, as a penance for such flagrant filial disloyalty, never to set eyes on Fabrice again if he survives. This would be a dilemma we could believe in if her father were anything other than an evil clown, a thoroughly nasty and betrayable fellow. Her husband likewise asks for adultery, makes it look like charity to his wife. The effect of this is to make Clélia's fidelity to her marriage and her vow appear first as a form of stiff-necked virtue on her part : not what she owes to her father or husband but what she owes to herself in an ideal relation to such figures —conceived as pure abstractions, of course, since the real thing ought to sink her high morality in a minute, and hurl her into Fabrice's arms. But beyond this, the lame and flamboyant obstacles to a happy end for the lovers—a vow to the madonna, in Stendhal, is a caricature of the notion of an obstacle—serve as vivid, unmistakeable signs, along with the predicted prison and the curious conversation by alphabets which Fabrice and Clélia conduct from window to window in the gaol. They point to this love, call down to its aid all the doomed loves it reincarnates. They place the story, and we know at once where we are, and why it works better than most of Stendhal's other attempts at blighted young passion. It is pure convention. There is not even a pretence that the troubles of these two are anything other than the token troubles they need to qualify for the myth. It is *Romeo and Juliet* with the feuding families represented by a kind of light algebra, we know what the marks mean. Stendhal's mathematics are at last made to play a tune.

There is, there always was, a cruel reading of such myths, they can be stripped down into a mean supposition. The obstacle, say, lay neither within the lovers nor beyond them, but between. One of them didn't love, and the rest was fantasy, the play is by Romeo with Romeo as the hero. King Mark didn't really care for Isolde,

Rome was just an excuse for Titus. Once, and only once, Stendhal allowed this interpretation of his own story into his fiction, in an inverted form and with wonderful results. What if Métilde felt about Stendhal not as Mme de Chasteller felt about Lucien Leuwen, but as Fabrice felt about Gina?

12. CONVERSIONS

'*Mais pourquoi ce monde? à quelle*
occasion? C'est ce que l'image ne dit
pas. Elle n'est qu'image'
VIE DE HENRY BRULARD

There is not much more. Stendhal works on another chronicle, with
a fine climax of poisoned nuns, gives up and thinks of transposing the
story into the eighteenth century. He writes the opening of a rollick-
ing, adventurish tale borrowed from Lesage, full of swordfights and
set in the age of d'Artagnan. 'It was in 1640; Richelieu, more
terrible than ever, ruled France . . .' (*Romans* 305). He starts a
light novel called *Féder*, a mixture of love story and old comedy, of
provincials in Paris, and abounding, ironically delivered advice
about how to get on in the world. Indeed Stendhal's theme in these
years is education of all kinds, young men and young girls are repeatedly fashioned by the tired consul's lonely wisdom. He returns
to Civita-Vecchia, dabbles in archaeology, falls ill, goes back again
and again to his plans for *Lamiel*. He begins a picaresque tale about
a port-urchin, seen from his window perhaps. *Féder* contains a sardonic and not altogether funny self-portrait : a painter who suddenly discovers that his only talent is for gross and belittling caricature.

Stendhal worked at *Lamiel,* on and off, from early 1839 until
shortly before he died, and yet what we have, although considerable
in quantity, is not even a draft. It is simply a set of ideas and scenes
and characters in search of a novel, and looking in rather unpromis-
ing places. Stendhal had *Gil Blas* on his mind, and the 1830 Revolution; he wanted to write a rogue's tale set then. Lamiel is a young

girl who adores the exploits of Mandrin and Cartouche, those French cousins of MacHeath, and one of Stendhal's plans for his book was to have her fall in love with a socially conscious criminal— 'I make war on a society which makes war on me' (*Lamiel* 1031)— and end up by burning down the law courts in his honour, her own charred bones to be found among the smoking ruins. An early mentor for her is Dr Sansfin, a gruesome comic hunchback who in many ways prefigures Groucho Marx: a votalile, eloquent, tricky and totally spurious Don Juan. He estimates his chances of sexual success at two women in every hundred attempted, and gets upset only when he falls below his quota. The best sequence in *Lamiel* as we have it is Sansfin persuading the local duchess, who has taken Lamiel under her quivering, aristocratic wing, that the girl, mildly ill, is close to death and that he, Sansfin, is the only doctor likely to save her. Meanwhile he administers noxious drugs to Lamiel in order to keep her at the necessary level of debility. His thought is to marry the duchess and become rich and powerful. He decides later that he is rich enough already, and would rather have the duchess as a mistress. She is bending an increasingly willing ear as as the theme fades out.

There are good things—Lamiel herself is charming, even on his worst days Stendhal could still make young people attractive—and other funny scenes: the night the duchess thinks the Revolution has come, and the old porter is afraid of being bitten. By the mob? No, by the bulldogs the duchess has imported to protect the chateau. Lovel, an English servant, is called out, as he alone is able to make his compatriots listen to reason. But it is all an idea, a project; nothing more. *Lamiel* is an interesting notebook.

Now as in an earlier low spell in Civita-Vecchia Stendhal turns briefly towards confession: now as then the confession tells us more perhaps about the novels than about Stendhal. The works I am thinking of are an odd stretch of diary written in a mixture of French and mangled English, and called 'Earline'; and an extraordinary amusement called 'Les Privilèges du 10 avril 1840'.

'Earline' is dressed up as notes for a novel, set in Rome among promenades, paintings, churches, sunshine, official soirées, balls, masks, a carnival. There is a husband, a son, two ugly sisters in the shape of a mother-in-law and a sister-in-law, and a cold, distinguished rival who is also a friend of the hero's. At the centre, the wraith of a woman, a face, eyes, clothes, a phrase or two which the would-be lover broods on with infinite attention. There was a day, apparently, when the time was right, when the hero should have made his declaration, carefully prepared and correctly mournful :

'I have to give you some bad news, you love me and I love you' ('Earline' 1506).

But he didn't, and he is unable to hide from himself that his love is rather something he wants to feel, a proof of a continuing capacity for finely strung emotion, than a passion imposing itself. Once back in Civita-Vecchia, he finds it difficult even to get himself to think of Earline. The affair pursues its willed and mildly hallucinatory existence for about a year, the lover returning to Rome and reading signs again like an early detective : what do her looks and her manners mean? A sense of humour, which is a sense of reality, never quite leaves these notes, though, and the lover calmly tells himself several times that the truth is harder and less malleable than he thinks it is : after all, either she loves him or she doesn't. He records a splendidly banal exchange, in which she apologizes for not having told him she was going to the Farnese's. *Scusate, caro Beyle.* The hero asks whether there is anyone in the drawing-room, and she says no. The dialogue, Stendhal comments, was very polite but certainly not very tender ('Earline' 1513).

It is a love story slipped into the interstices of a life, without, it seems, affecting that life at all. The love is woven into the most innocuous and meaningless encounters, it is a form of game which the world itself doesn't even have to know it is playing. And in this perspective Stendhal's pretence of planning a novel has a strange ambiguity and sadness. Of course, he has invented a few details, changed a few relationships, but 'Earline', in effect, is even less of a novel, in one sense, than the early 'Roman'. It echoes another piece of cerebration called 'Consultation pour Banti', in which Stendhal tried to console himself for his chronic timidity with Alexandrine Petit. There, he loved too little to conquer his shyness, as with Métilde he loved too much. But here, his love is a pure fabrication fanned by the desire to be in love again, and not even by the coarser but more concrete hope of getting Alexandrine into bed and help-ing his ambition along. In this sense it is *only* a novel, a dream of feeling bolstered up by every hectic memory Stendhal can call down on it. Alexandrine, Métilde, Clémentine are evoked repeatedly in these pages as if they could give Stendhal back what he felt for them. He tells himself he has returned to their days, that now is like then. *The Last Romance* is his title, or *The End of the Carnival*. There was a literal carnival going on, but the plaintive metaphor virtually drowns it : the party's over.

He writes a revealing phrase. A little real life, he says, has become mingled with his quiet, writer's existence, busy on *Lamiel*. '. . . real life, *id est* uncertainty about what will happen tomorrow' ('Earline' 1504). He is asking more of Earline than a guarantee that his old heart still beats, he is asking her to save him from fiction, from the safe places of the imagination. Where the unfortunate Visconti of *De l'Amour* gloried in the mind's capacity to make its own joys unaided, the mind is now seen as a prison, a sealed fantasy, a source of mere lies and evasions. Here and always, in his books and in his loves, Stendhal ultimately sought the novel he would *not* have imagined, the novel he would have come across in reality and not have spun out of his own insights and inclinations; the novel that would show the shape of art and the unsteadiness of life, that would simply *be there*, he would just have to find it, and then tell it or enjoy it.

The result is a fiction which has much less imaginative freedom than that of almost any other great novelist, which is hampered by a scruple and a modesty. On the other hand, it is never closed off, never complete, never literary, it regularly sends us back to reality. It is not, in Balzac's brave formula, in competition with civil life. On a copy of *La Chartreuse de Parme* Stendhal wrote, 'Would you prefer to have had three women or to have made this novel ?' (*Chartreuse* 1368). This is not a weak irony and it is not a consolation—literary pride, as Martineau puts it, avenging a failure in love ('Earline' 1626, Martineau's note). It is an unanswerable question, a last, wry facing of the fact that if books are poor things in bed, women don't offer much hope of immortality; a recognition that while art may give a life a reason, the daily quality of that life is made up of other, smaller things. It is the sense of these other things pressing on even the richest of imagined substitutes that gives Stendhal's novels their peculiar cutting edge.

The other things also have their day in the curious legacy drawn up in April 1840 : 'Les Privilèges'. I give the whole document here, Stendhal's belated bequest from a meticulous wizard of his own making.

'God gives me the following licence :
Article 1 Never any serious pain, until extreme old age; then, not

192

pain but death from apoplexy, in bed, during sleep, without any moral or physical pain.

Each year, not more than three days of illness. The body and what comes out of it odourless.

Article 2 The following miracles will be neither perceived nor suspected by anyone.

Article 3 The *mentula*, as hard and as moveable as the index finger whenever I wish. Its shape, two inches longer than the present article, same thickness. But pleasure by the *mentula* only twice a week.

Twenty times a year the privileged person will be able to become whoever or whatever he wants to be, provided that the creature exists. A hundred times a year, he will know whatever language he wants to know for twenty-four hours.

Article 4 If the privileged person, wearing a ring on his finger, clasps this ring while looking at a woman, she will fall passionately in love with him, as Héloise was with Abelard. If the ring is slightly moistened with saliva, the woman will become just a tender and devoted friend. If he looks at a woman and takes the ring from his finger, the feelings inspired in virtue of the preceding privileges will cease. Hatred will turn to benevolence, if one looks at the hating person while rubbing a ring on the finger.

These miracles will be allowed to take place only four times a year for passionate love; eight times for friendship; twenty times for the ending of hatred and fifty times for inspiring simple benevolence.

Article 5 Fine hair, good skin, excellent fingers never scraped, smooth light odour. The first of February and the first of June of each year, the clothes of the privileged person will become as they were the third time he wore them.

Article 6 Miracles for everyone who doesn't know him : the privileged person will have the face of General Debelle, who died in Santo Domingo, but without any imperfection. He will play whist, *écarté*, billiards, chess perfectly, but he will never be able to win more than a hundred francs. He will shoot, ride a horse, fence, to perfection.

Article 7 Four times a year he will be able to become whatever animal he wants to be; and afterwards turn back into a man. Four times a year he will be able to become whichever man he wants to be; also to concentrate his life into that of an animal which, in the case of death or hindrance to the first man he changed into, will be able to recall the privileged person to his natural shape. Thus the privileged person will be able, four times a year and for an unlimited period each time, to occupy two bodies at once.

Article 8 When the privileged man shall wear about his person or on his finger, for two minutes, a ring he has put briefly into his mouth, he will become invulnerable for whatever space of time he indicates. Ten times a year he will have the sight of an eagle and will be able to run five leagues in an hour.

Article 9 Every day, at two o'clock in the morning, the privileged person will find a gold Napoleon in his pocket, plus the equivalent of forty francs in change, in the currency of the country he is in. Money which has been stolen from him will be found the following night, at two o'clock in the morning, on a table in front of him. Assassins, at the moment of striking him or giving him poison, will have an attack of acute cholera lasting eight days. The privileged person will be able to cut short this pain by saying : I pray that the suffering of so and so may cease or be replaced by such and such a smaller pain.

Thieves will be struck by an attack of acute cholera lasting two days, at the moment they begin to commit the theft.

Article 10 When hunting, eight times a year, the privileged person will see a little flag a league away indicating to him what game there is and its exact position. The second before the animal moves, the little flag will be luminous; it is clearly understood that this little flag will be invisible for everyone except the privileged person.

Article 11 A similar flag will indicate statues hidden underground, underwater and in walls to the privileged person; what these statues are, who they were made by and when, and the price they will fetch when discovered. The privileged person will be able to change these statues into a ball of lead weighing a quarter of an ounce. This miracle of the flag and the successive conversion into a ball and into a statue shall be allowed to take place only eight times a year.

Article 12 The animal ridden by the privileged person, or pulling the vehicle which carries him, will never get sick, never fall. The privileged person will be able to join himself to this animal in such a way as to inspire its wishes and to share its sensations. Thus, the privileged person riding a horse will become one with it, and will inspire it with his wishes. The animal, linked to the privileged person in this way, will have three times its normal strength and vigour.

The privileged person, converted into a fly, for example, and riding an eagle, will become one with this eagle.

Article 13 The privileged person will not be able to back down; if he were to try, his organs would refuse to respond. He will be able to kill ten human beings a year; but no one he has spoken to. For the first year he will be able to kill someone provided that he hasn't spoken to him on more than two separate occasions.

Article 14 If the privileged person wanted to tell of or reveal one of the articles of his privilege, his mouth would not be able to make a sound, and he would have toothache for twenty-four hours.

194

Article 15   If the privileged person takes a ring on his finger and says : I pray that all noxious insects be destroyed, all insects within a radius of six metres from the ring will be struck dead. These insects are fleas, bugs, lice of all kinds, parasites, gnats, flies, rats etc.

Snakes, vipers, lions, tigers, wolves and all poisonous animals will take flight, smitten with fear, and will remove themselves to a league away.

Article 16   Wherever he is, the privileged person, having said : *I pray for my food*, will find : two pounds of bread, a well-done steak, a leg of lamb likewise, a plate of spinach likewise, a bottle of St Julien, a carafe of water, a fruit and an ice-cream, and a demi-tasse of coffee. This prayer will be granted twice in twenty-four hours.

Article 17   Ten times a year, if he asks, the privileged person will not miss what he wants to hit, whether with a shotgun or with a pistol or whatever weapon.

Ten times a year, he will be able to fence with twice the strength of his enemy or practice-partner : but he will not be able to inflict a wound causing death, pain or discomfort for more than a hundred hours.

Article 18   Ten times a year, the privileged person, if he asks, will be able to diminish by three-quarters the pain of someone or something he sees; or this creature being about to die, he will be able to prolong its life by ten days, diminishing the present pain by three-quarters. He will be able, if he asks, to obtain immediate and painless death for this suffering creature.

Article 19   The privileged person will be able to change a dog into a beautiful or an ugly woman; this woman will take his arm, and will have as much wit as Mme Ancilla, and Mélanie's heart. This miracle can be renewed twenty times each year.

The privileged person will be able to change a dog into a man who will have the style and presence of Pépin de Bellisle and the wit of M. Koreff, the Jewish doctor.

Article 20   The privileged person will never be more unhappy than he was from 1 August 1839 to 1 April 1840.

Two hundred times a year the privileged person will be able to cut down his sleep to two hours, which will produce the physical effects of eight. He will have the eyesight of a lynx and the lightness of Deburau.

Article 21   Twenty times a year, the privileged person will be able to guess the thoughts of people round him at a distance of twenty paces. A hundred and twenty times a year, he will be able to see what any person he wants to see is doing at the moment; there is a complete exception for the woman he loves most.

There is also an exception for dirty and disgusting actions.

Article 22   The privileged person will not be able to make any money, apart from his sixty francs a day, by means of the privileges set out above. A hundred and fifty times a year, he will be able, if he asks, to have someone forget him, the privileged person, entirely.

Article 23   Ten times a year, the privileged person will be able to be transported to wherever he wants to go, at the rate of a hundred leagues an hour; during the journey he will sleep.

Frédéric de Stendhal' ('Privilèges' 1525–1530).

Notes

Part One

1 *Pensées, Filosofia Nova*, Paris 1931, ii, p. 162. References to works by Stendhal not identified in these notes have been taken up into the text; editions and abbreviations as follows:

Armance		*Armance*
Le Rouge et le Noir	in *Romans et Nouvelles I*,	*Rouge*
Lucien Leuwen	Pléiade, Paris 1952	*Lucien*

La Chartreuse de Parme		*Chartreuse*
'L'Abbesse de Castro'		'Abbesse'
'Les Cenci'	in *Romans et Nouvelles II*,	'Cenci'
'La Duchesse de Palliano'	Pléiade, Paris 1955	'Palliano'
'Vanina Vanini'		'Vanina'
Lamiel		*Lamiel*

Vie de Henry Brulard		*Brulard*
Journal		*Journal*
Souvenirs d'Egotisme	in *Oeuvres intimes*,	*Souvenirs*
'Essaies	Pléiade, Paris 1955	'Autobiographies'
d'autobiographie'		
'Earline'		'Earline'
'Les Privilèges'		'Privilèges'

De l'Amour, Armand Colin, Paris 1959. *Amour*.
Rome, Naples et Florence en 1817, Juillard, Paris 1964. *Rome*.
Racine et Shakespeare, Jean-Jacques Pauvert, Paris 1965. *Racine*.
Romans et nouvelles, Livre de Poche, Paris 1968. *Romans*.
Translations throughout are my own.

2 *Pensées, Filosofia Nova*, i, p. 123.

3 Quoted in Jean Prévost, *La Création chez Stendhal*, Paris 1951, p. 53.

4   R. M. Adams, *Stendhal: Notes on a Novelist*, London 1959, p. xix.

5   Stephen Gilman, *The Tower as Emblem*, Frankfurt-am-Main 1967.
    Victor Brombert, *Stendhal: Fiction and the Themes of Freedom*, New York, 1968.

6   Brombert, *op. cit.*, p. 63.

7   Maurice Bardèche, *Stendhal romancier*, Paris 1947, p. 377.

8   *Pensées, Filosofia Nova*, i, p. 125.

9   G. Lukacs, *Studies in European Realism*, London 1950.

10 Prévost, *op. cit.*, p. 60.

11 Bardèche, *op. cit.*, p. 16. 'Il entend devenir poète comme on devient ingénieur . . .'

12 *Correspondance I*, Paris 1962, p. 816.

13 Jean Starobinski, 'Stendhal pseudonyme' in *L'Oeil Vivant*, Paris 1961

14 Victor Brombert, 'Stendhal, Analyst or Amorist?' in *Stendhal: a collection of critical essays*, Englewood Cliffs, NJ, 1962.

15 *De l'Amour*, Paris 1969 (Livre de Poche), p. 16. Del Litto's introduction.

16 cf. *Correspondance I*, p. 577.

17 *Promenades dans Rome*, Paris 1931, ii, p. 204.

18 *Histoire de la peinture en Italie*, Paris 1929, ii, p. 174.

19 *Ibid.*, ii, p. 135.

20 *Ibid.*, i, p. 241.

21 cf. Adams, *op. cit.*, p. 159.

22 *Le Rouge et le Noir*, Paris 1939, quoted in Martineau's introduction, p. xxxi.

23 P. G. Castex, *Le Rouge et le Noir*, Paris 1967, p. 79.

24 *Molière, Shakespeare, la Comédie et le Rire*, Paris 1930, p. 290.

25 quoted in L. Guichard, *La Musique et les Lettres au temps du Romantisme*, Paris 1955, p. 287.

26 *Ibid.*, p. 271.

27 *Ibid.*, p. 271.

28 *Histoire de la peinture en Italie*, ii, p. 362.

29 cf. G. Bertier de Sauvigny, *La Restauration*, Paris 1955.

30 *Histoire de la peinture en Italie*, ii, pp. 134, 135.

31 *Mélanges d'art*, Paris 1932, p. 170.

32 F. W. J. Hemmings, *Stendhal*, Oxford 1964, p. 24.

33 *Du Romantisme dans les arts*, Paris 1966.

34 *Mélanges d'art*, p. 141.

35 B. Drenner, preface to *Racine et Shakespeare*, Paris 1965.

36 Adams, *op. cit.*, p. 210.

37 *Du romantisme dans les arts*, introduction by Julinsz Starzynski, p. 10.

38 *Histoire de la peinture en Italie*, i, p. 203.

39 N. Richardson, *The French Prefectoral Corps 1814–1830*, Cambridge 1966, p. 9.

40 *Histoire de la peinture en Italie*, ii, p. 410.

41 *Ibid.*, ii, p. 413.

42 *Mélanges d'art*, p. 10.

43 quoted in Hemmings, *op. cit.*, p. 48.

44 *Ibid.*, p. 15.

45   *Ibid.*, p. 29.

46   E. Auerbach, *Mimesis*, Berne 1946, p. 401.

47   *Ibid.*, p. 410.

48   quoted in F. B. Artz, *Reaction and Revolution*, New York 1963, p. 229.

49   *Correspondance II*, Paris 1967, p. 890.

50   cf. R. M. Albérès, *Le Naturel chez Stendhal*, Paris 1956, p. 339.

51   Hemmings, *op. cit.*, p. 93.

52   *Mélanges d'art*, p. 165.

53   Hemmings, *op. cit.*, p. 72.

54   *Ibid.*, p. 89.

55   *Molière, Shakespeare, la Comédie et le Rire*, p. 224.

56   *Le Rouge et le Noir*, Paris 1939. Martineau's note, p. 592.

57   Castex, *op. cit.*, p. 88.

58   C. Liprandi, *Stendhal, le 'Bord de l'eau' et la 'note secrète'*, Avignon 1949.

59   Lukacs, *op. cit.*, p. 6.

60   Adams, *op. cit.*, p. 43.

61   *Le Rouge et le Noir*, Paris 1939. Martineau's introduction has a summary of speculations.

62   Hemmings, *op. cit.*, p. 125.

63   *Napoléon*, Paris 1930, i, pp. 47, 178, 183.

64   Castex, *op. cit.*, p. 118.

65   *Ibid*, p. 117.

66 Brombert, *Fiction and the Themes of Freedom*, p. 71.

67 Hemmings, *op. cit.*, p. 128.

68 Frank O'Connor, *The Mirror in the Roadway*, New York 1956, p. 54.

69 Prévost, *op. cit.*, p. 269.

70 M. Proust. *Contre Sainte-Beuve*, Paris 1954, p. 416.

71 *Romans et Nouvelles II*, Paris 1952, quoted in Martineau's preface, p. 1063.

72 Hemmings, *op. cit.*, p. 128.

73 A good recent guess is that of D. J. Mossop, 'Julien Sorel, the Vulgar Assassin', *French Studies*, April 1969. 'What is at stake is the whole semi-artificial personality he has built up in his effort to turn himself from a gentle timid youth into a Napoleon of energy and courage. He has reached a point at which he must either kill Mme de Rênal or kill himself, and to kill himself without killing Mme de Rênal would be to kill a dishonoured weakling.' Fine, except for the 'gentle timid youth'. But then this is one track of Julien's motivation; it doesn't exclude others.

Part Two

1 Paul Valéry, *Variétés II*, Paris 1930, pp. 85–6.

2 John Atherton, *Stendhal*, London 1965, p. 19. 'The structure of the *Vie de Henry Brulard* is comparable to that of the novels. All of them are directed towards an apotheosis that remains in the last analysis either unrealizable or secret. At the climactic moment the hero escapes our observation.'

3 Jean Prévost, *La Création chez Stendhal*, p. 43.

4 Georges Blin, *Stendhal et les problèmes de la personnalité*, Paris 1958, p. 545.

5 Paul Valéry, *op. cit.*, p. 117.

6 Georges Blin, *op. cit.*, p. 8.

7   cf. Roland Barthes, *S/Z*, Paris 1970.

8   H. de Balzac, *Etudes sur M. Beyle*, Geneva 1943, p. 73.

9   Harry Levin, *The Gates of Horn*, New York 1963, p. 133.

10 Erich Auerbach, *Mimesis*, Berne 1946, p. 410.

11 quoted in Léon Guichard, *La Musique et les lettres au temps du romantisme*, p. 287. *See* Part One, note 25.

12 Maurice Bardèche, *Stendhal romancier*, p. 12.

Part Three

1   Pierre Martino, quoted in *La Chartreuse de Parme*, Garnier, Paris 1942, Martineau's introduction, p. xxi. 'C'est le livre de la cinquantaine de Stendhal. Il enferme toutes ses expériences, les anciennes et les récentes. La mort s'annoncait prochaine, et il voulait passionément ressaisir tout son passé, le panorama moral et intellectuel de sa vie, les choses qu'il avait le plus aimées, les spectacles et les paysages préférés, ses plus grandes émotions, les rêves qu'il avait réalisés et ceux, plus nombreux, qui avaient dû mourir étouffés, ou même qui n'étaient pas parvenus jusqu'à la claire conscience. Richesse fébrile de la vision, hâte fiévreuse à la saisir . . . L'angoisse de vieillir et la peur d'oublier ce qu'il a été tourmentent Stendhal; il veut trop pour pouvoir tout; mais il finit par écrire le plus cher de ses livres, son livre, et c'est, avant tout, un hymne à sa vie, à la vie.'

2   Jean Prévost, *La Création chez Stendhal*, Martineau's preface, p. 10. 'En réalité rien n'a été perdu des dialogues pénibles et des scènes maladroites, ni des formules arides, ni des portraits figés . . .'

3   *Napoléon*, Paris 1930, ii, p. 13.

4   *Ibid.*, ii, p. 17.

5   *Correspondance II*, p. 762.

6   *Romans et Nouvelles II*, Paris 1952. Preface to *Chroniques Italiennes*, pp. 556, 557.

7   Jean Prévost, *op. cit.*, p. 322.

8   R. M. Adams, *Stendhal: Notes on a Novelist*, p. 255. 'He filled
    the opera house of his own personality with such melody that we
    shall never be done discussing him.'
    Jean-Pierre Richard, 'Connaissance et tendresse chez Stendhal' in
    Littérature et sensation, Paris 1954, p. 116. 'Parler de Stendhal,
    c'est chaque fois se condamner à l'impression que l'on n'a rien dit,
    qu'il vous a échappé et que tout reste à dire.'
    Paul Valéry, *Variétés II*, p. 139. 'On n'en finirait plus avec Stend-
    hal. Je ne vois pas de plus grande louange.'

9   H. de Balzac, *Etudes sur M. Beyle*, Geneva 1943, p. 76.

10 R. P. Blackmur, 'The Charterhouse of Parma', *Kenyon Review*,
    Winter 1964.

11 Balzac, *op. cit.*, p. 57.

12 Blackmur, *op. cit.*

13 *La Chartreuse de Parme*, Garnier, Paris 1942. Martineau's note,
    p. 625.

14 Jean Prévost, *op. cit.*, p. 32.

15 G. Lukács, *Studies in European Realism*, p. 73.

Bibliography

I. Texts

The standard edition of the complete works is Henri Martineau's:
Le Divan, Paris 1927–1937, 79 small volumes.

The Bibliothèque de la Pléiade (Gallimard, Paris) has:
  Romans et Nouvelles I (containing *Armance, Le Rouge et le Noir, Lucien Leuwen*), 1952.
  Romans et Nouvelles II (containing *La Chartreuse de Parme, Chroniques Italiennes, Lamiel, Romans et Nouvelles*), 1952.
  Oeuvres Intimes (containing *Vie de Henry Brulard, Journal, Souvenirs d'Egotisme, Essais d'Autobiographie, Earline, Les Privilèges*), 1955.
  Correspondance I (1800–1821), 1962.
  Correspondance II (1821–1834), 1967.
  Correspondance III (1835–1842), 1968.

Livre de Poche (also Gallimard) has:
  Le Rouge et le Noir, 1958.
  Lucien Leuwen, 1960.
  Lamiel and *Armance*, 1961.
  La Chartreuse de Parme, 1962.
  Chroniques Italiennes, 1964.
  Romans et Nouvelles, 1968.
  De l'Amour, 1969.

The following are good critical editions, all by Henri Martineau, of the major novels:
  Le Rouge et le Noir, Garnier, Paris 1939.

La Chartreuse de Parme, Garnier, Paris 1942.
Lucien Leuwen, Editions du Rocher, Monaco 1945, 2 volumes.

II. Criticism

The scholarly and critical literature on Stendhal is immense, and on the whole rather depressing. I have listed here only those books and essays about him which I found to be of quite exceptional interest.

R. M. Adams, *Stendhal: Notes on a Novelist*, London 1959.

Erich Auerbach, 'Im Hotel de la Mole', in *Mimesis*, Berne 1946.

H. de Balzac, *Etudes sur M. Beyle*, Geneva 1943 (a reprint of Balzac's article of September 1840).

Maurice Bardèche, *Stendhal romancier*, Paris 1947.

Georges Blin, *Stendhal et les problèmes du roman*, Paris 1953. *Stendhal et les problèmes de la personnalité*, Paris 1958.

P. G. Castex, *Le Rouge et le Noir*, Paris 1967.

Jean Dutourd, *L'Ame sensible*, Paris 1959.

F. W. J. Hemmings, *Stendhal*, Oxford 1964.

V. del Litto, *La Vie intellectuelle de Stendhal*, Paris 1959.

George Lukacs, 'Stendhal and Balzac' in *Studies in European Realism*, London 1950.

Jean Prévost, *La création chez Stendhal*, Paris 1951.

Marcel Proust, 'Stendhal' in *Contre Sainte-Beuve*, Paris 1954.

Jean-Pierre Richard, 'Connaissance et tendresse chez Stendhal' in *Littérature et sensation*, Paris 1954.

Jean Starobinski, 'Stendhal pseudonyme' in *L'oeil vivant*, Paris 1961.

INDEX